THE PITCHING STAFF

THE PITCHING STAFF

STEVE JACOBSON

Thomas Y. Crowell Company   New York   Established 1834

PHOTO CREDITS
Photo section follows page 110.
New York National League Baseball Club: page 1, 2, 3 (top), 4, 6, 7, 8.
Wide World Photos: page 3 (bottom), 5.

Copyright © 1975 by Steve Jacobson

All rights reserved. Except for use in a review, the reproduction or utilization of this work in any form or by any electronic, mechanical, or other means, now known or hereafter invented, including xerography, photocopying, and recording, and in any information storage and retrieval system is forbidden without the written permission of the publisher. Published simultaneously in Canada by Fitzhenry & Whiteside Limited, Toronto.

Manufactured in the United States of America

Library of Congress Cataloging in Publication Data

Jacobson, Steve.
  The pitching staff.

  1. Pitching (Baseball)   I. Title.
GV871.J32   796.357'22   75-6836
ISBN 0-690-00696-9

1 2 3 4 5 6 7 8 9 10

To **Harold Jacobson,**
who taught me honesty
and the deception of the curveball.

INTRODUCTION

Fielders fiddle impatiently with their gloves. The hitter twitches his bat in anticipation. But nothing happens until the pitcher throws the ball. As he stands imperiously on the mound, he's king of the whole damn world.

Pitchers are a breed apart, elemental men. When Harvey Haddix became a relief pitcher he recognized that the most interesting part of his career was coming in from the bullpen for the do-or-die confrontation. He or the batter—who was better? It's the ultimate distillation of the game. Mike Kekich, who had the arm of a star and the soul of a poet, once pitched a near no-hitter for the Yankees and was unsatisfied because too many of the White Sox hit the ball. Kekich said his ego craved to strike everyone out, to do the job without any help. Tom Seaver has never learned how to pitch an easy game. Every pitch is intended to be the perfect pitch.

Sometimes the king can stand on the mound and laugh at the hitters. If he has Nolan Ryan's fastball, he's a king. Once Ryan sent word through his catcher to Reggie Jackson, that every pitch would be a fastball. Ryan was matching his 100.8 miles an hour velocity against a great fastball-hitter.

Jackson lined to the left fielder. He couldn't get his bat around quick enough to pull the ball. Then he shook his head and he and Ryan laughed.

Once, in innocent wildness, Ryan hit the first batter's helmet and broke the second batter's arm. The third begged his coach not to make him bat. Ryan laughs about the recollection. He will never laugh at the memory of fracturing Doug Griffin's skull.

The ball is five ounces of rock-hard, leather-covered pain that can shatter a bone. The batter wears a helmet and if he's afraid, he can't hit. If the pitcher can remind him to be afraid, the battle is virtually decided. Once a batter was killed by a pitch in the big leagues.

The ball comes off the bat faster than any pitcher can throw it and the pitcher is the closest target. Herb Score's career was destroyed by a batted ball that nearly blinded him. Jon Matlack talks about preserving in bronze the bandage he wore when his forehead was fractured by a line drive.

Throwing a rock at a rabbit was a natural activity in the primeval world, but a hundred-plus pitches a game in forty games a year for ten years is something else. Once a hitter develops his skill, he goes on until age weakens him. The pitcher knows his next pitch might leave him with a terminal sore arm.

These factors link pitchers like an infantry platoon going into combat. They feel only other pitchers understand them and they're probably right. It makes them a team within a team. Pitchers usually room with pitchers. Pitchers run together in the outfield and pitchers go to dinner with pitchers. Pitchers drink with pitchers and party with pitchers.

Too long ago I was pitching for the Freeport Eagles. One game I pitched a two-hitter and struck out thirteen against some team from the Bronx whose names I never heard of and whose faces I couldn't distinguish. The feeling coming off the mound after the last out was a natural high. "It's the greatest feeling in the world to run off the mound and have people shake your hand," says Bob Apodaca of the Mets, who's still innocent enough to feel the spirit of the sandlots.

The owner of the Eagles gave me and the kid who pitched the second game of the doubleheader ten dollars each and bought us a pitcher of beer at Primavera's Tavern. The kid and I sat together, drank our beer, and compared how we'd pitched.

The next day, I was sure the wooden feeling in my leg and

the ache in my back were exactly the same as those Bob Feller experienced. That's universal. So was the sensation of the next game I pitched. I remember the fourth batter against the Eagles hit a home run with the bases loaded.

Some years later the San Francisco Giants held a tryout camp on Long Island. On assignment from *Newsday*, I borrowed a shirt—a little too small so I'd look bigger—and lied like anything about my age. I remember standing on the mound with the ball and looking around at the youths with caps perched atop bouffant hair-dos. They all wanted to do something to attract the notice of the scout. And they had to wait for me. I pitched to three batters. One hit back to the mound. One struck out. And one popped up. At the end, the scout said he'd call some players back for a second look.

He never called me. But I remember thinking, what if he did call? What if he offered Class D? I had a good job. I had already covered a World Series. But I would have gone in a minute.

FEBRUARY 21

The 1974 baseball season began today for the Mets. Tom Seaver signed his contract. He and the other pitchers reported to spring training in St. Petersburg, Florida. Seaver's contract makes him the highest-paid pitcher in history at $172,000. "Why not?" said general manager Bob Scheffing. "He is the best pitcher in baseball, isn't he?"

No doubt about it. And the Mets live or die on their pitching. That's why they're defending National League champions.

Scheffing had a chance to trade for Paul Blair with Baltimore and for Jimmy Wynn with Houston. But he wasn't going to break up that pitching staff to get a mere center fielder. The Orioles wanted pitching and the Astros wanted pitching. However, the Mets went to the seventh game of the World Series with their pitching, so Scheffing declined.

It's hard to argue with the man. He asks how many times has any other expansion team won anything, and the answer is none. Hell, the Mets have won twice in five years and the last time the Dodgers won anything was 1966.

The Wynn trade was the closest. "Somehow, I have a feeling we're better off that we didn't make that deal," Scheffing said. "I like the club we have. I think we have a good shot again, just the way we are."

Scheffing offered George Stone, coming off the best season of his career. The Astros wanted Stone and rookie Craig Swan, too. "I'm glad they didn't take Stoney," Scheffing said. "With him, our pitching looks strong. That's how we won it; that's how we can win it again."

Connie Mack used to say pitching was eighty, eighty-five, or ninety per cent of baseball, depending on how good or bad his pitching was that year. With the Mets, his evaluation seems a little conservative.

The sun is bright and warm and it feels good to step out of the car and stretch before checking in at the motel. It's Florida and winter is thousands of miles up the road.

More than that, it's St. Petersburg and it's the start of spring training and it's a wonderful feeling. It's spring the way it always was. It's starting everything fresh again. Inside a voice says, "Everything's going to be all right; they're playing baseball again."

Almost everything about the first days of training is hopeful. It's the time before the real competition begins; the time to forget that last season wasn't very good, because surely this one will be better. Every man's confidence is strongest in the first days of camp.

Now is the time a man can say he isn't throwing hard because he isn't in shape yet. He can say he isn't throwing as hard as some rookie because an older man needs a little more time to get ready—and it's an advantage that an older man knows his own body better than a youngster does. The veteran doesn't yet have to face up to the reality that he isn't throwing hard because he can't throw hard anymore.

For a few players there's the pressure one good season produces. "Spring is a great rejuvenation," outfielder George Theodore remarked. "It's a good feeling to come to camp. There's also the insecurity of having to do it again. Spring has two faces."

It's the fashion now for ball players to speak of the game as just one more form of work. Undoubtedly, it is sometimes. There are times when it's drudgery. And no salary figure makes a man feel fresh when he's tired. But spring training is almost fun. The Mets don't have to report until February 21 for pitchers and catchers and February 26 for the rest of the squad, but many of them were here beforehand. Some of them came early to jog on the beach. Some of them got in a few days of vacation in the sun. But more than any of that, they were here early because this was where they wanted to be.

"My wife can't stand me in January and February," said shortstop Bud Harrelson. "I'm here already. I enjoy being with the guys. I'm not queer, but I spend my life with these twenty-five idiots. That's why I was here two weeks early."

Harrelson and Tom Seaver and Rusty Staub of the Mets, and Joe Torre and Ted Sizemore of the Cardinals, who also train in St. Petersburg, all live in the same motel complex in Redington Beach. They illustrate the peculiar kind of kinship rival baseball players have that doesn't occur in other sports. There's time for kibitzing before a game and the two-day and three-day stays in a city give players in one uniform the opportunity to get to know players in another uniform as people, not just as rivals.

In the first weeks of spring training, before the onset of the interminable exhibition schedule, there's even time for a comfortable social life. Players and their families mingle on the beach and go to restaurants together. While the players are at practice the families are together. As much as the players are together during the season, they rarely see more than one or two of their teammates in social situations. Baseball families go whole seasons seeing other families only at airports. Now there's time to relax together and for the men to go off and play golf with each other after practice. "Once the games begin, there isn't time," Harrelson said.

Harrelson is painfully thin even before the grind of the season wears him down. The other players at the motel with him have to watch their weight from the other side. The children are acutely aware that Harrelson doesn't have to watch what he eats. Harrelson kindles the barbecue fire at five o'clock and his family eats at six. Then he makes his nightly ice cream run. The children call him "Uncle Bud" and the "ice cream man." Every night Sarah Seaver, three, asks, "Ice cream tonight, Uncle Bud?" And almost every night Uncle Bud takes all the orders.

FEBRUARY 26

Everybody is here except for Teddy Martinez, the reserve infielder from the Dominican Republic. Every year he says he has trouble getting a work visa. With his share of last year's World Series money, Martinez bought a car with an FM radio to drive at home. There are no FM stations in the Dominican Republic.

Every spring has its friendly reunions. Even on teams whose players know they're destined to lose 100 games. People who will be thoroughly sick of each other by July are genuinely glad to see each other in February. They spend their working lives together and there's a closeness that sharing victory and defeat produces that the world outside can never feel.

Some springs the reunions are better. This one is special for the Mets. They won the National League pennant last season after even they had abandoned any real hope. There are good times to talk about and smiles of recollection to be shared. They shake hands and ask, "Have a good winter?" Then they're into memories, and talk of how much better this season could be. If they could win in spite of eleven entries on the disabled list, just think how good they could be with everyone healthy.

"I was anxious to get here. I never was before," Harrelson said. "I had a good winter, but my last appearance was the thirteenth of February and I was on the plane on the fifteenth. I always loved baseball, but I never had this feeling before. I never felt the rush to be here."

The Mets rose up from last place at the end of August, when Tug McGraw was ready to resume being the best relief pitcher in the league and when the rest of the team was sound enough to play up to the pitching staff. Now they feel that the pitching staff should be better than ever.

Of the twelve teams in the National League, the Mets were eleventh in scoring. Only San Diego scored fewer runs, and the

Padres lost 102 games. The Mets' team earned-run average was the third best. Tom Seaver won the Cy Young award as the best pitcher in the league. For the third time in the last four seasons he led in earned-run average. He led the league in strikeouts and tied for most complete games. George Stone had the best winning percentage. More significantly, in the twenty-nine games that carried the Mets from last to first, they permitted as many as four runs only nine times.

Whatever the Mets do, pitching remains the foundation. They can't develop a hitter, but they do turn out pitchers. In his third season, Jon Matlack is expected to join Seaver near the top of the league's pitching. Jerry Koosman has shown himself his arm is sound again. Stone has proved he can win. There's no way McGraw will go through five months of struggle again. And Seaver is Seaver.

FEBRUARY 27

The Mets take no chances with their pitching. That's the family jewel box. Other teams have pitchers in camp early so they're ready to throw batting practice when the regulars arrive. "We don't do like other teams," Yogi Berra explained. "We don't pitch them until they're ready." Other teams have minor-leaguers around to throw live batting practice, but not the Mets. "The minor-leaguers are our stuff, too," Berra said.

That's been a point of contention here ever since the late Gil Hodges and pitching coach Rube Walker arrived in 1968. The hitters complain that they never get enough hitting in the spring. The pitchers say there is no place they'd rather be. The Hodges-Walker concept, now carried on by Walker, is that the pitchers work on four days' rest instead of the traditional three. And in between, they run like anything. Walker says the pitchers won't pitch as many innings on that schedule, but they'll pitch more effectively and they'll have more left down the stretch.

Walker's ruminations are very much in contrast to the theories of Johnny Sain, the best-known of all major-league pitching coaches. Sain believes a pitcher helps himself most by pitching and little if any by running. He also believes in autonomy—demands autonomy—for the pitching coach. The first point he establishes when he comes to a team is that there will be no second-guessing of the pitchers.

When Berra took over as Yankee manager in 1964, Sain was the incumbent pitching coach with a cult following on the pitching staff. Berra and Sain had rubbed each other the wrong way for three years under Ralph Houk and since Yogi was now the manager Sain had to go. He wouldn't stand for Berra's second-guessing.

Wherever Sain has worked since, pitchers have done better than ever before in their careers. Sain's pitchers were on three winners with the Yankees, with Minnesota, and with Detroit. Sooner or later managers would refuse to work with Sain. When he was fired in Minnesota, Jim Kaat wrote an open letter of protest.

Walker controls the pitching staff, but without the ego needs of Sain. He is basically a quiet, compliant man, not at all like the flamboyant and egotistical Sain. Sain was a great pitcher, and he has a gift for teaching the mechanics of pitching and helping a man with a new pitch. Walker was a catcher. He is very good at setting up a hitter and at spreading the work load, but he doesn't have a gift for teaching the mechanics and he isn't strong on boosting the morale of those pitchers who need it. Hodges was a strong silent type as a player, and he brought that characteristic along as manager. Walker was part of the package. But he is a warm, friendly man who holds the affection of his pitchers, all of whom appreciate how much Walker's work schedule can extend their own careers.

So the pitchers continue what they've been doing here. They throw hard for five minutes each day, even with the full squad in camp, popping the ball into the catcher's mitt as he crouches behind an arrangement of strings that approximates the strike zone. Branch Rickey pioneered the use of the strings as a teaching aid when he ran the Dodgers. Walker was a Dodger in the great years of the early 1950s and the experience left a deep impression.

A Walker development is the windbreak for chilly days like today. He had a batting cage covered with canvas and plastic sheeting so a pitcher could throw from a pocket of still air instead of from a wind-swept mound.

The hitters stand unprotected at the plate against the best batting practice serves of the coaches, Berra, and the pitching machine. Hitters hate the machine especially because there is no motion that enables them to anticipate the release. They hit too many balls on the handle and that makes their winter-soft hands sting. The cold makes the sting worse. "It used to be warmer here," third baseman Wayne Garrett said. He's a Floridian.

Today is Wednesday. There will be no live batting practice until Friday.

Berra was asked, "What's good about the first day's work?" Cleverly, Berra shrugged. "It's only the first day," he explained.

Berra assigned reporting weights to all the players with the threat of fines of $100 a pound for being overweight. He said there have been no fines. He is trying to avoid "fat cats," he said.

Seaver doesn't need the threat of a fine. He's a remarkably disciplined human being. When he says that he hasn't had a beer or a dessert since Christmas, nobody doubts him. He never forgets that a chocolate sundae in the winter is that much more he has to burn off in the spring. He's so disciplined it's frightening. But that's why he's the best pitcher in baseball. Some people consider him self-centered. Admirers regard him as goal-oriented.

Spring training has a large component of boredom too. There are calisthenics and there are the fielding drills. The pitcher tosses the ball to the plate from the mound and a coach raps another ball on the ground, either to the mound or to the first baseman. If the ball is to the first baseman, the pitcher has to cover the base in the recommended manner, breaking toward a point along the baseline and then making a left turn toward the base so as not to cross the path of the runner.

It's the same drill the Mets used when they were assembled for their very first spring training in 1962, when nobody imagined how bad they were going to be. The drill is the same, but the personnel is different and they do it better. But there is one original Met; Bob Miller, who has traveled from Wizzleton to Wazzleton in the intervening years. He's back for a second tour.

Miller joined the 1973 Mets late in September, too late to be eligible for the playoffs or the World Series, but in time for the excitement. What he didn't have to go through was the Mets' five months of decline from their high hopes of the spring to the despair of August, when last place looked a whole lot more realistic than first place.

For some unknown reason Casey Stengel always called Bob Miller "Nelson." Stengel was always identifying people with someone else in his own past. Bullpen coach Joe Pignatano, also a Met in 1962, remembers Stengel's nickname for Miller and uses it in the drills. At one point this morning, Miller, now thirty-five, handled the ball at first base and a rookie said, "Waytago, Nellie." Yogi Berra calls him "Bill Miller" after some long lost hopeful pitcher for the Yankees.

"I don't want to go through another year like last year," Seaver said. "It's the greatest physical and mental strain to keep telling yourself you got a chance to win when everybody gets back. You got to keep telling yourself you're going to make a big run when you're all together. Until then you have to work twice as hard to keep yourself above water. The reward is greater, in a sense, because of that. You had enough discipline to keep yourself in contention. In a season that's so long, discipline is one of the primary attributes of an athlete. Our season is so long. It's such a drain."

Unlike all the other games, baseball is an everyday life. There's no week in between to let down and build up again. In the last month of the pennant race—a phenomenon unique to baseball—the game was never really over. As soon as one game ended, the mind shifted to the next day's game.

"It's good to see everybody together today," Seaver said. "It brings back good memories. Today we're starting toward a goal. We may not see it until October, but still, today is the first day."

Just before the regulars arrived to make the work day longer, Seaver played in a pro-am golf tournament and won a set of clubs. Just what he always needed. The $172,000 pitcher gave the clubs to Pignatano, a $20,000 coach.

Miller begged to be excused from the running at the end of practice. "I just washed my feet and can't do a thing with them," he said. Request denied.

FEBRUARY 28

The newspapers here have a story almost every day of some staid meeting on a campus being disrupted by a naked student. The Mets had their first streaker this morning, inspired no doubt by the prospect of more headlines. He wore bright red shoes, a bright red hat, and eyeglasses. He ran toward the clubhouse door as if to run out into the crowd of waiting spectators and make a spectacle of himself. Then Ray Sadecki turned and ran down the row of lockers to his own stall. The room filled with giggles.

Minutes later a pretty girl stuck her head through the door and it looked as if the Mets were about to be streaked. But she took her look and backed off, leaving the Mets to discuss who and what had been seen.

At the side entrance to the clubhouse, there was the station wagon from the Wilson people. The Rawlings, MacGregor, and Louisville Slugger people will be around shortly. Their appearance is one of the highlights of the spring. In ones and twos, in various stages of dress, the Mets made their way to the wagon to see what's new and different or old and familiar in gloves and shoes.

Hardly a man has a soul so dead that he can see a box of professional model gloves and resist slipping one on his hand and popping his fist into the pocket. There's a whole world of fantasy in that one gesture.

Late in the morning Jackson Todd held a contract on the top of the station wagon and signed his name on the bottom line. Todd is one of the minor-leaguers here to pitch batting practice and to learn what he can from the exposure to the big-leaguers. He's twenty-two and pitched half of last season at Memphis—believe it or not—in the Texas League. It was his first season as a professional. "He may be another Tom Seaver, I don't know. I never heard of the boy," said Harry Cagney, the Wilson representative. He signed Todd on the advice of pitching coach Rube Walker. "We're not too strong on the Mets," the Wilson man said. "Rube has given us good help."

For the company, it's all an investment in the future and competition against the other manufacturers for signatures. Todd signed a two-piece contract, which means a glove and a pair of shoes each year. Each piece is worth forty or fifty dollars. If Todd makes the big leagues, the standard contract is for four pieces a year. And if he makes enough of a name for his name to be put on a glove, it would be worth $1,000 to $5,000.

The company's intention is to have the right name on a contract before the player does something sensational. It's like catching lightning in a bottle, except the risk isn't very great. Wilson's dream come true, Cagney said, was Denny McLain. "We signed him at eighteen," Cagney recalled. "The year after he won the thirty-one games, we ran his name on what we called the '31 Series' and sold a ton." McLain got more than the standard endorsement fee for that.

It's part of Jackson Todd's dream just to sign the contract. "I guess it means they have faith that I could make it to the big leagues," Todd said. "I suppose it's a fantasy to think of seeing my name on a glove some day. It would be like a dream come true. Having your name on a glove means you've achieved something you set out to do."

Realistically, Todd is here as cannon fodder, to throw strikes for the hitters while taking the burden off the real pitchers, but every Jackson Todd that ever was is entitled to have his own idea of what might happen. Maybe he'll get into a game that runs into extra innings and pitch so well Berra will want to give him another look, and another. That's how Jim Bouton made the Yankees in 1962.

"I'd like to make the team," Todd said. "If I get a break and throw well in the Grapefruit League and impress somebody, I could make the team." Nobody refers to the exhibition schedule as the "Grapefruit Circuit" except the Florida Chamber of Commerce, team publicity men, and rookies who see everything as a chance to make the team.

There are a couple of spots open on the pitching staff, two or three. Berra figures on going North with nine pitchers and maybe adding another when the schedule fills out in early May. Count them this way: Tom Seaver, Jon Matlack, Jerry Koosman, and George Stone are starters. Tug McGraw is set in the bullpen and probably Bob Miller because he has experience and is right-handed. Harry Parker and Ray Sadecki are the swing men. That's eight.

The most likely prospects among the newcomers are Craig Swan, a starter, and Bob Apodaca, one of the new breed of pitchers raised as a reliever. Rarely does any player make the team entirely on the basis of spring training. For the most part, his status is determined by what he did last season. He can look so bad that it's decided he needs more time in the minor leagues, or he can do so well that he revises the reports. What a man usually has to do is play up to the evaluation of his last season. Reports were good enough on Swan that Berra gave him a start in September and good enough on Apodaca that he was thrown into a tight relief situation in the heat of the pennant race. Both did poorly, but the evaluations weren't hurt by that.

Buzz Capra has a shot, but he's had three shots with the Mets and never really impressed. They'd like to make a trade for him. Hank Webb is a possibility, but what the organization really wants is for him to show his head has caught up with his arm and start the season well at Tidewater. Tommy Moore also has to leave a good impression behind when he's sent out.

In the next rank is John Glass, who once was paired with Nolan Ryan but has since acquired a reputation for having an arm that needs to be treated like glass. Randy Sterling and Steve Simpson are here out of courtesy. And the nonroster pitchers—Jackson Todd, Augie Garbatini, Tim Juran, and Gary Manderbach—are here to work and learn.

For each grouping, spring training has a different objective. Tom Seaver is going to pitch opening day if he can raise his arm, no matter how he pitches here. The hopefuls have to demonstrate they can stay. Most of the others can leave good impressions to be instantly recalled if they do well in the minors. But you can't tell them it's that cut and dried. They have to dream, too.

Tonight there was a dinner in the ballroom of the St. Petersburg Hilton to honor the area's most successful athletes. Tennis player Betsy Nagelson, who recently turned professional, was one of the guests of honor. (A note of interest: The hotel's shell, fourteen stories high, went up from floor to roof in fourteen days. Some of the sinks in the bathrooms are chest-high.)

Berra and Seaver made presentations to the local heroes. "They're there because they won something," Berra, the speechmaker, explained earlier. "You make a presentation and say, 'Congratulations.'"

Seaver, who completed work for his degree in public relations at the University of Southern California over the winter, takes chores like this more seriously. He always has the proper thing to say. "We came here to look for jobs," he reflected on his first spring training and the spirit of all spring trainings. "Some of us came 3,000 miles. . . . We came to beat an older fellow out of a job . . ."

MARCH 1

Today the hitters get to see what the pitchers are throwing for the first time and the pitchers get to pitch to batters instead of practicing on the sidelines. The hitters welcome something more than the arm of coach Joe Pignatano, but they aren't ready for the kind of stuff Seaver and Matlack can throw for a few minutes or the velocity of Craig Swan, who pitched in winter ball. The pitchers are glad to have the taste of competition any pitcher-hitter situation creates. Most pitchers who've been around any length of time develop a game to challenge themselves even when they're pitching batting practice. "It's pleasing to throw and not have somebody standing next to you," Seaver said.

According to his station, the first pitcher on the mound this year is of course Seaver. When you get down to it, Seaver is the manager of the team. He doesn't push his weight around but . . . The manager is restricted, so to speak, in the communications arts. He often whispers a request to Seaver to make a loud-voiced announcement to the team. It's a team founded on its pitching staff and Seaver is the main man of the pitching staff. When a game is rained out, Seaver keeps his place in the rotation and everybody else shoves over. When Seaver is ready, Seaver pitches. When Seaver isn't ready, Seaver doesn't pitch.

That condition drove Gary Gentry to distraction for four years. He complained loudly and often that Seaver, who dressed in the adjoining locker, was permitted to work out of situations while Gentry was always relieved. But Seaver had earned his status and Gentry, two seasons after being traded to Atlanta, still hadn't.

Seaver warmed up and then took the mound for five minutes. Rusty Staub waited to be the first hitter like a man trying to take a cold shower without getting wet. "Man," Staub said, "do you think I'm going to be able to hit against that? No chance." Staub swung very late at the first pitch. "I'm standing a little far away now," Staub said to Seaver. "I'm a little chicken."

Seaver's motion flowed, a factor that he says interests him most in the early days. He was so pleased he requested and received another minute of pitching after Berra had looked at his pocket watch, the hallmark of the manager/coach, and said it was enough.

Until the exhibition games begin on March 9, the Mets work from ten in the morning until one-thirty or so in the afternoon on the Payson Field Complex, named appropriately for Joan Payson, the rich lady who owns the team. The complex is out toward the beach areas where a number of the married players are living, and working there beats fighting the traffic to the downtown area where the games are played.

The complex is composed of a sprawling clubhouse with rows and rows of lockers under a big roof arched like an airplane hangar, and four fields fanning out from a central observation tower. The fields are named for Bob Scheffing, the general manager; Joe McDonald, minor-league director and heir-apparent when Scheffing retires; and for Nelson Burbrink, director of player development. One field is unnamed. It was named for Whitey Herzog when he was a big man in the farm system, but when he moved on to manage the Texas Rangers, the field became as anonymous as a piece of Russian history.

If you look closely at the signs on the field, the corner of each says, "by Choo Choo," and thereby hangs a little piece of history. Choo Choo Coleman—Clarence Coleman, actually— was a catcher on the original Mets, when they were inept and engaging and nowhere near as actuarial as they are today.

Coleman hardly ever said anything, much less addressed anybody by name. He called everybody "Bub." Most of that first year Coleman roomed with Charlie Neal, an infielder whose once exciting career was near the end of a rapid

THE PITCHING STAFF 15

downhill slide. The second spring Coleman greeted Neal as "Bub" and Neal said, "I bet you don't even know who I am."

"Sure I do," Coleman drawled. "You numba foah."

Another time broadcaster Ralph Kiner was struggling through an interview with Coleman and, grasping for anything, Kiner asked, "What's your wife's name?"

Coleman replied, "Mrs. Coleman."

Seaver remembers pitching to Coleman at Jacksonville in his first season as a professional. One game Seaver was in trouble, and Coleman went to the mound and made an extended commentary to the pitcher. Seaver says he understood hardly a word of it, but responded by pulling his game together.

Seaver was succeeded on the mound by Swan, a burly six feet, three inches with a tendency to gain weight if he isn't careful. The pitchers have nicknamed Swan "Baby Huey" for an overweight cartoon bird. He had something of a jump on the others because he played winter ball in Puerto Rico. He went there to make up the time lost when his Triple A season was interrupted by a midseason appendectomy. "The doctor said it was the biggest appendix he had ever seen," minor-league director Joe McDonald said.

Swan looked awkward. He threw in sections like a golfer who'd taken a whole lot of lessons and was trying to remember all of them.

"I concentrated on how many strikes I threw, how it felt," Seaver said. "I'm very pleased. I feel like I have a sense of rhythm. I call it a plus day."

Seaver has his sense of security. "I have a time schedule for myself," he said. "I know where I should be. I don't have to impress anybody. I don't have to rush myself."

He also remembers very well what it was like his first spring training with the major-league club, when he still had to earn his spot on the team. He wasn't sure until the weekend before opening day. It's Seaver's nature to observe and retain everything. "If the new players' approach is the same as mine was," Seaver said, "they're trying to throw hard already.

16 THE PITCHING STAFF

They're trying to throw hard to impress the manager and the scouts. You shouldn't do that yet."

Certainly not. "The first day you're trying to get it over the plate, that's all," Swan said, as if anybody could believe him.

Ray Sadecki was to have pitched too, but he went home early. He was sick. "Officially sick," he explained.

When they weren't pitching to hitters, the pitchers practiced pickoff throws to first base on Diamond Three. They found unfamiliar V-shaped lines chalked on the mound as part of an experiment involving the balk rule. When a left-handed pitcher tries to pick off a runner, he must stride to the first base side of the line or be charged with a balk. The intent is to formulate a new rule to keep lefties from cheating. Left-handed people are always being accused of something devious. There's also a line for righties to clear in throwing to third base, but that's one of those plays that hardly ever occurs except in the rule book. It smacks of tokenism.

One observation is that if a lefty pitches off the third base end of the rubber, only a contortionist could step across the line. Jerry Koosman raised a more practical consideration. "There'll be a lot of meetings on the mound," he said. "I'll tell my infielders to gather round me and accidentally wipe out the line."

As usual, the last thing everybody did was run windsprints—seventy-yard dashes in one direction with a walking return. About twenty of them. The pitchers always run more than anybody else. Seaver kicked chalk from the foul line on Rube Walker, the portly pitching coach. Everybody loves a fat man even if he is a slave driver.

In the cool of the clubhouse, where they took off their uniforms and pools of sweat formed under them as they caught their breath, there was talk of the dinner last night. There was still considerable speculation as to the identity of the main course. Some of the veterans remember the dinner the Chamber of Commerce gave them the spring after the miracle of 1969 and the cocktail party with hors d'oeuvres of such exotica as armadillo and moose. There were no such attractions this time. "It's the armadillo and moose crisis," Tug McGraw explained.

MARCH 2

The gas shortage is as bad here as anywhere. At first it appeared even worse. St. Petersburg is bigger and more spread out than an outsider realizes. Its population is listed as 216,000, but it plays bigger. The Mets live all over the place. Reporters, too. The only way to get to work in the morning is by car.

Piniellas County law permits gas to be sold to even-numbered license plates on even dates, and so on, which cuts down the waiting time but doesn't make gas any more available. A man has to get up early in the morning if he's going to scout for a station selling gas, wait in line for forty minutes, and still be at the workout on time. A signboard at a roadside smoked-fish stand where a queue for gas regularly forms says: "What do you think of Johnson's Great Society now?"

But for a team with 40-odd players, plus staff and front office personnel and newsmen and wives, a sophisticated scouting report has been compiled. The 76 station at Tyrone Boulevard pumps gas until 1 P.M. The Sears station only operates early in the morning. The Humble station just before the bridge pumps gas only in the afternoon. So we can all get by. Some of the Mets worked out effective car pools. Matlack, Stone, McGraw, Miller, and Kranepool live with their families at the Friendly Native in St. Petersburg Beach. Often the five go to practice in one car.

St. Petersburg's reputation, although it has changed in recent years, is still mostly inaccurate. St. Pete's is still identified as the world's largest old-age home, sort of an elephant graveyard. It does have a staggering proportion of old people, to which it caters. Webb City bills itself as the world's largest drugstore, a claim that goes unchallenged. It's special attraction is a mermaid show.

A drive through the downtown area can make an impatient Northerner gnash his teeth at the seventy- and eighty-year-old drivers moving at less than walking pace and the elderly pedestrians crossing the streets with no idea of what it takes to stop a moving car.

The green benches that used to line Central Avenue downtown and set the image for the city are largely gone, but many of the street corners have ramps cut into the curbs for rolling access and many of the drug and variety stores advertise blood pressure tests for as low as twenty-five cents. One shop out toward the beach bills "Beauty Parlor" and "Colonic Irrigation" on the same signboard.

Sometimes it seems ludicrous, but then sometimes it's pathetic. Drive or walk through downtown and observe the crowds at the Traymore or the Orange Blossom or the other cafeterias that are a way of life to the old people with fixed and inadequate incomes. By 5 P.M. the dinner lines have formed to take advantage of the "early bird" special low prices. The nicest residential areas show great numbers of "For Sale" signs on small, substantial homes. Many of the signs indicate that the home has outlived either its owner or his finances. It can be depressing to a young bachelor, but I wonder how many ball players, with their enormous incomes, ever give a thought to those people.

But St. Pete isn't all depressing. One of the most remarkable sights anywhere is the daily game between the Kids and the Cubs, not one of whom is younger than seventy. The players run and slide as hard as they can while spectators hold their breath at the thought of what might befall the man who hits a triple. They are games played by men who haven't come to St. Petersburg to die, but to live out their remaining years. The prospect of dying in the arms of the third base coach doesn't seem to frighten them. "I can't think of a better way to go," said one man who seemed to speak for the rest. The games are enormously encouraging. So is a walk under the trees in the nearby park where golden-agers hold hands as they stroll.

There many changes in St. Pete that indicate a revision in the city's point of view, not the least of which are the presence of an X-rated film house and several topless bars. One bar on the beach features a young lady working topless and wearing men's boxer-shorts, about the size Rube Walker wears. I pointed this out to my wife: "You're not going to believe this, but look over there." Not long ago the idea of a topless place in St. Pete was absurd.

There are young people in St. Pete and some lovely and lively resort areas along the beaches. St. Petersburg Beach, Passagrille, Madiera Beach and Redington sit on a chain of enlarged sandbars that runs ten miles along the Gulf of Mexico. Some of these beaches are lined with hotel/motel developments and some remain private property. Many of the players who've been here before find places at the beach. It's constantly amazing that some players earning $50,000 a year will live in cramped, dank apartments behind other apartments with none of the feeling of being at the edge of the sea.

Theoretically, the players aren't paid for the spring training period. They don't get their semi-monthly paychecks until the season begins, but with their annual salaries, it's not the same as not being paid. Besides, the players who live away from the hotel receive $280 a week in expense money.

Players here without families live, with a few exceptions, in the team's headquarters hotel, the St. Petersburg Hilton on First Street South. The beaches are 150 blocks and a thirty-minute drive to the west. Exhibition games are played at Al Lang Field, across the street from the Hilton, but the Mets are more like limited partners in the use of the field. They share it with the St. Louis Cardinals, who found St. Pete as a training site long before the Mets were conceived and before even the Yankees, who preceded the Mets to St. Pete discovered the city. Actually, it was the St. Louis Browns who first trained in St. Pete, in 1914.

The Cardinals use Lang Field as their training camp, which leaves the Mets, like the Yankees before them, somewhere else. For the period before the exhibition games, the Mets enjoy the spaciousness of Payson Field, 100-or-so blocks toward the beach. Once the games begin, they shift to Huggins-Stengel Field on Fifth Street, just a short drive from

Lang Field. It's a first-class setup except that the Mets have to go back and forth between the field and the clubhouse by taxi. But that stage of training is still a week away.

McGraw gave his own little fashion show this morning as he undressed to dress for the workout. He took off his trousers, revealing a bikini-cut pair of mesh shorts with blue trim. "Hey, Seaver," McGraw called, "do you think Rusty will like these?"

McGraw strolled toward Staub. "If I get in a hurry, I can slip it out through the net." Such style consciousness stamps McGraw as a dandy. The trend among the new breed of players is no underwear at all.

MARCH 3

The hitters take their turns in the batting cage. When the air is warm, they try to cheat a few extra swings. When it's cold, they're generally happy to turn the cage over to the next man. Between pitches, a coach with a fungo bat slaps ground balls to the infielders, dozens of grounders to one man at a time, to one side or the other, trying to extend the man's range, and not hitting the ball too hard.

It isn't forgotten that Gil Hodges hit a hard shot that broke Jim Fregosi's thumb before he ever played a game for the Mets. Hodges called it "a National League ground ball." One new development this spring was the aluminum fungo bat used by Coach Eddie Yost. But the players didn't like the "ping" sound the ball made on the bat so Yost went back to the old wood bat.

When the batter takes his last swing he runs around the bases. The outfielders stand in the outfield and wait for a batter to hit a fly ball. Sometimes pitchers stand out there too.

Back in 1965 Johnny Keane tried to change the order of things with the Yankees in order to have the infield drill and hard outfield throwing at the start of practice, just after the players had stretched their muscles in the warmup calisthenics. But it never went over. Cincinnati once had an organized set of exercises they did in the outfield before exhibition games, and opposing players asked, "When's the kickoff?" That didn't last, either. Baseball players don't like to be seen as oddballs by their peers.

The improvements that have been made are in the better use of time. The players get the same work done in less time under more efficient managers, and then are free to play golf or rest in the shade earlier and with a better disposition. More affluent and progressive organizations have adopted the multiple field setup the Brooklyn Dodgers pioneered twenty-five years ago at Vero Beach.

From the outside it all looks rather uninteresting. After all, what is there to see? A gaggle of pitchers strung behind a mound taking turns fielding balls batted by a coach. A succession of unrecognizable players taking turns in the batting cage. And then everybody runs. Still, it must be human nature to enjoy watching somebody else exercise. It's like the old Peter Arno cartoon showing a portly old gentleman lounging in his easy chair with a martini in his hand while his butler lifts weights. "Once more, Jeeves," the gentleman says, "and then feel my muscle."

Maybe it's just sitting out there in the warm sun or just the idea of something for nothing because there are always a couple of hundred people around to watch the Mets train. Many of them prefer to bring a folding chair and sit where they like instead of sitting in the small grandstand. There's a refreshment stand and it's usually busy. The Mets do their part by handing out a list of names and numbers.

In the clubhouse the contrast with the old days is greater. Players are treated more as if they were people and less like rubes who never wore shoes other than baseball spikes until they got to the big leagues. The lockers are large and the room is airy and clean and, surprisingly, doesn't smell bad at all, considering all the sweaty bodies in it.

Two trainers, Tom McKenna and Joe Deer, are always available and a doctor, Peter Lamotte, usually is. Lamotte is recognized as an outstanding orthopedic man at Roosevelt Hospital in New York and doesn't need the retainer from the

Mets to make a living, but he enjoys the association and the glamor. The players enjoy him, too.

This is Lamotte's last spring. James Parkes is to replace Lamotte in about a week. Lamotte is moving on to set up a kind of resort hospital in Hilton Head, S. C. where Billie Jean King is the resident tennis pro. "The best hospital in America," Lamotte promises. He has always been a conservative and cautious doctor with the players. "You'd take an X-ray of a cold," trainer McKenna tells him. Lamotte is not the type of physician who advises players to rub dirt on an injury and stay in the game.

Before pitching, each pitcher gets a rub and a muscle stretch from the trainer. Some teams require pitchers to ice their arms after pitching. The Mets don't.

Somewhere along the line a nutrition expert—perhaps it was Casey Stengel—decided that it was like shoveling sand against the tide to make players sweat off weight in the morning and then parade them past a lunch table of bread and cold cuts. So there are no sandwiches for lunch in the clubhouse, not even for the reporters who make no promises about getting into shape. What the Mets have is the weight-watchers' delight table prepared by Chef George, a timeless little man who rolls when he walks like a sailor at sea.

Lunch begins with a different soup every day, clam chowder every Friday. Then there are celery stalks, carrot sticks, cottage cheese, wedges of tomato, and hard-boiled eggs. Dessert is a banana or an apple. By the time the Mets leave camp, George estimates, he will have served 168 quarts of condensed soup and 2,500 eggs. And the Mets will hopefully be in good shape.

It's a pretty effective system. Hunger is soothed just enough so the players can survive until dinner, which most of them eat before the sun sets. Some of them stop for a hamburger and a beer on the way home from practice. Some of them know they can't get away with it. "I'll pass that up until later in the spring when I can afford it," McGraw said.

This spring the sight around the clubhouse is a personalized T-shirt in almost every locker. Early arrivals Seaver and

Harrelson had them made up. Coach Joe Pignatano is known universally as Piggy. He wears one with the head of a pig and the legend: "Pigs Is Beautiful." Jerry Grote's shirt is appropriately lettered "Red Ass."

Grote's identification as an irritated man has its roots in events in his early seasons with the Mets. In 1967 he threw a towel out of the dugout to protest an umpire's call and caused himself to be thrown out of the game when he was the last remaining catcher. An outfielder was pressed into duty behind the plate and the game was promptly lost on a passed ball.

Wes Westrum fined Grote $100 for the indiscretion and later that night fined Grote again for missing bed check. Grote was in the coffee shop debating a writer on the inequities of official scoring.

Grote isn't likely to be thrown out of a game when he's the last catcher today. More important, he's grown into a pretty solid handler of pitchers and an important part of the pitching staff. He hasn't yet posted a sign over his locker proclaiming patience as a great virtue. Everybody would be disappointed if he did.

MARCH 4

Florida weather is a fraud. Everybody comes here with the bill of goods sold by advertising agencies. Take summer clothes; that's what we want to wear. Leave the winter clothes at home. Be free. Bull! Fortunately, those of us who drove down from the North have heavier jackets stuffed into a corner of the trunk. Today is another day to wear them. Seaver remembered having his eyebrows singed in his first spring here when he lighted an old-fashioned oil heater to take the morning chill out of a bungalow.

The wind whipped across the field and there was no protection from it. The few spectators who showed up huddled in their folding chairs, trying to crawl deeper into sweaters and light jackets.

But it's remarkable how a man can forget about the cold if he's working hard enough. The aches that grip muscles all over are about gone for the pitchers after two weeks. Now it's a matter of building up the strength to throw hard. At this point the secure pitchers are throwing fastballs at three-quarters speed and spinning curves instead of snapping them.

But only the owner of the arm knows what is three-quarters speed. And a sense of security is in the eye of the holder. George Stone is one of those to whom security comes hard. Stone had a 12–3 record last year, his first really good year in the big leagues, and now they're asking him to do it again. Stone was the first batting practice pitcher today. "His arm feels better," Berra said. So that was why Stone looked so grim in the clubhouse the other day.

Sadecki replaced Stone on the mound. "George, did you leave anybody on base?" Sadecki asked.

Seaver replaced Sadecki and proceeded to break some bats with a fastball that bores in even at three-quarters speed. "You don't use an S-2 against Seaver," said Theodore, tossing away a thin-handled bat and picking up one with a thick grip. "You need a 'Jackie Robinson.'"

Berra's smile gleamed constantly as he watched Seaver. "Whenever anybody asks me who looks good," Berra said, "I tell them, 'Seaver.'" He crinkled with self-appreciation. Not every manager can be so lucky as to start a season with a pitcher like Seaver. When Don Sutton was asked what he would do with the money from his $114,000 Dodger contract, he said, "Invest in Seaver."

McGraw replaced Seaver and that was another thought to warm Berra despite the weather. When McGraw found himself last August, he put together a dazzling stretch of nineteen games in relief, winning five and saving twelve and compiling an earned-run average of 0.88. If he and Seaver have normal seasons, the Mets will be close. Guaranteed.

McGraw threw well and enjoyed it until Berra told him his five minutes were up. "No way that was five minutes," said McGraw, who is listed as a vice president of a watch company in New York. "Better get a Clive watch," McGraw said. Bob Miller replaced McGraw.

"I try to stay relaxed and get in a good groove," McGraw said. "When you're fighting for a job, every time you throw a ball, you try to have something on it. Every time they hit one good in batting practice, you don't like it. You try to get everyone out."

McGraw is one of those rare people who can have great success, make a lot of money and still retain not only the memory but the feeling of the struggle. He's been a premium relief pitcher since 1969, earns close to $90,000, but still relates to people on other levels. By the standards of a newspaper man who works the dressing room after the games, McGraw is a decent human being whether he wins or loses, which is the real test.

He's often most interesting when life isn't going well. Anybody can laugh when he's winning. When the struggle is hardest, McGraw shows his darker sense of humor. Instead of blaming the people who write about defeat, as if they had caused it, McGraw is willing to put his insides on display.

He has fresh recollections of the spring of 1967 when he was coming off a fine season at Jacksonville, then the Mets' top farm club. He had a bad spring and was sent back to Jacksonville. Wes Westrum was the manager of the Mets then and everything McGraw did displeased the manager. Westrum couldn't accept McGraw's effervescence. He didn't like the way McGraw bounded off the mound when he ended a tough inning. He didn't like McGraw's soul-searching when he did poorly. He told McGraw he had to take the bounce out of his walk; it just didn't look professional.

"I used to run my sprints as hard as I could," McGraw reflected. "I tried to do it all better than the other left-handers in camp, to impress Westrum. Now I try to go out and do my thing to get ready."

Now the Mets are working on two fields, spreading the work to get more of it done in less time. Webb is impressive with his lanky build and snapping delivery. "If he could just wake up," Berra wished. "He has good stuff."

Webb has periodic lapses of control, mental and physical. "He's working on something," Rube Walker said. The pitching coach displayed an ironic smile.

All this batting practice business isn't as simple as it appears. The pitchers can throw just so much. The coaches are older men and they can throw safely just so much. And now Joe Fitzgerald, the batting-practice pitcher, is having trouble. He hit Jerry Grote, of all people, with a pitch. It didn't help Grote's disposition. Some people observed that it didn't hurt either.

"Joey will be all right," Berra said.

"We'll keep him away from Grote all spring," Walker said. "As soon as Grote says, 'Get the fucking ball over,' Joe freezes up."

The day wound up with an enjoyable simulated game, the Eddie Yosts against the Roy McMillans, with about fifteen players on a side and the machine pitching to both sides. Sometimes they played five outs or six outs to an inning so Berra could set up situations that might never crop up in a straight intrasquad game. Often the best line drives were caught by the extra outfielders. "When you're going bad," Rusty Staub observed, "you think there are that many out there all the time."

The game turned out to be a showcase for Benny Ayala, the outfielder who didn't ripen in three years on the farm but was at his best in winter ball when Berra made a trip to Puerto Rico. Ayala's strength is the talk of the camp. He's a hitting phenom and the Mets haven't had one of them since Ron Swoboda was a pup. The problem seems to be Ayala's glove. Today he made a leaping catch of a misjudged fly ball. He also hit two home runs.

"They got one more guy than we do," Harrelson complained.

"Yeah," Staub said. "He's the left fielder and he keeps hitting the ball over the fence."

MARCH 5

Beautiful warm sunshine. That's what the tourists pay all that money for. It's even good for working.

It was a day in which the batters could hit without stinging their hands. It was a day for the pitchers to get loose and come off the field drenched in sweat. It was a good day to compare and contrast Swan, Webb, and Moore, the three rivals for one pitching opening.

"All three have good arms. All three have good ability," said Rube Walker, careful not to offend anybody. "I expect all of them to make it. We want to see who gets ready quickest."

Webb has the most stuff but the least command of it. He's twenty-three. Swan, also twenty-three, is the most together. He's had two encouraging seasons as a pro, plus a good winter season in Puerto Rico. When Ayala was leading the Puerto Rican league in home runs and runs batted in and was hit by a pitch, ending his season, it was Swan who threw the ball. The fact that Ayala's arm wasn't broken by the pitch indicates either that the Mets' luck has changed or that Swan wasn't throwing very hard.

Moore, twenty-five, is somewhere in between. He's been a professional since 1967, but was an outfielder for the first three seasons. He was impressive enough as a pitcher to be called up to the Mets the last two seasons, but not impressive enough to be kept long.

He had a spell with the Mets in May when everything was against him. Moore was called up because the Mets needed another starting pitcher, and he was told he'd start in Chicago. His start was rained out. He was postponed until Montreal and that game was rained out, too. When he finally got his start in San Francisco on May 28, he got his block knocked off. He was sent back to Tidewater on June 9.

"I had a 9–11 record, but I read it different," Moore said. "I guess you get that from everybody. I didn't get any breaks.

There were two or three games I lost that I could have won. And I had a hell of a time getting myself back together after being up with the Mets and pitching so little."

Moore has blue eyes, fair hair and a blond mustache. He's a trim five feet, eleven inches and 175 pounds. He looks more like an athlete than the bulky Swan or the gawky Webb. Although pitchers merely have to be able to pitch, Moore looks as if he could play another position. That sets Moore apart from the division in the clubhouse that seems to have the pitchers stocked in one row of lockers and the infielders and outfielders in another as if by natural selection.

"You can see the differences between the groups," Moore said. "You see the pitchers hang together in one group and the infielders and outfielders in other groups. But the pitchers seem to hang together more than the others. I couldn't understand it when I wasn't a pitcher.

"Now I can see why the pitchers can't understand the other side of the clubhouse. The pitcher thinks nobody who isn't a pitcher can understand his situation."

In each case, the other man's job looks easy. All the pitcher has to do is throw the ball. He doesn't have to be a hitter. He rarely has to field a ball. But then a pitcher looks around and sees that all the outfielder has to do is wait for the ball to be hit to him while the pitcher has to labor through the heat of July and August to throw 120 pitches. The outfielder sees no reason in the world why his pitcher should hang a curve. The pitcher makes the batter hit the ball on the ground and sees no reason in the world why the shortstop can't get to it.

In an earlier life Berra was a great catcher with the Yankees and a greater second-guesser. He said all pitchers were "crazy." He said they were "all babies."

"I've sat around when the pitchers complain about some of the plays made behind them," Moore said. "They ask how an outfielder could miss a fly ball. I have to explain it's a hell of a lot easier to follow the ball on the way out than it is from the outfield looking in. Pitchers don't understand those things. I do."

He also understands what it's like to be hit on the mouth by a pitched ball, what goes on in the mind of the batter after an experience like that and what goes on in the minds of the observers. He was hit by the pitch the spring after he hit .285 with sixteen homers and eighty-five runs batted in and was jumped from Class A to Double A. The Mets always did have a shortage of hitters, but then they remembered Moore had led his two leagues in outfield assists. "They said I was falling away from the plate," Moore remembers. "In a month they decided I was bailing out and should be a pitcher." When he was asked if that judgment helped his career, he shrugged.

Moore has a curiosity about life and a willingness to record the things he sees. He went to Cerritos Junior College in California but he's taken his education beyond that. Last fall Moore and his wife, Pam, went on a picture-taking safari from Kenya to Nairobi to Tanzania. Few big-leaguers involve themselves in trips like that, and Moore isn't the only ball player married to a stewardess with a travel discount. "The trip broke us," he said, "but it was something we had to do then or maybe never."

The difficult realization now is that Moore's career is close to a now-or-never stage, too. He's discussed that with some of the others he sees as rivals—Capra, Webb, Swan, Apodaca, Glass. They were all teammates at Tidewater last year. "We discuss being against each other," Moore said. "We throw it into conversation. It's always in the back of your mind and in your heart."

From time to time the Moores and John Glass and his wife go to dinner together and they think about it. "I don't root against the others, even to myself," Moore said. "Maybe both Glass and I will take a job. Maybe we'll take somebody else's job. I just know what I have to do is most important."

It must be the only way to think when life is in the hands of the general manager, the manager and the pitching coach. Today Moore pitched fourteen minutes of batting practice, which meant treading the fine line between trying to impress somebody and not making the established Mets bitch that he was trying to make the team at their expense.

"I wish I knew what [the brass] think," Moore said. He

smiled faintly under that mustache. "But then," he said, "I guess it's better not to know."

Pitchers who felt secure enough to make a joke circulated a petition against Rube Walker. They claim brutality. While Berra was running another simulated game on one field, Walker was running the pitchers through a separate game on another field—and running and running them. If the batter—against a pitching machine—didn't run all out on every fair-hit ball, including pop flies, Walker called his side out.

At one point, Seaver simulated a tantrum. He threw a belly slide into third base, yanked the bag out of the ground and threw it at Walker. That's a classic display of Seaver's sense of humor. It was a friendly, harmless little prank played on the teacher, one that Burt Standish would have found suitable for Frank Meriwell.

When the game ended with the score 5–4, Walker ruled it was a tie, "and everybody runs." So instead of the winners strolling to the clubhouse laughing at the losers taking a lap around the field, everybody took the lap.

MARCH 6, ST. PETERSBURG

It's a comfortable clubhouse. The disappointment these people endured for most of last season brought them close together. It's an unusual group to begin with. They're tame, mature to the point of often being dull. There isn't the dirty-shirter atmosphere the Pirates produce or the salt of the Athletics. But it is comfortable.

Sometimes there are elements of some 1940s movies of a college team or a fraternity house. The dominant visual feature of the clubhouse is a mock advertisement taped over Jerry Koosman's locker showing Linda Lovelace endorsing a mouthwash.

On one side of the aisle of lockers Rusty Staub recalled in horror how Seaver operated around the barbecue at their motel the other night. Seaver was in charge of cooking the steak. It was done on one side and Seaver went to turn it. He touched it with his bare hand. His right hand. His pitching hand.

The thought of Seaver touching that steak with his meat-hand horrified Staub. Seaver again gingerly touched the meat and flipped it over, sending Staub into a frenzy. "If you get a blister there, I'll kill you," Staub said.

It was Seaver's joke, teasing Staub, but completely out of character. Tom Seaver doesn't mess around with the meal ticket. Pitchers learn that at an early age: wear long sleeves, stay out of drafts and constantly search yourself for traces of pain.

Barring some kind of freak accident like running into a wall, hitters play out their careers to ripe old ages. Pitchers spend their whole careers knowing that when they're blithely sliding down the bannister of life it can turn into a razor blade. Maybe that's why pitchers have a reputation for being tightwads. Waiters used to run from Warren Spahn, who spent a lot of years at the top. On the Mets George Stone is known for a keen sense of thrift.

The arm just wasn't designed for the load pitchers put on it and nobody has been able to revise the construction in all these years. Some precautions pitchers take are wholly superstitious. But then who knows what goes on in a pitcher's arm that causes it to break down?

Seaver has learned to sleep off his throwing arm and when he got married, he taught Nancy about that, too. Seaver sleeps with long sleeves. When he hunts, he shoots left-handed to protect his right shoulder from the recoil.

"You make your living with that one arm," said Staub, a student of the game. "you want to make it last as long as you can. I sleep on my left side. When I'm with a girl, she's at my left side."

McGraw has been detected wearing a tank top around the motel. "Poor judgment that day," McGraw said. "I was trying to be stylish. I don't wear a tank top on the day I pitch, but I probably never should."

Seaver has said McGraw "only has about forty-eight cards in

his deck." That is the consensus regarding McGraw's occasional frivolity, which is generally attributed to all left-handed pitchers. But McGraw has learned some things, too.

"I always hold the baby in my right arm," McGraw said. "It pulls the arm down. A pitcher can dream up all sorts of things; but Rube says, if you think that's causing the problem, it's part of the problem."

Matlack doesn't own a short-sleeved dress shirt, although Berra requires the Mets to wear neckties and jackets on the road no matter how hot it is in St. Louis in August. Matlack sleeps with long sleeves, too.

"Old wives' tales or not, they're part of my rationale," Matlack said. "I cut firewood and do things around the house that could hurt me, but I consider that out-of-season activity. I'll even wear a T-shirt out in the cold. But in season, if I fall asleep with my arm behind my head while I'm watching television and my arm falls asleep, it scares me to death."

Once a pitcher has had a sore arm and can't pitch, or has to pitch in pain, he never forgets it. No matter how good he feels, the morning after he pitches he checks the functioning of his arm and asks himself which muscles ache. He looks for a "good soreness." If it's in the muscles of the back and shoulder—and isn't too severe—that's good. If the joints hurt, that's not good.

Any time Seaver feels abnormal, he goes right to the trainer or the doctor, more for reassurance than treatment. "Any little click that lingers for more than a day, anything I can't run out, I see somebody," Matlack said.

Matlack had his first experience with a sore arm while he was at Tidewater. He phoned his parents and couldn't pick up the phone with his left hand. "I overheard the trainer and the doctor talking about exploratory surgery if they couldn't find anything on the X-rays," Matlack recalled. "I don't know if it was serious talk, but it was scary to me."

Seaver, twenty-eight, can't fully straighten his pitching elbow. Neither can Matlack, twenty-four. "I don't think any pitcher who's been around at all can straighten his arm," Matlack said. "We all talk about it. You see a pitcher the next day after he's pitched and you ask him, 'How do you feel?' It's like saying hello."

Before practice, Dr. LaMotte delivered his annual lecture on the dangers of pep pills and other drugs. He also threw in a warning on VD. Actually, a sore arm is worse.

During practice Hank Webb went to the clubhouse to change into a dry shirt and encountered a newsman who wanted to chat. Webb lingered. Herb Norman, the clubhouse man, waited a few moments and offered a well-intended suggestion. "You know what they think," Norman said to Webb. "If they catch you in here, they're liable to tell you to pack and go home."

"They don't trust me," Webb lamented. "I'm paranoid." It's true. They don't trust him.

MARCH 7, ST. PETERSBURG

Tom Seaver slumped on a stool in front of his locker, pulled at the elastic at the cuff of the sleeve of his rubberized shirt and perspiration trickled out to pool on the floor at his feet. it was hot and he had worked hard in accordance with his well-developed routine for three days before pitching. He had pitched seven minutes on the mound, seven on the sidelines, and seven on the mound again to approximate the routine of pitching in the game on Sunday. His face was flushed and drawn. Suddenly he looked older than he's ever looked.

Seaver was always a young pitcher in people's minds. People who remember the Mets of 120 defeats only too well remember seeing Seaver when he was a phenom at Jacksonville in 1966, remember the spring of 1967 when he made the team. The scoreboard at Jacksonville had billed him as "Super Rookie" and his Jacksonville teammates carried that along to the Mets as "Supe." He had a layer of baby fat and players who killed the afternoons watching children's television saw a resemblance to Spanky in the "Our Gang" comedies.

He sold himself on the marketplace to the highest bidders after the dazzling success of the amazin' Mets in 1969 and became a one-man industry of books and endorsements and Sears Roebuck catalogues. He lived by the line of the Jacksonville manager, Solly Hemus, who coached on the original Mets and likened Seaver to Robin Roberts, a great pitcher of the fifties. "Seaver," Hemus said, "has a twenty-year-old arm and a forty-year-old head. Usually we get them the other way around."

Seaver learned to pitch efficiently. He knew what all the parts of his body were doing all the time. He developed brilliant control for a man who could throw so hard. He developed a motion that put into play the muscles in his thick thighs. At the height of his motion, he dips his right knee in the manner of a golfer cocking his knee in his backswing. Seaver gets down so low that he wears a sponge pad to protect his knee.

"I use my legs because they contain the biggest muscles of the body," he says, "the adductor longus, the sartorius, the semitendinosus. I let the legs absorb the strain. That takes it off my elbow and shoulder."

And he plays practical jokes. Usually they are simple and without harm or subtlety and directed at people like Rube Walker, the teacher, or Jerry Koosman and Rusty Staub, Seaver's near-equals in the pecking order. The other morning he tacked a clipping to Staub's locker. The banner headline read. "Plane Crash in France Kills 345." The story beneath it said that the crash of a DC-10 near Paris had set the record for death in a single air crash. The point of the joke was that Staub loves to cook and he loves to hit, but he hates to fly.

Staub read it and cursed. "You did it, didn't you, bastard," he said to Seaver. "I was trying to think who was sick enough to do that. You'd better check your food when you eat at my place again."

There was little rancor in Staub's response and less surprise. Everybody who flies long enough gets to think about the reduction of the odds each time. Some of them, like Staub, dwell on it longer.

But there was none of that mischief in Seaver as the sweat spread beneath him. He will be 30 in November and suddenly he has passed the line from youth into the middle age of baseball. It's his eighth season in the big leagues and it would be an accomplishment in itself if he were to have eight more.

At that moment he was tired. "I enjoy work less and less every year," Seaver said. "I'd like to take a pill and be in shape." Seaver has always been the embodiment of the Protestant work ethic. He was born to some wealth, but he has always worked harder than anybody. He liked work. But not any longer. The chore of convincing himself the Mets still had a chance last year seems to have left a fatigue he can still feel.

"Physically and mentally and emotionally I had had it," he recalled. "You could feel the pressure on airplanes, in hotels, everywhere. The only days of relief I had were when I'd get to the park and pitch."

He was able to immerse himself in concentrating on the game. There is none of that now, just the labor of trying to get ready and finding that the body needs more time at twenty-nine than it used to. "I must be getting there because I feel worse every day," he said.

There's another dimension to his life now, something a lot of ball players discover at some point of their development as human beings. Seaver is a father and being a ball player takes away from that.

"I don't enjoy swimming any more," he says. "It just doesn't interest me. The only time I go in the pool is to take my daughter in. Yesterday I got her to kick her legs.

"I've been out to eat once here. In the season I'll be coming home at eleven-thirty or twelve at night. Here I get to eat dinner with her every night."

When he first reached the Mets, Seaver was a married man of one year. Nancy used to wait up for him after night games. Now when he comes home, Nancy is asleep. Life is changing, some of it is slipping by. Today, he planned to play golf when his energy was restored. The games begin Saturday. It may be the last time for golf until October. When the other players get the three-day break at All-Star time, Seaver will be pitching in the game in Pittsburgh.

Hopefully, he will throw better then than he threw today. Even Sunday will have to be better than today. "I'd hate to be in a game situation, as bad as I felt today," he said. It will be three innings or thirty-five pitches. He'll be trying to throw low strikes, trying to refine pitches instead of trying to set a hitter up. He'll throw a curveball because he needs to throw curveballs, rather than trying to make the batter hit it on the ground. "I'm not ready to commit myself to a game situation yet," he said. He hopes to reach that peak for his last two starts of the spring. "If not then," he said, "then hopefully on opening day."

MARCH 8, ST. PETERSBURG

Pitchers have been announced for the first two exhibition games and revealed for the third. Matlack, Koosman and McGraw are to open the schedule tomorrow, Saturday, against the Cardinals, with Seaver, Stone and Apodaca against the Cards on Sunday. It's a revealing arrangement. Matlack and Koosman are regulars in the rotation and McGraw is the first man in relief. Seaver and Stone are regulars and Apodaca is linked with them. That doesn't indicate how things will work out, but it is a line on how Berra and Walker will try to make them come out.

Monday, Swan will start against the Dodgers. He's the first choice of the rookies to make the team as the fifth starter. Tommy Moore is supposed to pitch the last three innings with an outside chance for the same job. But it's simple enough to see: they're looking for a starter and they're giving Swan the first chance to start in quest of it. The regulars play the first few innings and Swan will be tested against them. Moore will pitch when the scrubs are in the game.

In the middle is Harry Parker, redefining his role on this staff. He's a useful pitcher. His curveball is exceptional, best on the team. But he's neither a starter nor a reliever. More generously, he's either a starter or a reliever. He began last season as a starter and won his first five decisions. But he didn't start after July 1. When Stone came on strong, Parker went to the bullpen. He did good work there, too, but when McGraw found himself, Parker was pushed into the background.

That's the nature of the man, it seems. He doesn't stand out in a crowd. He appears to be a bright fellow. He's thirty credits short of a degree in mathematics at Tulsa University, but he seems reluctant to make an observation or reveal an opinion. Just when it seems he's about to make a point of interest, he backs off.

He smiles readily enough, showing a Terry-Thomas gap between his front teeth, but humor doesn't flow around him. He's condemned to be identified by his won-lost record and earned-run average, as befits a math major. "I've gotten one letter since I've been down here," he said. "My sister-in-law wrote the other day."

At age twenty-six, after nine seasons as a professional, after two brief shots at the Cardinals and one full year with the Mets, he's willing to accept his role. He liked that one year, beginning with making the team in spring training and winning the award as the outstanding rookie in camp. And it wasn't a bad year. He won eight and lost four and his five saves were second only to McGraw's twenty-five. When McGraw was floundering, Parker was the best they had in the bullpen.

That earned a little bit of security for him. "The difference is the point of view," he said. "I have time to get in shape. Now I have more time to work on things. Last year I had to peak early. I could have pitched the first couple of days here."

"I had no choice. The coaches and manager didn't know me last year. I feel now like I've shown them something. The pressure last year took the fun out of being here. I felt I had to have it together in batting practice."

Fun is fun according to who's measuring. Parker's fun is quiet evenings at home with his wife. She doesn't care to spend much of the summer in New York.

But merely surviving can make for a lot of hours spent counting the names on the roster and wringing hands. "I'm sure Swan and Moore are the same way I was. You can't deny somebody else the right to play to his full potential—but you'd like to beat him. If you get shelled a couple of times as a rookie, you know you're in big trouble. I knew that when I came here. Every game was a big game for me. If there's any tightness in those two, they're not showing it."

Parker remembers, as they all do, the moment he knew he'd made the team. It was very late in the spring. The losers on the last cut were to stay behind to continue training with the Tidewater club. The winners were to go on to Fort Lauderdale with the team. "I knew I'd made the club when I saw a sack lunch in my locker," Parker said. "The guys who didn't have one weren't going. Nobody told us." The sensation then, Parker quickly summarized, was "good." He didn't eat the sack lunch. "I usually don't eat a sack lunch," he said.

Parker is one of those people who always looks back over his shoulder and sees something gaining on him. "I'm not going to take anything for granted," he said. "Once you've got everything figured out in your mind, you've got it figured wrong. Unless you're a Seaver or somebody, you can't plan very far in advance in a baseball career."

His $9,000 share from the World Series is marked for the start of a new home in Tulsa. The completion of the work for the degree will have to wait a while.

The day was warm and cheerful enough to bring several of the wives and children out to the workout. You can always pick out the baseball wives among the spectators here. They're always in a cluster, and when do you ever see three or four good-looking women in their twenties together in St. Pete? Besides, when the tourists here are in their twenties they wear jeans and bare midriff shrink tops. Baseball wives feel they have to be dressed for display wherever they go.

Mark McGraw, twenty-one months old, played tug-of-war with Phyllis McGraw as a ball player in uniform trotted past. "Daddy," Markie cried out.

Another player ran past and Markie repeated the call. "That's not Daddy," Phyllis McGraw corrected.

Tug McGraw, mindful of the attention the Kekich-Peterson wife swap created the spring before, observed, "Something could be made of that if this were the Yankee camp."

MARCH 9, ST. PETERSBURG

It was easy to tell today was special. The players were changing their sweaty clothes at Huggins-Stengel Field after the morning workout and the orange cabs hadn't yet arrived to take them to the opening of the exhibition season at Al Lang Field when M. Donald Grant presented himself at the clubhouse.

M. Donald Grant is chairman of the board of directors by virtue of his position as manager of Mrs. Payson's money. He's a stockbroker of some considerable success and has the kind of air that suggests the question: "And where are the customers' yachts?" He's tall and spare and silver-haired. He looks formal even when he comes into the clubhouse wearing white shoes and slacks, a polo shirt and a white golf hat with the Mets emblem, which is part of the uniform of the non-uniformed brass. He likes to talk of the players as "members of the family," and leaves most of them with the impression that he sees them as children.

They refer to him as Mr. Grant. Harold Weissman, the publicity man, refers to him as Don Grant, and so do some newsmen. But "M. Donald" seems more suitable. Mencken once explained that the amount of the impression was equal to the square of the number of initials. It's hard to visualize a man who has an initial in front of his name getting his hands dirty.

Grant makes appearances in the clubhouse during the season to congratulate the team after a stirring victory and sometimes to give a pep talk. Last July when the Mets were at their low ebb, Grant, in his stockholder's gray suit, gave the pre-game talk that thrust Tug McGraw's "Ya gotta believe" battle cry into everyday use. McGraw had used it before, but it was easy to see his great overuse of the expression as faintly mocking.

Grant rallied the troops like Washington at Valley Forge, he told them he believed in them and in Berra, who was under fire, and Scheffing, who was also under fire. Grant himself was under fire in the press at the time.

And some of the troops believed him. "A man that high up in business, you'd have to take him at his word," Harry Parker said. Remember, Parker is a math major, not a business major.

The Mets responded to Grant's talk by winning two in a row and then breaking even for six weeks before taking off on their September rush to the pennant. Word of Grant's uplifting talk reached the pressbox during the game that night and Grant wasn't around for questioning by newspaper men after the game. When I called him at home after the game, he first suggested that he be called at the office in the morning. Then he hung up. Grant has been in the league since 1962. He has been president of the club a long time. He does not yet understand—or perhaps doesn't care—about deadlines or see a function of his own with regard to the press.

Today Grant just walked around the room, friendly-like, taking special pains to stop at Seaver's locker. Seaver is a favorite of Grant's. Who knows? Someday Seaver may own a ball club himself.

Grant crossed the clubhouse to say a few words to Bob Miller, who was in the same room at the start of the first exhibition schedule twelve years ago. "I hear you're coming along good, young man," Grant said. Miller said he had thought Grant knew his name. "We met last year," Miller said.

The clubhouse hasn't changed much during Miller's long time in the diaspora. "Looks about the same," he said. He says he doesn't remember very much about those early days, except that on the first day trainer Gus Mauch told him not to cut his toenails in the trainer's room.

Even after Grant left, there was a feeling of anticipation around the clubhouse. The first exhibition game is a kind of opening day. The first several games are always a relief until the monotony of the exhibition games sets in.

"Today is the first time you find out where you are," said Jon Matlack, the opening pitcher. "You find out if you're ready to concentrate on your breaking ball or if you need more conditioning. If you get a guy set up for a certain pitch and you feel right, you might try to make it. Or you might throw a change when it's not the right situation because you want to work on the change. You play it by ear."

The players kidded about not being ready for things like pop flies on the first day with bright sun and clear sky. "Staub said no fly balls," Matlack said.

The infield is AstroTurf, this being the domain of the St. Louis Cardinals, who have AstroTurf on their home field in St. Louis. The Mets hadn't played on the artificial surface yet this spring. The infielders didn't relish the prospect of handling ground balls today.

Matlack pitched his three innings well and went off to do his fifty pickups and fifteen laps. Koosman and McGraw did well, too, and the Mets beat the Cardinals, 4–1.

Everything came off as planned—even the clothes of the two male streakers who emerged from the overflow crowd and cavorted on the field before escaping over the center-field fence. Everybody who'd been abreast of current events knew there would be streakers at the first game—even in St. Pete. They did their thing with McGraw pitching and two out in the bottom of the ninth inning. If you had to pick which Met pitcher would be involved, you'd have to name McGraw. "I can see the headline tomorrow," McGraw said. "Mets 4, Cards 1, Streakers 2."

And leave it to a pitcher to have paranoid feelings about it. McGraw had a count of three balls and one strike on Stan Papi when the streakers streaked. "Did they have to pick that time?" McGraw asked. "Did they have to come when I had three balls on the batter?" McGraw walked Papi before getting the last out.

Surely there will be more streakers before the season is over. Even the left-handed pitchers will have to get used to the distraction. "If they're gonna do it," Yogi Berra appealed, "they could at least have a couple of good-looking girls once in a while."

MARCH 10, ST. PETERSBURG

Across the street from Al Lang Field, a flotilla of sailboats drifted on the gentle breeze across sun-bright Tampa Bay. In the stands, fans held their scorecards as shades against the sun and even the slight breeze was a welcome relief.

No streaker today. The streaker is a contribution of our time, our kind of protest and cry for attention. It's an anachronism at Al Lang Field—especially on the kind of day that makes everything seem just as it's always been. That's a special quality of baseball. Especially in spring training and especially at Lang Field. Baseball retains its leisurely grace, oblivious to the change of the world outside. The gray hair and wrinkled faces here are a link to times when baseball really was the only game. Lang Field sets the scene as if Norman Rockwell painted it for the cover of some since departed magazine.

It's an old stadium, full of the dark green colors that were standard before pastel became the vogue in the cookie-cutter new parks. Tall, slim, steel columns of green support the corrugated roof, and the outfield fences are ringed by tall palm trees. An overflow crowd huddles in the shade of the scoreboard. In the grandstand on this Sunday afternoon there were a number of flat skimmer straw hats, the kind that are hardly ever seen any more in a major-league ball park but which Connie Mack used to wear all the time. In the conversation in the stands you can hear mention of Walter Johnson and Babe Ruth, as if Tom Seaver and Joe Torre on the field were interchangeable with any players at any time or any place.

Lang Field is within walking distance or a short cab ride from the downtown hotels where so many of the older tourists stay, because that's where they've always stayed. The Cardinals used to stay at the sprawling Vinoy Hotel on the bayfront with its pitch-and-putt golf course and genteel air. When Bob

Gibson reported to his first spring training, he went to the desk of the Vinoy and was told there was a room reserved for him at the home of a black family. A few blocks closer to Lang Field is the Soreno Hotel where the Yankees used to stay. Elston Howard reported there as the first black man to play for the Yankees and was given a note directing him to the home of a black doctor.

That part of St. Pete has changed. At the Hilton, all the Mets can stay under one roof. That the black players with families—the Mets have never had many black players—prefer to stay in the skimpy hotel quarters while the white players with families find resort apartments is another issue.

What hasn't changed much is that there are still a lot of people with very little to do in St. Pete. They aren't working, they don't play golf, and a lot of them don't have very much money. For them, baseball is inexpensive and so comfortable. "A simple pleasure, like what life used to be," said a guest of the Vinoy. He said he was sixty-nine but that looked to be his baseball age.

There's a game at Lang Field almost every day in March, with either the Mets or Cardinals as home team, and John Hennessey is there often. "Have you ever been at the Vinoy?" he explained. "There's nothing to do in the daytime."

In the stands, a small boy is sitting next to an elderly man. Perhaps the boy is a grandson visiting on his Easter vacation and it's his first ball game. "It was a chance to bring the little fellow today," said H. Hitchcock of nearby Clearwater. "It kind of makes you feel young again."

Not everybody involved here needs to feel young again. Some of them already are. "I got a wake-up call at five this morning," Rube Walker complained.

Joe Pignatano, who was standing nearby, corrected him: "Five-fifteen."

On his way in last night, Pignatano spied the wake-up sheet on the front desk of the Hilton. When the clerk wasn't looking, Pignatano wrote some names next to some very early times.

Seaver, Stone, Apodaca, and Simpson pitched in the game and the Cardinals beat the Mets, 6–5. Seaver pitched a nice three innings, allowing one run and reporting no sign of the tenderness in his shoulder. Apodaca's three innings were perfect. Simpson gave up a run in his inning. He was the "backup" pitcher, in case somebody needed help. It was an opportunity, but it wasn't flattering.

Simpson got the opportunity because Stone's three innings' worth of pitches were used up in two innings. The first two batters hit a triple and a single, and the third drilled a shot into Stone's midsection for an uncomfortable out. He hit the next batter and was touched for two more singles with the last two outs coming on the bases. As general manager Bob Scheffing put it, "He ain't fooled anybody yet."

MARCH 11

As if life weren't difficult enough for Craig Swan and Tommy Moore, just pitching in their first game of the spring, they had to do it with a handicap. Neither of them was permitted to throw a slider today and that was an effective pitch for them in the minor leagues. They had instructions to work on a curveball instead.

"It's too early for a slider," Rube Walker said. "It's too easy to hurt yourself with it if you're not ready. And I want them to work on their other stuff. Swan, he'll cut out throwing the curve altogether, if you let him." It was like getting two little boys to take their awful-tasting medicine because it was good for them.

Swan, a right-hander, needs a curve to get left-handed hitters out. His fastball and slider aren't enough to get him by in the big leagues. Moore, also right-handed, needs another pitch, they think. He wasn't told of the restriction until he went to the bullpen to warm up.

Harry Parker already throws the curve quite well. It's his

best pitch. He was able to pitch the middle three innings of the ten-inning 3–2 victory over the Dodgers and consider it exercise. "I got to work more on my curve," he said. He grinned.

That left Moore and Swan to examine their efforts and read whatever they could find into it. "It was good for him, not necessarily good for me," Moore said.

Swan pitched his three innings with two hits and an unearned run. Moore's three innings lasted only two innings. He wasn't charged with any runs, but he gave up three hits, walked two, and fell behind, three-and-oh, on another. If Swan pitches well his next time, then today can be included as a plus. If he pitches poorly next time, he'll be even. Moore will have to overcome this one or slip off among the pitchers who don't pitch.

"It pissed me off to come out after two innings," Moore said. "I thought I needed to go out there one more time. I felt myself trying to bump up on a couple of pitches."

Pitchers in Moore's situation often try to throw the ball harder than they can. The effect is a fastball that flattens out and a curve that hangs high, instead of breaking down.

Swan was just as uncertain. "I was kind of excited," he said "I threw too hard." Both hits were off curves that hung. "I hope they don't continue not letting me throw the slider," he said.

All the explanations and instructions are very esoteric. What counts most is results, which do not call for long years of baseball experience to interpret. "My wife doesn't know the difference between a slider and a curveball," Swan said. "I think she did know, but she forgot. She knows, if they don't get any runs, that's good."

Tomorrow Swan and Moore will talk and compare impressions. After running his laps in the outfield, Swan went back to Huggins-Stengel and didn't see Moore pitch.

They'll talk about the concept of the slider, and how Moore wasn't given his instructions until he got to the bullpen. There always seems to be some kind of gap in communications around the Mets.

"They don't tell me anything," Moore said. "They just tell me to go and pitch. Is that good or bad? I don't know."

What Moore did know was that he hadn't pitched to a batter for five days, and two innings wasn't time enough to get both a new pitch and himself in order. "I know what he means," Parker said, remembering his own experiences of last spring. "When you got to pitch to stay and they won't let you pitch . . ."

Parker could think analytically about his curveball needing work. "I'm lazy with it now," he said. "That has to be my first priority."

Calling anything a first priority is a luxury to Moore. "That's for veterans," he said. "This is the hardest pitching staff there is to break into. A rookie, you've got to go out for the first fucking time and throw your brains out."

In one of those little breaks that crop up, Bob Miller got to pitch two innings and did well. "Just fastballs and some palmballs," he said nonchalantly. He was the backup pitcher and might not have pitched at all, but Moore was cut short and a run in the last of the ninth sent the game into extra innings. The Mets scored in the tenth and Miller had a winning streak—two in a row as a Met, dating back to the next to last day of the 1962 season.

John Glass took two cortisone shots in his shoulder. Once he could throw the hell out of the ball, but he has had a sore arm and that's like having a prison record. His arm may be perfectly sound, but people will always consider him suspect merchandise.

"You're supposed to report everything," Glass said, "and once you do, you're on the shit list. Every scout in the world knows two years ago you had a bad arm."

George Stone's elbow hurts. He said it was a kind of bruise. "I didn't warm up enough," he said.

MARCH 12

Hank Webb remembers when there were two Bob Millers on the team: the righty we have back again and a lefty who just faded away. Webb remembers how the Mets won 40 and lost 120 games that year and how a pitcher named Craig Anderson lost two games in one day. "It was the kind of thing that made the Mets great," Webb said. "They had the ability to be so inept. Everybody related to them. Everybody wanted to see somebody as inept as he was." Webb understands things like that. He's a semester short of a degree in sociology from New Paltz State in New York and on paper he's no dummy.

When the Red Sox' skinny outfielder Juan Beniquez hit Webb's pitch in the third inning and the cowhide cover tore open, the first reaction was to blame Webb. "I thought it was a joke," said Bud Harrelson, who fielded the flapping ball at shortstop. "I thought, 'I'll be a son of a gun, he threw the rosin bag.' Hank Webb was pitching. I was sure it wasn't a ball."

It was in keeping with the image the Mets have of Webb. They talk about how Webb needs to concentrate more. They accuse him of being naturally left-handed and Webb is right-handed.

A year ago he was driving to spring training from his home on Long Island. He got from Copiague to Brooklyn, had a flat tire, and was two days late reporting.

After last season, too much of which was spent waiting for a chance that never came to pitch in a game with the Mets, he was asked if he wanted to make up the lost time by playing winter ball. Webb said it sounded like a good idea, so farm director Joe McDonald asked where Webb would like to play. "Where are the best beaches?" Webb is said to have replied.

Inevitably, he is likened to Dick Selma, the pitcher who was nicknamed "Mortimer Snerd," for Charlie McCarthy's hayseed companion. Selma was rooming with Danny Frisella one spring when the Mets' hotel was the Colonial Inn. Frisella had brought with him from San Francisco a lead weight that had been used on a fishing net. The weight was just about the size of a baseball, and Frisella used to stretch the muscles of his arm with the lead ball in his hand. One day Frisella went for a haircut and left the ball in the room with Selma, who was always experimenting with his motion or a new pitch or something. When Frisella returned, Selma had all the pillows propped up at the head of the bed and was working on something new. "Watch this," Selma said to Frisella, then threw his pitch. It missed the pillows and the headboard and went right through both sides of the wall into the next room, leaving a hole as clean as that made by a World War II German 88.

Selma and Frisella rearranged the furniture in the room to cover the hole and finally wound up hanging a picture at waist-height over the hole. When the chambermaid inquired, Selma explained, "We just like it that way."

Webb is fully aware of the line on his concentration. "Some people project their ideas into your head," he said. "They don't know what they're thinking about; how can they know what you're thinking?" Then he shrugged and said, "So many people have said that. They're not trying to make me paranoid. There must be some validity." There is a suspicion that Webb deliberately plays the flake to be in some kind of vogue. "No," he said, "to be in vogue today is not to be in vogue."

Webb had had a cup of coffee with the Mets last season but it was more like a demi-tasse. He spilled it. He was recalled from Tidewater on April 27 and sent back on May 11. His first pitch was a home run. He pitched only once more after that. There is some merit to his argument that he shouldn't have been brought up if that was all the Mets intended to do with him.

With those two weeks shot, Webb compiled an 8–9 record at Tidewater, but he says he actually pitched better than that. "I was 6–6 and gave no earned runs in my last six games and ended up 8–9. No earned runs," he said.

What no earned runs? "Well, hardly any," Webb said. Then he laughed. He remembered one game in which he gave up seven unearned runs . . .

After pitching the first three innings of the 3–1 loss to the Red Sox, the smile was rueful. Webb was the starter, which means something, but the first two Boston runs were charged to him, which means something else. The first two hits were scratchy and can be written off, but when Webb was put to the test, he failed. With runners on second and third, he could have escaped from the jam and helped himself. Instead, one run scored on a sacrifice fly and another on a single. "I don't think I did as well as most of the rest of us," he said.

MARCH 13, DAYTONA BEACH

One of the nice things about being a pitcher is that you don't have to take the long bus trips on the days you're not scheduled to pitch. You get your workout on a double-time schedule and are finished for the day. One of the not-so-nice things is that if it's your turn to pitch, you make the trip when anybody who's anybody has a way out of it. The Yankees used to joke that Yogi Berra never made a trip to Fort Myers.

In the spring almost all the trips are bus trips. They are unpleasant reminders of the days in the low minors when all the trips were by bus. They are long, inconvenient times spent sitting in one place punctuated by tasteless lunches from paper bags.

The bus and the lunches left Huggins-Stengel Field at seven thirty this morning for the four-hour ride to Daytona Beach and the game with the Expos. Ted Martinez played shortstop and Lute Barnes second base, and Jon Matlack, Jerry Koosman, and Tug McGraw pitched.

Don't blame the pitchers for the 4–3 loss. Teddy Martinez played Bud Harrelson's shortstop position and made two errors, causing three unearned runs off Matlack. Koosman and McGraw pitched comfortably and well.

Having Matlack and Koosman pitching in the same game produces an interesting comparison and contrast in careers and personalities. The future that once was bright and shiny for Koosman and will never be realized is now the hope for Matlack. That's what being a pitcher means. Matlack is twenty-four and the number two pitcher behind Seaver. Koosman is thirty. When Koosman was Matlack's age, he threw, the ball jumped, and the hitter blinked. When hitters are that good at that age, they just get better as they mature, like good wine. Koosman had to completely remake himself as a pitcher. When his arm broke down, he had to remake his head as well.

"You can't conceive how intricate pitching is until you start to lose it," Koosman said. What Koosman lost was the kind of super stuff Seaver has. He won nineteen games in 1968 and was narrowly beaten out for Rookie of the Year by Johnny Bench. Seaver, who was Rookie of the Year in 1967, won sixteen games in 1968. That year, Koosman set Met records for victories, ERA, and shutouts and was the winning pitcher in the first home opener the Mets ever won.

There were exaggerated stories of how Koosman used to pitch to his brother in the barn in Appleton, Minn., and the tale of how he was overlooked in the free agent draft and uncovered while pitching in the Army. It seems that his catcher at Fort Bliss in 1964 was the son of an usher at the Polo Grounds, where the Mets played their first two seasons. The catcher wrote of Koosman in letters home, the usher contacted the front office and the Mets followed it up. Red Murff, the scout who found Nolan Ryan in a small Texas town, signed Koosman on his discharge from the Army. (Note that Murff asked for a little more porridge and now does his scouting for the Expos.)

"Koos was just a crazy country boy then," recalled minor-league pitching coach Bill Connors, who was a pitcher teetering between making the Mets and recognizing the end of his career at the time. "He would just go out there and throw," Connors said. "He wasn't thinking, just throwing. If somebody was a fastball-hitter and cracked one nine miles off him, Koos would watch the ball sail out and then throw up another one harder than the one before. You couldn't tell him anything."

There were older pitchers on the Mets then and, in the brotherhood of pitchers, they gave him the best of advice even though he was moving them out. Koosman is the first to admit he didn't listen. With slight difference in style, it was like the time Duke Snider, near the end of his fine career, offered hitting tips to eighteen-year-old Ed Kranepool and was told, "You're not doing so good yourself."

"Bob Shaw and Don Cardwell would always try to give me advice," Koosman said with the wisdom of his age. "Cardwell, he could really pick out the little things I would do wrong right away. But many times with young pitchers you won't listen to them. You tell them, 'I'm not like you. I don't have the same delivery. I throw differently.'"

Before Koosman could follow up on his success of 1968, he found the things that happen to pitchers had happened to him. He was breezing along on a chilly day in Montreal in late April when he heard a funny sound. It was his elbow recommending that he find a different way to pitch or find a different way to make a living.

After an idle month, Koosman came back to pitch brilliantly as the Mets performed their miracle of 1969. But he suffered repeated arm problems and missed a lot of pitching time the next three years. When he pitched he was reluctant to throw hard. Once a pitcher has a sore arm, he never forgets it. What he has to do is find a way to put the memory aside. Koosman kept saying that adversity was making him a better pitcher—when his arm was better, he'd have mastered the breaking stuff to go with his fastball. He does see himself as a slick young man. Other people were saying his arm was already sound—not as strong as it once was, but good enough.

Last year, Koosman put it all together again at the right time. He won five of his last six decisions, plus one in the playoff and one in the Series. Nobody ever doubted his competitiveness. "I pitched the best ball of my career last season." Koosman said. "There were only three or four times where I didn't have it."

There were those things he learned. He can pitch inside to right-handed hitters as well as any lefty around. "He's the meanest lefty I ever hit against," says right-handed Ron Santo, who spent a number of years trying to solve Koosman for the Cubs.

Yet, Koosman won fourteen games and lost fifteen last year.

He hasn't won as many as he's lost since 1970. "He can throw hard again, but he doesn't think he can," says Bob Gibson of the Cardinals.

MARCH 14, ST. PETERSBURG

Every day seems to build a better case for Bob Apodaca. He goes about things on the mound in a positive manner all the time. He fields a ball and makes the difficult throw to second for the force instead of settling for the timid out at first. "He takes charge," Berra said.

Apodaca finished up with two scoreless innings as the Mets beat the Tigers, 3–2, and that gives him a string of five scoreless innings this spring. That reinforces the judgment of last September when he was thrown into the heat of the pennant race.

Apodaca may be the last one to realize what he's doing here. He's friendly and smiles often, but he speaks so softly and the smiles appear to be forced, as if he were afraid to tell himself he was making the team. Maybe there's the memory of what happened in September that keeps him from positive thinking or maybe it's the fact that his whole career is built on rejection. Baseball is full of people who worry when they're going bad—and when they're going good, worry that it can't last forever. "I always have doubt creeping into my mind," Apodaca said.

Apodaca is gradually being accepted into the court of his peers. He has a nickname. They call him "Daca." Seaver appears to have arrived at the contraction. At least, he uses it often, biting on the first letter.

Apodaca is slightly built in a time when pitchers are the giants of the team. He's five-eleven and 170 pounds and is a sinkerball thrower on a staff of power pitchers. Maybe some of his shy demeanor comes from growing up in a Mexican-Portuguese family in Los Angeles. Maybe some of it comes from the fact that he had a dream shattered once before.

It was only three years ago that he was completely rejected. He went from Cerritos Junior College to Los Angeles State, majored in police science, and, after four years of school, the free agent draft came and went and nobody wanted him. Even in junior college he failed to impress. That's when he learned about worrying. "Then the coach said I had too many minuses," Apodaca recalled. "He said I couldn't hit or run good enough to be an infielder, so he was making me a pitcher. That's when my dream of making the major leagues almost ended, because I wasn't a pitcher."

He became enough of a pitcher to be named to the league All-Star team both years at LA State, but several of his friends were selected in the 1971 draft and Apodaca stayed home. He found games where he could, and scouts from several teams dropped by to watch him pitch. "I sat by the phone for a week," Apodaca said.

Then the Mets farm in Visalia ran into a pitching bind. The manager called the minor-league office in New York and begged for a pitcher, any pitcher who could pitch immediately. There was Apodaca waiting at home just a couple of hours' driving time downstate and the Mets decided he was worth a chance. "I knew they'd release me in a month if I was only mediocre," Apodaca said.

He promptly started and pitched well. Then he pitched well again. And by the time the season ended he had a 7–1 record and was established as one of the better prospects in the organization.

By his third season, Apodaca was getting attention as a relief pitcher with a 1.80 earned-run average. But the Mets were in the midst of their pennant run so they told him to go home for a month until the winter league opened. Nine days later Harry Parker hurt his hand and Apodaca was rushed from Los Angeles and shoved into a game against Pittsburgh in the ninth inning. The Mets were three and one half games behind. Apodaca pitched to two batters, walked both, and one scored. And Apodaca, with his earned-run average of infinity, was not called on the bullpen telephone again.

"I thought about walking those two batters in Pittsburgh whenever spring training was mentioned." Apodaca said. "I keep asking myself if I can get major-league hitters out." To give Apodaca something more to think about, his wife is home in Paramount, Calif., expecting to give birth to their first child any day.

Seaver started and was hit for two runs on four hits in the first inning before settling down. Stone did well for three innings and his arm appears well again.

MARCH 15, ST. PETERSBURG

There are still nineteen games remaining, but things have begun to shake out in the pitching derby. Swan and Apodaca have opened up a gap on the field and Moore and Webb have fallen behind. Swan pitched three strong innings in the 3–1 loss to the Red Sox, striking out four and allowing two hits. Now his first appearance, which Berra called meaningless, takes on significance.

There was a touch of luck involved this time. Both Boston hits were in Swan's first inning. Luis Aparicio singled; with two out, Carl Yastremski also singled, but Aparicio turned too far around second base and was the third out.

In Moore's three innings, he walked three and gave up two runs. While Swan had Bud Harrelson at shortstop, Moore had Ted Martinez, who didn't come up with the infield single that began the two-run inning for Boston. Then Moore had the challenge of pitching to Rick Miller, a big-leaguer last season, with two runs in scoring position. That's the kind of test the decision-makers look for. Miller singled two runs home.

The pre-judgments are being supported. Berra and Rube Walker say they are equal-opportunity employers but some people have more equal opportunity. Swan and Moore have pitched in the same games both times. But Swan has started against the regulars with regulars behind him. Moore has finished up with the scrubbinies in the game. The distinctions are subtle but meaningful.

When Berra was asked about Swan and Apodaca having taken the inside track, the manager muttered something that sounded like "ubble, gubble, unless the roof falls on them." He also said, "It's just the first week." That's a disclaimer that leaves room for a change of mind or an injury. No manager wants to have to re-examine a player who thinks he's already disqualified.

Another aspect of the pitchers' work was involved in the treatment of Benny Ayala, the fading phenom. He has four hits in twenty-four at bats. The pitchers are probing and may have uncovered the fatal flaws: the breaking ball outside and the fastball inside. Ayala hit a home run yesterday, but his critics point out that it was off a high change-up that he's not likely to see again.

"They've been pitching him the hardest of our players," Berra said. "That's good. If he learns to handle it, good. If he doesn't learn . . . ," Berra made a flicking motion that looked like an upside-down wave goodbye.

The Boston pitcher was Juan Marichal, now thirty-five years old after fourteen seasons with the Giants. He has won more games than any active pitcher, one more than Bob Gibson, but is struggling to hold a job and his $140,000 salary. Only one of his last four seasons was good.

He doesn't have the good fastball he used to throw but he still has his high-kicking motion and the hitter never knows where the ball is going to come from. Sometimes he throws over the top—overhand—sometimes sidearm or someplace in between. Sometimes he doesn't draw his arm all the way back but comes forward quickly, before the hitter expects it. That gives him what the hitters feel must be a thousand pitches.

Often pitchers can fool the hitters in a new league with that kind of stuff for a while. He baffled the young Mets for three innings. A new league can be a new lease on life. Certainly, the old lease wasn't going to be renewed by the Giants. Charlie Fox had Marichal in the bullpen and the Giants wanted to cut his salary by $30,000.

MARCH 17, VERO BEACH

This is the place mass production baseball got its start. Branch Rickey invented the farm system with the Cardinals and honed it to perfection with the Dodgers. The players live in barracks left over from the Navy in World War II. Wherever you look on the several fields there are people in Dodger uniforms playing baseball. The numbers on their backs are astronomical. The Dodgers do things like running sprints against the clock, and they actually work in the sliding pit on nearly extinct arts of the game.

Jerry Koosman, Tug McGraw, and Hank Webb pitched today. Koosman gave up three runs in the first inning and then worked three scoreless innings. McGraw gave up four runs in one inning. And Hank Webb balked, a lapse of composure he couldn't afford.

McGraw isn't advising anybody "Ya gotta believe" this spring. After the windup he had last season, he believes more than ever; he just doesn't say it. Not even for big money. "I haven't used the phrase a single time this year," he said.

In an era of total exploitation, when Tom Seaver has sold his name to a whole publishing industry, McGraw turned down several thousand dollars–he isn't saying just how much—to say "Ya gotta believe" in Eastern Airlines commercials. He agreed to do promotional work for the company but not anything connected with the phrase.

McGraw wasn't about to stop the airline from exploiting it, even if he had wanted to. Eastern is using the line without McGraw's smile and strong jaw. It was just an expression that had been used often before but last year it was attached to something that, in retrospect, bore belief.

But it was last year's phrase. "It has served its purpose," McGraw has said. "I guess it sticks in your throat after a while. You gotta believe it."

This year's phrase will never get out of spring training. It demonstrates the difference between something spontaneous and the product of a publicity man who's looking for something with alliteration or at least rhyme. "You gotta believe more—in '74" is the party line.

McGraw's refusal to sell his part of the expression he says was born in desperation, and the way he survived the circumstances that spawned it, are strong indications of his growth the last few years. For all of his blithe spirit, McGraw's emotions are a delicate balance. They are still very close to the surface, a violation of the ball player's code. By definition, a professional is not supposed to display his emotions; better still, he shouldn't have any emotions.

Especially a relief pitcher. McGraw spends his whole working life walking a tightrope across one Niagara or another. If he makes one mistake the ball game is lost. The rules of the game insist that a relief pitcher put past failure out of his mind. If he doesn't have confidence, he doesn't have anything. McGraw has too much emotion. He can think himself into a slump. A lot of people wonder how he can keep coming into sudden-death situations and be so effective.

The most endearing thing about McGraw is that he reacts to his performance. Like most of the rest of us, McGraw is elated by his own success and depressed by failure. His wife, Phyllis, says she can tell how the game has gone with little more than a look and the sound of his voice when he gets home from a game.

"When he's pitched well and the press has been all around him, he's all out to here," she said. She spread her hands to indicate the glow she could see around her husband. "When he's done poorly, his chin is around the ground," she said.

When he's been bad, he remembers it the next time he pitches. Seaver observed McGraw's slump last season and said he thought McGraw was looking in the wrong place for the solution that was inside him all the time.

McGraw is too complex to change on demand. He's still torn between his mother and father, who have been divorced since he was a little boy. When the Mets play in San Francisco, where he grew up, he has Lou Niss leave tickets for both of

58 THE PITCHING STAFF

them. He makes sure his father's tickets are on one side of the field and the tickets for his mother and her husband are on the other.

One time in 1969, the legendary championship year, McGraw's father didn't keep a breakfast date at the hotel and Tug waited so long he missed the bus. He spent a long time before the game curled up in his locker with tears on his cheeks.

Hodges called McGraw into his office and spoke to him about handling himself as a man. For those few minutes, McGraw had a father and pulled himself together. He performed brilliantly the rest of that year. In the clubhouse after the Mets won the final game of the World Series, Tug poured champagne over the head of Frank Edwin McGraw, Sr. Tug said it was the happiest day of his father's life. He may have been speaking for himself at the same time.

Five years later, with 300 relief appearances and a reputation as perhaps the best relief pitcher in baseball to his credit, Tug hasn't changed that much as a person. He's learned to keep his emotions from extremes, but he hasn't subdued them entirely.

When he fell into a deep slump last season, saving only two games from mid-May to mid-July, McGraw had very little reserve remaining. The team depends on him to preserve the few runs it makes. Even the best relief pitchers have off-years. Some have had alternately good and bad years. He had never been through a time like that before. A pitcher like Ray Sadecki, who has been through bad times, learns to ride them out. He understands that his existence doesn't change from day to day.

But McGraw bounced back. In a remarkable stretch that involved nineteen appearances and forty-one innings pitched, he saved twelve games, won five and posted an earned-run average of 0.88. Almost as $2 + 2 = 4$, the Mets came back from last place in the last month and got as far as the seventh game of the World Series.

MARCH 18, ST. PETERSBURG

The first time the Mets and Yankees play each spring is an event. The other five times they meet will be ordinary exhibition games—unless one team is embarrassing the other. The first time they ever met in Spring training the Yankees were the World Champions riding the crest of their dynasty. Nobody really knew how awful the Mets were, except maybe Casey Stengel.

Stengel, who had been fired by the Yankees after the 1960 World Series, saved his one professional pitcher, Roger Craig, to start that game. The Mets played it as if it were a regular-season game—or something more. Stengel carried on in the dugout from start to finish. And when the Mets won the game, Stengel carried on in the clubhouse and the pressroom as if the season were a success, right then. That night the New York *Daily News* put it in big type on page one: "Mets Beat Yanks."

Now the cycle has come all the way around. The Mets are up and the Yankees are down, but hardly any of these Yankees were around when the situation was reversed. Practically the only exception is Elston Howard, the Yankee coach. When he was an All-Star catcher on championship Yankee teams, Howard regarded the Mets with total disdain. To him Choo Choo Coleman was worth only a laugh as a human being.

Now Howard is on the defensive. Of all things, the Yankees will be playing this season and next in Shea Stadium as unwilling and unwelcome guests of the Mets. "I'll tell you what," Howard said. "I'll bet you, if we get off to a good start, we'll outdraw them." He did not look for somebody to hold the money.

Now this game has its touch of a neighborhood rivalry. Ron Blomberg of the Yankees took his first look at Jerry Grote since last season and pronounced, "You're uglier." "It's fun," Blomberg said. "It's a rivalry. You can't get away from that."

By coincidence, of course, the pitchers turned out to be Matlack for the Mets and George Medich for the Yankees.

Medich is at the brink of becoming the number one man on the Yankee staff and if Matlack continues to develop as he did last year, he'll be close to Seaver. The game was scoreless until the Mets scratched out the only run of the game in the last of the eighth.

Matlack was dazzling with five strikeouts in five innings. Apodaca pitched two more scoreless innings; he hasn't been scored upon yet.

But the rivalry seemed to be lost on Medich, who pitched five innings for the Yankees. "I would have preferred to have done it against the Orioles or the Red Sox," he said. "To establish dominance." And that man is going to be a doctor.

MARCH 19, ST. PETERSBURG

The same qualities that make Seaver a great pitcher—intelligence, extremely hard work, singleness of purpose, and total confidence—may someday be his downfall. Seaver pitches his ass off every time he pitches. It's the same whether it's a scoreless game or he has a five-run lead, which the Mets don't give a pitcher very often. Seaver never learned to pitch an easy game. He doesn't know how to let the batter hit the ball.

In his wisdom, he will throw a type of pitch in a comfortable situation that the batter will never see when he can turn a game, but it will always be aimed at the black edge of the plate. Seaver once put his name on a book entitled *The Perfect Game*, which focused on the night in 1969 when he took a perfect game into the ninth inning. He's constantly trying to pitch a perfect game. "He's always trying to throw the perfect pitch," former Met Danny Frisella once observed. He's like Rick Martin in "Young Man With a Horn"—forever searching for the note beyond his reach.

Seaver has struck out 200 or more batters six consecutive years. Only three other men have ever done that and nobody has done it more than seven times. Striking out all those batters is a hell of a lot of work. Not only does it demand more pitches, it demands more taxing pitches even if Seaver does pitch on four days' rest.

"That's why he wears down at the end of the year," Ed Kranepool suggested. From August 15, when Seaver's record was 15–6, he won four and lost four while the Mets were winning twenty-nine and losing fourteen.

A more pointed illustration came in the first game of the playoff against the Reds. For seven innings Seaver was absolutely magnificent and the Mets had a 1–0 lead. But in the eighth inning he gave up a home run to Pete Rose that tied the score, and in the ninth Johnny Bench hit a home run to beat Seaver, 2–1. Both were hit off inside pitches. Seaver works on the inside of the plate and a hard pitch on the hands is the most difficult pitch for even the best hitter to handle. But that same pitch, if it isn't inside quite enough, or if it isn't quite hard enough, is the pitch the hitters take downtown.

Bob Gibson, who has made a nice living getting the best hitters out with a baseball, says there was no way Seaver should have thrown a pitch a hitter like Bench could have pulled at a time like that. Bench can hit a home run off an outside pitch, too, but the risk is that much greater with an inside pitch—especially when Seaver had already pitched eight punishing innings on top of a 290-inning season. But when he's throwing good, Seaver feels he can strike out any hitter.

"It's one of the most difficult things, to realize during a game when you begin to lose something," he said. "I missed my spots on those pitches. Human error." But that's the point. Even Seaver is subject to human error.

He is a great self-analyst. When he went through a difficult period a few years ago, he wondered if he hadn't fallen into a pitching pattern that was too predictable. He did some rethinking and quickly emerged as a dominant pitcher again.

Now he says he's done his rethinking already. He says he's thinking of changing speeds more than he has, but he's always had difficulty throwing a change of pace. If he mastered it, it would give the hitters a lot more to think about and it would conserve some of Seaver, too.

The specter of the decline of Robin Roberts is always present. When Roberts was at his best, all he threw was a fastball. It moved so well, he had such good control and he was so strong, that fastball was all he needed. People told him he should develop another pitch but while he was still winning he never did. He was a twenty-game winner six times in a row with the Phillies, who gave a pitcher less help than the Mets do. But the last time was at the age of twenty-nine and he was never a dominant pitcher after that. Roberts didn't master anything other than a fastball until his career was apparently over and he made a comeback with Baltimore. Seaver is twenty-nine.

A mark of Seaver as a pitcher is that he's been able to recognize early in a game when he doesn't have his best stuff and to adjust. That's how he's managed to be such a consistent winner over his seven seasons. The others on the team all feel that no matter how bad things are going, Seaver's turn is going to come up and he'll give them a game to stop the slide. "My pride comes in winning games," he said. "I'm paid to win without good stuff. In many ways, that's more rewarding. There's more mental work, more pitching than striking out thirteen."

Now Seaver is conscious that it's harder to get in shape than it ever was. "It seems to take a little longer," he said. "It takes harder work. The work begins to fatigue me more than it did. I'm trying to do a little more work, a little more running and exercise."

Maybe he's reached a point in his career where he should revise his style. There are some pitchers who are constantly working on a pitch so they have it ready for the year they need it. Warren Spahn perfected a screwball years before he needed it. A good change would make Seaver's fastball better, so would a better curve.

Seaver is always studying something on the field. "By watching Sadecki, I've learned how much you can do with a curve," he said. Seaver has developed a sinking fastball as a companion to the explosive rising fastball he throws on the best days. "If I have to pitch an entire season with the sinking fastball, I will," Seaver said. "I throw it fifty per cent of the time already."

Seaver has all of this filed away in his mind under the category of Food for Thought. "They have valid points," Seaver says about criticism regarding the Bench home run. "I've thought about it."

He doesn't think he's reached the Robin Roberts point yet. "I'm not going to change what I do for a living based on that one experience," Seaver said. He also said, "There's a human, emotional element." The emotional element in Seaver still tells him "Right on, full speed ahead."

Yesterday he threw five good innings against the Reds. Maybe he can get through the spring without his usual shoulder tightness.

In a "B" game, George Stone pitched $5\frac{1}{3}$ innings against the Cardinals without an earned run. Maybe his arm has come around.

MARCH 21, ST. PETERSBURG

Ray Sadecki is scheduled to pitch in a "B" game tomorrow and that's just about right for him. For some pitchers, the "B" game is the wrong place to be. It means being relegated to a meaningless game, in which a pitcher can only look bad and never good. A generation ago the Brooklyn Dodgers used to have a tall left-handed pitcher named Paul Minner who hated "B" games because he usually had to play first base and didn't get a chance to display himself as a pitcher.

But Sadecki can ride over all those objections the way he handles his weak eyesight or the Polish jokes in the clubhouse. He wears contact lenses when he pitches and he wears them in the shower. He doesn't take them out until he returns to his locker and has his eyeglasses in his hands. One afternoon the rain began to fall as the Mets were leaving the clubhouse and Tug McGraw took his leather sun shade—really just a headband with a visor—to Sadecki's locker and announced that it was a Polish rain hat.

Sadecki is thirty-three and it was ten years ago that he was a twenty-game winner for the pennant-winning Cardinals. After the next season he was traded to the pitcher-hungry Giants for Orlando Cepeda, who won the Most Valuable Player award for St. Louis in 1967.

Sadecki never won more than twelve games for the Giants. The rumor was that the biggest Polish joke in San Francisco was Ray Sadecki. He learned to live with the jokes and the disappointment and now the Polish jokes on the Mets are mainly the ones Sadecki tells. Koosman is most often the butt of the jokes, not because Koosman is Polish—he isn't—but because Sadecki tells them. Koosman and Sadecki are very close.

At banquets Sadecki likes to tell about the time Koosman dreamed he was eating a giant marshmallow and woke up to find his pillow was missing. He likes to tell about the fictitious opening of Koosman's farm equipment dealership in Morris, Minn. "There was this big banner stretched across the main street," Sadecki says, "that said: 'Jerry Koosman stands behind all his farm implements except the manure spreader.'"

On the Mets, Sadecki is admired for his competitiveness and for his sense of humor. He is one of those rare pitchers who can sit without pitching for two weeks and give a creditable performance on demand. He is willing to stay ready and wait his turn. Harry Dalton, the general manager of the Angels, calls Sadecki "a staff-saver."

When the Cardinals first signed him for a bonus of $50,000, which was a lot of money in 1958, Sadecki opened a coffee shop in downtown St. Pete. "Then the business moved out to Thirty-Fourth Street," Sadecki says. "I sold the coffee shop and business has moved back downtown again."

One thing he is not, is a good spring training pitcher. "I get embarrassed," he said. "The best thing for me is the "B" games. My salvation is that people have tolerated my poor springs. One year I had my usual lousy spring and in my first game in the season, I threw twenty-one pitches against the Phillies and struck out five."

There are two ways to pitch spring training. One is to try to get all the batters out. The other is Sadecki's way. "I've tried it both ways," Sadecki said. "I can be cute and get hit all over the park. The next time I can walk four batters in a row. My job is to get in shape and be ready for the season. That has to be frustrating to the kids."

He's a good athlete. He can run, he can handle a bat and he can field this position. The last time he pitched here, he made a two-base throwing error and the other pitchers have been reminding him of the throw ever since. "There's a good reason," he explained to pitching coach Rube Walker. "All I've done so far is work on catching the comebacker and putting it in the bucket behind the screen."

MARCH 22, ST. PETERSBURG

At what point are you supposed to stop rooting for an athlete to make a comeback and accept the fact that he's had a fine career and it's over? I certainly don't root for Bob Gibson to make more money. But if you dig baseball, you have to want Gibson around. You wince when Dave Schneck and Benny Ayala hit home runs off him in an exhibition game and the Mets get eight runs to beat the Cardinals, 10–0.

Gibson is thirty-eight and he's had a brilliant career. He's won 237 games, more than any other active pitcher. What lament could there be? Except that he's the prototype of the pitcher, the hand-made model from which the Grand Prix racers are fashioned.

His style on the mound is exciting. He gives a big motion with a flamboyant follow-through like the flapping of a giant bird. And at his age he's still an unreconstructed power pitcher, although he works the outside of the plate with his fastball now. But he's tall and his body is hard and lean, and what teammate Joe Torre calls "that fucking fire" is still in his eyes.

Besides age, Gibson is fighting the effects of a torn knee cartilage and surgery early last August. At the time of the injury he had won eleven games, eight of his last twelve decisions, and the Cardinals were in first place. "When he was hurt, I knew it was over," catcher Ted Simmons said this morning.

While he was out, the Cards won twenty and lost thirty-one and finished second to the Mets. Gibson recognized that his absence was more than just the loss of an effective pitcher. "They think they can't win the pennant without me," Gibson said. "I don't think that's the case physically, but there is the factor of what's in their minds."

What's in their minds was exemplified by the work Gibson did to get himself back onto the mound before the season ended. "I heard on the radio one day in the clubhouse that I'd never pitch again," he said. "I said, 'Then what in the world am I wearing myself out throwing on the sidelines for?'"

Simmons and other Cardinals visited Gibson in the hospital and didn't like what they saw. "He looked sixty years old," Simmons said. "There was no way he could come back."

Then Gibson began to pressure the team to let him pitch, but what good to a team in a pennant race was a pitcher who couldn't pitch? Finally, Gibson was announced as the pitcher for the next-to-last day of the season. The team was desperate. "I told my wife to buy all the souvenirs of that game she could because this was his last game," Simmons said.

Gibson pitched six innings, allowed one run, and was the winning pitcher. "I didn't want to go all winter not knowing if I could pitch again," Gibson said. "It was enough reassurance. I wasn't ready to let go, but I would have adjusted to it if I couldn't pitch any more. I'd just do something else, that's all. I wasn't ready then, but that's life."

Gibson would have thrown himself into something. He's done some radio and television broadcasting and owns a piece of a radio station in Omaha. He's also on the board of directors of a new bank in Omaha. Call it a color-blind bank. "I got the idea when I first tried to buy a home," Gibson said. "I was making $50,000 and couldn't get a loan. I got excuses." Gibson and Bill White, then a teammate, made it their business—uncomfortable or not—to show their black faces in previously all-white restaurants in spring training once the barriers began to come down.

Now there's another twist to his life. He and his wife of nearly twenty years were recently divorced. That means his two teen-age daughters who for years suffered with him the indignities of driving through the South to spring training and being told to use the weeds instead of the restrooms won't be around much this season.

Gibson is defiant when he talks about fighting age and injury. He's less defiant about the effects of the loss of family. But that makes the clubhouse his home more than ever. It will intensify his competitiveness on the field.

Joe Torre talks about going to the mound in an All-Star Game to speak to Gibson after years of being ignored because he was on another team. He found Gibson barely communicative. To him, Torre was still on another team in real life and Gibson didn't need friends on other teams.

"I like the competition of pitching," Gibson said. "I'm like that off the field, too. It's not a good way to go through life. I love an argument."

With a salary of $150,000, the competition still turns him on. That's what made a year of playing basketball with the Harlem Globetrotters totally unacceptable. Torre says Gibson doesn't play because he loves to compete; Torre says Gibson plays because he loves to win.

I remember the scene in the Cardinals' clubhouse after the seventh game of the 1967 World Series against the Red Sox, in which Gibson pitched his third complete game win. He was exhausted and in trouble in the eighth inning, but pitched out of it. Later, shortstop Dal Maxvill said he knew Gibson would overcome. "I went to the mound and looked in his eyes," Maxvill said, "and those babies were gleaming." Who can say when he'll be too old to win?

MARCH 23, ST. PETERSBURG

The picture I have of Bob Miller the twenty-three-year-old is a pale-faced youth with a voice that quavered as he sat on a

68 THE PITCHING STAFF

table in the lusterless clubhouse of the Polo Grounds and answered questions after losing his eighth or ninth or tenth consecutive game. A kind of terror seemed to surround him.

Twelve years later Bob Miller says, "I knew from the first day it was going to be a fun year."

I don't think anybody on the team knew it was going to be a fun year from the first day. That remained for the newspaper men who were there and felt the lunacy of the situation. One early day Stan Issacs of *Newsday*, after meeting with all the unidentifiable faces, asked coach Solly Hemus, "How's Walter Plinge doing?" And Hemus said Plinge was doing just fine. There wasn't any Walter Plinge on that team, but how was Hemus to know? And what difference did it make?

For the players there was a whole lot of uncomfortable times, especially for the younger ones who didn't understand that treating the nature of their losses with lightness was a whole lot more comfortable than it would have been for the press to take them all seriously. Of all the employees of the Mets, only Stengel seemed to recognize the folly immediately.

But Miller is thirty-five now and he's the most traveled player in history. He's been with twelve teams, the Padres and the Mets twice. Only Lindy McDaniel, among active pitchers, has appeared in more games. Miller has had his degree of success. He's been on five championship teams and pitched in three World Series.

He remembers walking into the Mets' clubhouse in 1962 and seeing faces he didn't recognize, people culled from eight National League organizations in the expansion draft, plus some picked up from the American League. "Who on the Mets could have made you feel at home?" Miller said. "It was all a grouping of outsiders. Nobody was a Met yet."

Miller had been a bonus player with the Cardinals. The Mets drafted him for $125,000. He found Jim Hickman and Chris Cannizzaro from the St. Louis organization and that made them friends in the way ball players find friends. At least they knew his name. Red Ruffing, the pitching coach, didn't know who Miller was. Stengel called him "Nelson."

"I sat in the clubhouse with the press guide figuring out who the people were," Miller said. "My uniform didn't fit. This year it does." The press guide in 1962 wasn't very good either. The Mets had an expansion publicity man, too.

With some probing, Miller recalled his early impressions of Casey Stengel. It was the first time Miller or any of those players had heard Stengelese in person. Stengel said "butcher boy" when he wanted a ball chopped on the ground to advance a runner. He said "back up the moving van" when he meant a player was about to be shipped out. "If you took time to think about his expressions, you could figure them out," Miller said.

When the club got to the Polo Grounds, there were billboards at each foul line that promised a boat to the player who hit the signs most often. To some players that meant trying to pull the ball when the situation demanded a ball to the opposite field. Stengel said, "If you want to go to sea, join the Navy." Stengel was an old Navy man. And when players cursed their luck, Stengel said, "Bad luck, your ass. You make your own luck. You'll have bad luck all your life."

The team was full of names that made sense to Mrs. Payson, who had owned a little piece of the Giants before they left town. Miller remembers Richie Ashburn, Gus Bell, and Gil Hodges, who had the names of stars. He remembers how Ashburn used to drive to practice in a 1934 car wearing Bermuda shorts and a cab-driver's cap, both of which just weren't done.

That was the spring Stengel looked out the clubhouse door and saw that someone had left the bats and balls on the ground after finishing with the pitching machine. In great anger Stengel tracked down the culprit and arrived at the locker of Lloyd Flodin, a long-forgotten catcher who never made the team. Stengel directed Flodin, who was completely undressed, to get the equipment. Flodin refused. Stengel insisted in a stronger voice. "Go fuck yourself," Flodin replied. "That's not my job." Stengel repeated his demand and added a very strong threat. "Let me get a towel," Flodin said. But Sengel wasn't going to wait that long. Out went Flodin to get the bats and balls and the intersection of Fifth Street and Fifteenth Avenue, St. Petersburg, Fla., had its first streaker.

"It's amazing how bad we were," Miller said. "I didn't think anybody could be that bad, especially with the names we had. We were all sure we were better than the Cubs and the Phillies."

One of the first jolts came at the expense of pitcher Jay Hook, an engineer who knew exactly why a curveball curved, but couldn't get batters out with his. Stengel let Hook absorb a fearful pounding in an exhibition game. Ten runs in one inning as Miller recalls—actually eight runs in the first five innings and eight more in the sixth. Hook wept afterward. "None of us expected to lose 120 games, Miller said. "Nobody will ever do that again."

Miller lost his first twelve decisions. He won his only game that year in the 159th game of the season. But as Miller says he remembers it, it was a fun year from the beginning.

MARCH 24, TAMPA

John Glass looks so young. His face is round and his hair is fair and he has freckles just like Huckleberry Finn. But he's twenty-six. That's not young for a man who's still a minor-leaguer and has a reputation for hurting himself.

Berra and Walker waited while Glass got in shape and waited when his shoulder got sore and waited while the cortisone shots did their job. Then they put Glass in the game against the Reds in the sixth inning and couldn't wait for him to get out of the eighth inning. When he came out of the game he looked old and very tired. "I'll never catch up," Glass said afterward. "It's not uphill for me any longer, it's all downhill."

It looked like the classic case of the showcase for Glass against the Reds. The Mets have no place for Glass; the Reds are hungry for pitchers. If he pitched well before the eyes of the Reds, they might be interested in making a deal. "We're not trying to showcase him," general manager Bob Scheffing said before the game. "It's just his turn to pitch."

It was the first time Glass had pitched since the previous

September at Tidewater. Nobody told him it was his turn. "I didn't find out I was going to pitch until I read the paper this morning," he said. Physically, it probably didn't make any difference whether Glass knew he was going to pitch or not. Maybe he would have gone to sleep an hour earlier, maybe not. It's a nice courtesy most teams give their pitchers, but Glass isn't one of the Mets' pitchers, is he?

"Maybe somebody—like Atlanta—is coming to look at me," Glass had speculated wistfully. "I know the Braves need pitchers because they have guys that I'm better than who passed me up in the minor leagues."

If it were a showcase, Glass looked like nice goods for two scoreless innings after George Stone left the game with a 5-3 lead. They gave Glass another three runs to work with in the seventh. Glass got two outs in the eighth before the roof fell in. By the time Berra and Walker brought in Bob Miller, Glass' big-league career had disintegrated in a barrage of seven Cincinnati hits and seven runs.

Once, long ago, two young pitchers from Texas named Lynn Nolan Ryan and John Dudley Glass held cigaret lighters to two baseballs and put the charred remains on the desk of Gil Hodges. The balls were inscribed "Texas Heat" for the fire they threw.

Glass was close to making the team in 1968 before he hurt his arm near the end of spring training. He was the last selection by Montreal in the 1968 expansion draft, and in 1971 he hurt his arm again. The Expos released him and the Mets claimed him again. He had the second-best earned-run average in the International League last season, but doesn't have the heat he used to throw.

He has a wife, a son and a daughter and no idea of what he'd do for a living if he weren't a pitcher. "Let's face it." Glass said. "The Mets have passed me by for so long that I know I'm never going to pitch for them. Eight years, four major-league rosters, and I've never pitched a day in the big leagues. I've done just about everything I can to reach the big leagues. Maybe that's why I haven't been able to do anything else."

From the outside, baseball looks like a nice six-month job. But for the struggling people like John Glass, it's six months of pitching in the minor leagues, plus winter after winter in Puerto Rico or Venezuela or Mexico trying to earn a little more money, trying to learn a little more baseball and grasping at the opportunity to show somebody the talent that's there.

He's tried to go to school whenever possible—at Hill Junior College, East Texas State, and Memphis State. "I tried to go to school wherever I was playing but it's hard because the season lasts too long, so sometimes I'd end up pitching winter ball. You've got to feed the family. Let's face it, the whole idea is trying to feed the family."

MARCH 25, LAKELAND

There's a lot that can be learned about a man by observing his family. Sometimes it seems to be an invasion of privacy for a newspaper man to be living in the same motel as the Matlacks. But then, they have nothing to hide.

Jon is at the brink of becoming one of the best pitchers in the league and being paid appropriately. But Jon and Dee were married when there was no assurance they'd ever get as far as spring training in the big time. They spent four of his five seasons together in the minor leagues when the money wasn't very good at all.

There were lessons she hasn't forgotten. She doesn't have to dress for the evening to go to the supermarket. She doesn't have to flaunt her husband's success. She can kid George and Diana Stone about their Louisiana drawls—"Say frawg, Diana" —and make it very gentle. She can tell about the time she stood behind the screen on a night John was the losing pitcher for Raleigh-Durham and threw plum pits at the umpire for the calls he made against her husband.

Matlack spends a lot of time with his children and he often swims in the pool with his own and other children. So do Stone, who has no children, and McGraw, whose children are too young to be in the pool by themselves. In the pool games, Stone is "Sea Monster" and McGraw is "The Tickle Shark."

Much of the hell-raising and the practical joking of the clubhouse has a bite that isn't all humor. That's not Matlack's element. "I like to raise hell, play practical jokes, like the other guys. But I don't get half the fun out of it that they do," he said.

His makeup is reflected in his daughters—Kristin, not yet five and Jenny, not yet three. They have two new friends this spring. Yesterday they also had a box of candy. With a piece of chocolate marshmallow in one hand and two pieces in the other, Kristin climbed the flight of stairs to ring my doorbell and offered the candy to my two children.

Nobody had to remind her of the value of sharing. The atmosphere in the Matlack house had already taught her. There seems to be a great unselfishness about the father, too. Some people see that as a weakness in an athlete. The good ones, they say, think only of themselves. I don't want to think that's necessary.

On the pitching staff, Matlack and Seaver are the closest. They see each other socially in the off-season, too. Their approach to pitching is similar and Seaver appreciates Matlack's interest in learning. But there's a softness to Matlack that Seaver doesn't show. Matlack is much more aware of the feelings of people around him and he makes no attempt to create or maintain an image.

"We're close, although I used to be scared to death of him," Matlack said. "I heard he was like a hostile animal, an ugly person who would spit on rookies. Now, if I have a problem, I go to him. It took me a couple of days to get up the nerve to ask him anything. Then he was always willing to help. That shattered the big bad-guy image.

"I guess I came along at the right time to ask him for help. Before that he didn't feel he had progressed to the point where he could stand on solid ground in helping someone else."

When Matlack's turn came up to pitch in the seventh game of the World Series against the Athletics, the Mets were satisfied. When it was over, even though he lost, Matlack was satisfied, too. I saw the possibility before the Series began," he said. "I told Dee when we won the playoffs that I would pitch the first, fourth, and seventh games and I was glad. I told her I hope to hell I can walk away from the Series and know I didn't let anybody down."

Matlack didn't let anybody down. In his three games he compiled an earned-run average of 2.12. That he won one and lost two can be laid to the conditions that exist for any man who pitches for the light-hitting Mets. Pitching against Catfish Hunter and Ken Holtzman of the Athletics didn't help either.

Matlack's teammates were pleased to have him going for them. Even if he wasn't Seaver, their number one, they feel Matlack could be a number one. There are pitchers who are constituted to be the main man on a pitching staff and others who can be effective if someone else is carrying the burden of leadership. The classic example some players give is that Rick Wise was a big winner for St. Louis last season as long as Bob Gibson was number one. When Gibson was hurt in mid-August, Wise stopped winning. The way Matlack pitched down the stretch, winning seven of his last nine decisions while Seaver was having a hard time, moved Rusty Staub to say, "Matlack pitches like he's been around more than just two years."

Matlack is six feet, four inches and a slender 205 pounds, and he seems to be just growing into his body. He is a power pitcher. Hitters don't like to hit against him. Yet in two seasons he has won twenty-nine and lost twenty-nine. "I don't consider myself only a .500 pitcher," he said. "I've never won a major award. I've never been Rookie of the Year, been named to the All-Star team or won the Cy Young Award. It could take time—or it might never happen."

Seaver has earned all that recognition. Physically, Matlack is not far behind. "For the first time I feel I can handle any situation mentally," Matlack said. "Last year I was in games I should have taken command of like he does. He wins games he shouldn't. He gets down to one key situation, maybe in the early innings, and he does it so decisively, it sets the tone of the game.

"He may win 12–1, but there may have been a situation in the second inning when the game was scoreless and he blew out a hitter when he could have changed the game. I have to be able to do that, too. I think I'm closer to it."

On the way to play the Tigers at Marchant Stadium in Lakeland, the bus driver got off the highway at the wrong exit and drove about aimlessly for a few minutes until Sadecki suggested a stop at an ice cream stand for directions. Sadecki called to three boys on bicycles, "Hey Shoot-fire . . ." The boys were standing next to a sign that offered peanut butter milkshakes. When they got to the ball park, Matlack took his string of eleven innings without an earned run to the mound. He was driven out by the fifth inning, having allowed seven runs and ten hits.

On another front, the Mets got word that former teammate Ron Swodoba had been released by the Braves. "I'm broken up about Swoboda," McGraw said. "He was my first roommate on this club." McGraw was always the first to encourage Swoboda when he was down, and Swoboda always had a pat on the back ready when McGraw needed it.

MARCH 26, ST. PETERSBURG

Today was one of those rare days at cut-down time when the celebration wasn't at someone else's expense. Tomorrow there will be long faces. Today only smiles.

Bob Apodaca stood around the clubhouse accepting congratulations on the birth of his first child. And then Buzz Capra accepted congratulations on being sold to the Braves.

The Braves are desperate for pitching and Capra will get more opportunity with them than he ever got with the Mets. And if Capra is gone, then Apodaca knows he's that much closer to making the team. It's appeared to be a certainty for some time, but then Apodaca isn't one to jump to that conclusion.

Before he heard about Capra, Apodaca said he'd like to visit his wife for a few days, "but I guess it's best I stay here and work to make the team." When the competition was revised, he asked for the time off. Before leaving, he gave Berra three more scoreless innings to remember in a 4–0 loss to the Phillies.

That brought Apodaca's total to thirteen innings without a run. "It's too good," Berra said with an eye for the imponderable. "I almost wish he'd get knocked around once."

Craig Swan was also boosted by the departure of Capra, but Swan didn't pitch as well as Apodaca. He gave up all four runs.

Happiest of all was Capra, who is twenty-six and at the brink of never-never land after shuttling between Tidewater and New York for three seasons. "I've been with the Met organization for five years and it's tough to leave," he said, "but I'm happy about being sold. Every year I came here and I had to pitch my way on the team. There were times I thought it should have been the opposite, that I should have been given the chance to have to pitch my way off the team."

The Mets have starting pitching and Capra isn't constituted to be a relief pitcher. "Over here they think I'm too small to go nine innings," he said. He's five-nine and baseball teams often make decisions based on that much evidence.

"You'll be able to play plenty of golf in Atlanta," Tug McGraw advised Capra, "and they don't have one pitcher on that staff." If he does pitch, Capra can expect more runs from the Braves than the Mets give anybody. Today's was the second straight shutout of the Mets.

Capra was so elated he planned to drive to join the Braves immediately at West Palm Beach. He said he would leave his wife in St. Pete until the end of the month. "Because I've paid the rent until the end of the month," he said.

Harry Parker said his arm doesn't hurt as much. He's been

told the X-rays showed the pain was caused by a muscle strain and was not in the joint.

MARCH 27, ST. PETERSBURG

This one hurt. For many of the Mets it was like looking into a mirror and seeing into the future—maybe a number of years away—and seeing what they didn't want to see. In *The Boys of Summer*, Roger Kahn wrote that athletes die twice. The first, and most painful, time is when they are told they can't play ball any more. Jim Beauchamp died today.

You could see the uneasiness in the players as they moved restlessly from the dish of sliced carrots on the table to the water cooler and out onto the little porch in front of the clubhouse. And you could feel the tension when they passed Beauchamp's locker, where a little green bottle of aftershave proclaimed that there was once a man occupying this space.

Beauchamp wasn't a very important factor in the winning or losing of games for the Mets but he was a part of their lives. He drank beer with them. His wife played tennis with their wives. Now most of them will never see him again. But more than that, the ones who could spare the thought could identify with him. Beauchamp spent eleven seasons in the minor leagues before he made a full season in the big leagues. Once he was considered a super prospect, but he tore up his shoulder in the Texas League and there aren't many big-league jobs for a man who can't throw. He was a right-handed pinch-hitter and he accepted his role. In his Oklahoma twang, he said "peench-hitter" the way the family pronounces their old French name "Bee-chim." He made it through last season because the Mets had so many injuries. He made it through the winter because the Mets weren't sure George Theodore's hip had recovered. But if they had kept Beauchamp until tomorrow, they would have had to pay him two months' salary.

Bob Scheffing thinks a lot of Beauchamp. He said he would have offered him a minor-league managing job, if he had one open. Instead he offered to create an instructor's job in the organization. Beauchamp said that was nice, but he needed time to think about it.

"It's not the end of the world," Beauchamp said after the meeting with Scheffing and Berra. Then he went back to his apartment to think and to tell his family that he has had six years in the big leagues and at thirty-four there won't be any more.

"What do you tell the kids?" Bud Harrelson said. "You get home and they ask you, 'Did you win today, daddy?' Do you tell them, 'Daddy doesn't play baseball any more?'"

For every one who goes, there's one who stays. On the porch, Dave Schneck didn't try to suppress a grin, nor could Swan in the clubhouse. They were supposed to pick up the champagne on the way home. They and their wives had planned a small private party for this evening. It isn't official yet that they and Bob Apodaca have made the team, but it's generally accepted.

"I think I got the team made," Swan said. Jerry Grote, the number one catcher, has caught him the last two times and Swan takes that as a good sign. "The other guys didn't get too much of a chance," he said.

Maybe when it's all official there will be handshakes from the pitchers who will be going back to Payson Field to join the Tidewater team. Maybe not. "I'd like it," Swan said, "but I won't be looking for it."

Tommy Moore looked wistful. He tried to be encouraged by what happened to Capra. "I'd like to have a chance to go to the big leagues in New York," he said, "but if not, I'm happy for Buzz. Maybe something else will happen for me."

If there were condolences for Moore and Glass and Simpson and the others, they were well hidden. "You got to look out for yourself," Schneck said. "Maybe it's a good friend leaving but still, in the back of your mind, you look out for yourself."

"Poor son of a bitch—I don't think anybody said that about me."

MARCH 28, ST. PETERSBURG

Officially, the squad cuts came. Steve Simpson, Randy Sterling and Hank Webb were optioned to Tidewater. They can be recalled at any time if they do well. John Glass and Tommy Moore were outrighted to Tidewater, which means they have to go through waivers by the other twenty-three teams before they can pitch for the Mets.

MARCH 31, FORT LAUDERDALE

Then the Mets broke camp. The team flew to Fort Lauderdale for the last exhibition game in Florida and the families headed to more distant points. Phyllis McGraw and Susie Miller flew to California. They planned to rejoin their husbands later. Diana Stone and Dee Matlack formed a two-car convoy and headed toward Philadelphia where the Mets open the season.

Diana Stone took her small fluffy dog, Pooh, in her car. Dee Matlack took Kristin and Jennifer and an independent calico cat named Bingo in her station wagon. Pooh was afraid of Bingo.

APRIL 2, COLUMBIA, S.C.

An odd conglomeration of a game. The Yankees, Mets, and the University of South Carolina team. Then the Mets beat the Yankees in a regulation game. The game was at South Carolina because the Yankees made a promise to Bobby Richardson. The former Yankee second baseman is the South Carolina coach now, and he is resisting the urging to enter conservative politics.

Richardson played with the Yankees from 1955 to 1966, acquired a reputation as a very clever player, and was exposed to the wisdom of Johnny Sain, at least by osmosis. After coaching here and being responsible for every facet of the game, Richardson said: "I heard the things Sain used to tell the pitchers, but I forgot what he said. It was amazing to me to learn how little I knew about pitching."

APRIL 3, NORFOLK, VA.

One of the minor encouraging scenes of the spring was the sight of Yankee pitcher Steve Kline accepting handshakes after pitching seven good innings as the Yankees beat the Mets, 4–1, in the rain. Kline missed almost an entire year with a sore arm and now he's ready to begin a season as a whole pitcher again. The word Kline heard with the handshakes was "excellent." It was a word for every pitcher with an uncomfortable feeling in his arm or in his mind. It tells every pitcher that a sore arm doesn't have to be the end of the world.

This was the best Kline has pitched since he hurt his elbow last April. Nobody could tell him what the problem was, but he knew it hurt too much to pitch. One suspicion was that a bit of the bone in his forearm just below the elbow was pulled away by the stress of throwing. The uncertainty was as painful as the injury. "I hate to be melodramatic," Kline said, "but eleven months is a long time to think about something."

George Stone pitched five innings and allowed all four Yankee runs, but only after an error at shortstop had paved the way. After such an uncertain beginning, Stone has had a pretty good spring. Apodaca and Sadecki added two scoreless innings. It seems that the pitching staff is going to come out of spring training in pretty good shape. Parker is the only one with a questionable arm.

Seaver put the last polish on his preparations for pitching opening day in Philadelphia. He threw for twelve minutes and ran in the rain. "I ran until I was soaked and then ran some more," he said.

Diana Stone and Dee Matlack turned up unexpectedly at the Mets hotel here. Diana wanted to see George pitch tonight. Dee welcomed the detour. The Matlacks spent three summers here in the minor leagues. They arrived just in time for the game. Dee had a flat tire and had to unpack luggage, daughters, and cat to get to the spare. That's why they drove in convoy.

APRIL 4, RICHMOND, VA.

Training is over. The last exhibition game was rained out. The next game counts, and that's an exciting prospect. No other sport has an "Opening Day," in capital letters.

The Mets have Tom Seaver, who's started every opening day since 1968, pitching the first game. That's encouraging to begin with. Just beginning fresh is pleasant to the Mets. They won in an awful struggle last year and they feel this season can only be better.

And then there's the excitement of Seaver pitching against Steve Carlton of the Phillies. "I would pay to see Seaver and Carlton pitch against each other," said Mel Stottlemyre, who will be pitching opening day for the Yankees.

Seaver won two of the last three Cy Young Awards in the National League and Carlton won the other. It's Seaver's power and control against Carlton's curveball, which may be the best around. In the last four years, he's lost nineteen, won twenty and twenty-seven, and lost twenty. Seaver thinks Carlton hadn't matured as a pitcher yet.

Seaver pitched against Carlton last opening day and won, 3–0. Seaver says he would pay to see—the rematch—as a student of the game. As a pitcher he says he won't permit himself to be involved in the identity of his opponent.

Seaver has developed self control to the point where he sometimes seems all too bloodless. "Every time I go to the mound I try to think the same," he said. "I can't think I have to work harder against the other team's number one pitcher. If I did, then could I work less hard against the number five pitcher?"

Seaver anticipates the luxury of a fan's excitement in watching Jon Matlack pitching against Carlton or Bob Gibson. "I used to feel that stimulation against Gibson," Seaver said. "I thought of myself going against one of the premier pitchers in the game. Now my emotions go around myself. I think more about me than the other pitcher.

"Once the game begins, it's not a name on the mound for the other team, it's a human being who's going to tire. He's going to tire before me."

Of course, when he's pitching against Carlton or Gibson the determination is strong on both sides. The matchups are frequent. Good pitchers usually are matched against good pitchers. Their turns aren't adjusted to fit somebody else's schedule, but it usually works out that the best pitchers are spotted around the same lulls in the schedule.

There are exceptions. Sandy Koufax and Juan Marichal rarely pitched against each other even though the Dodgers and Giants were almost always in the same pennant race. Koufax would open the big series on Friday night and Marichal's turn would come up on Saturday. "Some pitchers would rather pitch against the other team's third pitcher than the first," Seaver said. "That's another discipline you have to teach yourself."

Sometimes the confrontations are memorable. Stottlemyre remembers pitching against Denny McLain in 1968, his thirty-one-game season, when McLain won his first sixteen decisions on the road. "It meant nothing to us in the standings," Stottlemyre said, "but I beat him, 2–1. I've pitched bigger games, but I don't remember them as well."

Opening day takes on some of that tone, but Seaver looks at it differently. "It's different now to me than it ever was," he said. "Before, I didn't want to admit it was a thrill and an honor to me, but it was. Now it means getting started."

"Everyone gets psyched up," Stottlemyre said. "Anyone who tells you he doesn't is lying."

"It turns me on," Seaver said, "but when you're a pitcher, the first game you pitch is the one you think about. The pitcher who pitches the third game, that's his opening day."

APRIL 6, PHILADELPHIA

It was going to be a terrific opening day. The afternoon began with Hugo Zacchini, of the circus Zacchinis, being shot from a cannon behind second base in a high arc into a net at home plate. *Boom.* Hugo tumbled through the air as planned and delivered a baseball from his shirt to be used as the ceremonial first ball. "Jesus Christ!" several of the Mets said. Usually they don't even watch pre-game promotions, but there was no telling what kind of damage Zacchini might do to himself.

The Mets even scored four runs off Steve Carlton and at one point had a 3–1 lead, which is generally plenty for Seaver. But after 111 pitches he was losing his edge and said he had enough. After seven strong innings by Seaver, they took a 4–3 lead into the eighth inning and Tug McGraw came on to pitch.

McGraw was immediately dazzling, striking out Greg Luzinski and Willie Montanez, both dangerous hitters. Luzinski never twitched at a called third strike and Montanez managed only a feeble last-instant swing. McGraw was so elated to be starting off this season like he ended last season that he leaped off the mound as if it were the last out of the game.

With Wayne Garrett leading off the top of the ninth for the Mets, the streaker appeared. In boots, goose pimples, and rolls of fat. It was great fun at the time. "He was the first one I'd ever seen," Garrett said. "He was so cold he was blue. It was funny." McGraw watched from the dugout and didn't think it was funny.

While the streaker was being caught and wrapped in a raincoat, a fully-dressed fellow ran on the field, and then another. McGraw then went into the clubhouse to keep warm, but it was a long delay before returning to the mound on a cold day.

This pitching business is very tenuous stuff. "After a while it pisses you off," McGraw said. "The delay gives you a chance to think about how you're going to pitch, but it slows you down and annoys everybody."

The first batter McGraw faced singled and the next sacrificed. Next up was Mike Schmidt, who hit .196 last season. McGraw missed with his best pitch, a screwball. Next McGraw threw a fastball, low and over the plate, and Schmidt hit it far over the wall. Instant victory for the Phillies and sudden death for McGraw.

"Tug sat there so long, he's got to get tight," center-fielder Don Hahn said. "That inning before, they couldn't touch him. I could see that from center field."

"I think those people on the field might affect a pitcher," Schmidt added. "The pitcher has momentum before that. His concentration has to be hurt."

That wasn't what McGraw chose to remember. He already had the memory of the streaker in the ninth inning of the first exhibition game in the back of his mind, and now this. An alibi is not something McGraw needs to establish with 161 games left to play.

"I'd just as soon not concentrate on the streaker," he said, stiffling his sense of humor. "I have to evaluate what I did. If I think about the streaker, it'll blur the image when I refer back to this game." He couldn't even enjoy a laugh.

APRIL 7, PHILADELPHIA

The Mets won today, 9–2, which looks easy on paper, but for seven innings they trailed 1–0. The Mets scored four runs in the eighth and five in the ninth. When Matlack got into trouble in the eighth, McGraw got out of it. When McGraw gave up a run in the ninth, it became almost a boost because he got out of his own jam.

"The game was important because pitchers can be temperamental, we all know that," McGraw said. "If you start off the year getting shut out, it puts a negative feeling in your mind.

Then we come back and score and you can't wait to get out there and pitch again."

APRIL 10, SHEA STADIUM

The home opener must have been a special day because M. Donald Grant was in the clubhouse after the game. "Good work, young man," he said to Bob Apodaca.

It was a special day because the Shea Stadium ground crew greeted the new season by raking the snow off the field and the infield tarpaulin. It was the day the Mets were presented with their National League championship rings in the shivering cold. And it was the day Bob Apodaca got an out in the big leagues. Not only did he get an out, he got the last two outs in the ball game, which is why he's here.

Word came that Tug McGraw had a fever and wouldn't be available. On opening day McGraw sagely advised Apodaca, "Time to get nervous." This time he went to Apodaca and said, "I'm not in there today, big guy."

"That's when the butterflies started," said Apodaca, who isn't very big.

Then it was time for all the thoughts that had been simmering in the back of Apodaca's mind to come to a boil. He was uncomfortable with them. One by one, the Mets of last season had been called to home plate before the game to accept the mementoes from National League president Chub Feeney. Apodaca, who didn't qualify for a ring, stood in the dugout and felt out of place. "Then I thought, there has to be a new player in there sometime," he said.

Jerry Koosman, who had been splendid, took a 3–1 lead into the ninth inning against the Cardinals and then ran out of luck. A fly ball dropped for a triple when the mud gave way under Don Hahn in center field. Koosman got an out and then gave up a bloop single and an infield single and it was time for help.

With the tying run on second base and the winning run on first, Berra called for Apodaca, who throws a sinking fastball Jerry Grote says feels like a lead weight in his glove. Walking to the mound, Apodaca was alone with his thoughts. "All that was in my mind was, 'Don't let them down.' " he said. When he got to the mound he asked Grote how to pitch to veteran Tim McCarver, who was waiting to pinch hit. Grote said to throw that sinking fastball and be ready for McCarver to hit through the middle.

McCarver hit Apodaca's second sinking fastball back to the mound. Amid the swirl of bodies around second base, which could have befuddled a rookie into throwing the ball into center field, Apodaca picked out the shortstop to start the double play that ended the game. The Mets won, 3–2. Apodaca got a save.

Then a part of the traditional blue and orange pre-game floral horseshoe belonged to Apodaca. He had the handshakes of congratulations in the big leagues for the first time.

"Now I don't ever have to think about Pittsburgh any more," he said. "I'd like to think of this as my debut. It's the greatest feeling in the world to run off the mound and have people shake your hand."

APRIL 11, SHEA STADIUM

In a brief pre-game ceremony, Apodaca was named the winner of the award as the outstanding rookie of the spring. Then he and Swan made plans to drive to Tidewater—Norfolk, actually—after the doubleheader to pick up household goods left there last year and to return tomorrow on the open day.

Apodaca was in such a good frame of mind reliving yesterday's success. Last night he phoned his wife in California and played games with her. "I gave her the situation when I came into the game and I told her McCarver hit a home run. She said, 'Oh, no.' Then we both laughed."

McGraw was still sick so Berra had to look for somebody else to protect the leads in both games against the Cardinals. He's still looking. Craig Swan blew a lead and lost the first game. Bob Apodaca blew a lead and lost the second game. And Seaver had no fastball again.

Seaver came into the clubhouse after warming up as Sadecki was passing through in search of a cigaret. "How did you crank up?" Sadecki asked.

"So-so," Seaver replied. He had a pained expression.

He left after five innings, having allowed six runs on ten hits and three home runs. Two of them were hit off fastballs. Swan and Apodaca can be expected to blow a few leads before they're adjusted to the big leagues but Seaver is Seaver.

The press isn't permitted into the clubhouse between games. Recently the Mets have responded to urging by building a small, bare room for between-game interviews with players who aren't required to stay around for the second game. Seaver came out to discuss the situation. He smiled and even tried to tell a joke.

"Everything physically feels fine, that's what makes it a little puzzling," he said. "I just don't seem to have any life on my fastball."

He told a story about an Air Force colonel who wasn't doing his best work. A psychiatrist asked him when he last had sex. The colonel said, "1957." "No wonder," said the psychiatrist. "I guess so," said the colonel. "The time now is only 2130." The only application to Seaver seemed to be an attempt to keep his spirits up.

His fastball was such that Rube Walker trotted to the mound in the fourth inning to ask Seaver if he were hurt. When Seaver isn't hurt, which is what he said, when he's throwing as hard as ever and the ball isn't going so fast, there are ominous implications. Walker says he isn't concerned. Jerry Grote says he isn't concerned. So then Seaver must be the only one concerned.

What seemed to disturb him most was the home run Joe Torre hit off a pitch at chin-height. That's where Seaver's fastball should have its greatest rising action. "For him to get the good part of the bat on it," Seaver said, "the fastball must be dead as can be."

This was his second start and the second time he didn't have a Seaver fastball or an explanation either. Since Walker is not strong on mechanics, Seaver is the man the other pitchers go to for explanations.

"I can see where it might puzzle him," Grote said. "He always has everything figured out. He's got it down to a science. He has no explanations for this. I don't think there's any reason to be concerned." Grote said it with his eyebrows squeezed together and his voice a bit higher than normal. The unsaid word appeared to be "yet," as in, "let's see how he does next time."

Berra said he wasn't concerned, either, as long as Seaver said he wasn't hurt. "He's the one who knows," the manager deferred.

The conclusion to be rejected was that some of Seaver's overwhelming fastball might be gone except on the very good days. Seaver knows that every pitcher has a bad outing in spring training and he went through clean. Just because the schedule says the season has begun doesn't mean his body knows it. "Maybe this was it," he said. "I'm a few years older now than I was. Maybe the fastball comes a little later now."

APRIL 14, SHEA STADIUM

Another doubleheader and another double loss. The season is beginning to take on a familiar and unpleasant look. If they keep losing them two at a time, they'll be out of it in no time at all.

Blame the bullpen again for both games, which were lost in the manner of the original Mets. This time it was Yogi Berra standing knock-kneed and naked—instead of Casey Stengel, lumpy-legged and naked—listening to Bob Miller's explanations. It could just as well have been Easter Sunday of 1962.

They'd tie the first game with a dramatic home run in the eighth inning and Craig Anderson—or somebody—would lose it in the eleventh. They'd get a lead in the second game and Willard Hunter—or somebody—wouldn't be able to save it. Miller could have been the starter in either game—and probably was.

Now Miller is a relief pitcher. After Apodaca and Swan failed last time, Berra gave Miller a chance at the prestigious end-man role in both games. He pitched two good innings in the first game in relief of Jon Matlack, who pitched seven good innings. McGraw got through the tenth on Rusty Staub's throw to the plate and lost it in the eleventh.

Miller did so well that Berra called for him in the second game when Jerry Koosman needed help in the eighth inning, after he had thrown as hard as he could remember "for three or four years." Miller got out of the eighth allowing the second of Koosman's runs on a fly ball. In the ninth Miller got an out, gave a single, got an out and then gave up three hits and the tying and winning runs.

"Welcome to the Mets," Miller said with old memories revived. It was the end of his eleven-year winning streak.

It was also the fifth loss by the Mets, all of them lost in the eighth inning or later, and all by the bullpen. The Mets are supposed to have a good bullpen.

APRIL 16, MONTREAL

It was a long time after the game before Seaver put his butt down underneath the bilingual "Bienvenue/Welcome" sign on his locker. He threw down the parts of his uniform as he took them off. He slung the towel over his shoulder and tromped to the showers. He tromped back and then off to the trainer's room and back again. He tossed his empty beer can into the trash basket. And when he did perch on his stool and pick at his fingernails, questioners really weren't welcome no matter what the sign said.

"I can still pitch," he pronounced unwillingly, leaving everyone to decide for himself how much he thought Seaver believed it himself. Of course Seaver can pitch, but how well?

He pitched a nice game, but the standards he has set for himself are painfully high. "He came damn close to having a hell of a day," said Ron Fairly of the Expos.

But when you got right down to it, Seaver didn't have a hell of a day. He couldn't get a fastball past Fairly when a strikeout was needed. Fairly's single broke a 1–1 tie and Seaver lost, 4–1. He had a 1–0 lead for six innings and a 1–1 tie after seven. It was his second "nice try" in three starts.

Of course, there were mitigating circumstances. "Considering the weather conditions, I pitched a pretty fair game," Seaver said. "I guess there's a lot of ifs."

If it had been a warm day instead of forty degrees with a strong wind blowing across the mounds of sooty snow, then maybe Seaver would have demonstrated his fastball. "Today I was worried about hurting my arm," he said. "It gets awfully tight on a day like today."

If Teddy Martinez had come up with a grounder.... But if Bud Harrelson hadn't pulled a muscle, Martinez wouldn't have been at shortstop. If the plate umpire had called "strike three" on either of those pitches to Ken Singleton in the Expos' eighth.... But if Seaver had been able to get a one-ball, two-strike fastball past Fairly, he wouldn't have gotten the hit that broke the tie. And if Bob Bailey hadn't hit a home run, the game wouldn't have been tied in the first place.

It was the three home runs the Cardinals hit in Seaver's last start that pushed him to the painful self-examination. "After that game I came to a lot of conclusions," Seaver said. What he called conclusions were the questions that formed in his mind:

"Am I washed up at twenty-nine? Have I lost my fastball at twenty-nine?"

Merely conceding that he had asked himself those questions was a display of emotion few of us had ever seen in Seaver. He'd shown anger before and plenty of pride, but certainly not fear. And here it was.

But it was on display for only a moment. "Then I decided that game was just one of those things," Seaver said. "I'm not a kid any more. Maybe it takes me longer to get ready now. That was another conclusion I came to." Maybe he's right. It's awfully hard to doubt after three games when a pitcher has been as good as he's been.

At the same time that Seaver was looking for flaws on the videotape, hitters around the league were studying the box scores and the brief game accounts from the wire services that run in papers around the league. "I noticed the three home runs the Cardinals hit and I read where two were off fastballs," said Singleton, who was a Met in 1970 and '71. "I had to think maybe he's slowing up a bit, maybe an inch or two off the fastball."

That's an interesting ball player's description, whatever the derivation. It relates the fastball to the point where the batter starts his swing. When a pitcher loses a foot off his fastball, the hitter has his bat well around when the ball reaches the plate. When he's throwing a super fastball and the ball is on the inside part of the plate, the batter has to get the bat around that much faster or he's jammed by it. He gets only the handle of the bat on it. That's what Seaver does with his super fastball.

Singleton said he saw only one super fastball from Seaver, the three-and-two pitch that walked him in front of Fairly's hit. Singleton said it was the hardest pitch he's seen this season. "He can really air it out for one pitch," Singleton said. "Maybe he can't air it out like he used to for a whole game. He's thrown so many pitches, a man has to wear down a little." That's just what everybody is afraid of, especially Seaver. Today didn't answer any questions. It just left questions still standing.

APRIL 17, MONTREAL

The Mets were on the short end of a 7–4 score today. Now they are getting into the gray area of psyching themselves one way or the other. Last year they psyched themselves into believing. "Everybody has to make up his mind to turn things around and start playing the way we can," Stone said.

That brings it all around to what some of the pitchers feel is their responsibility on this team. "Each game is important, but when a team is in a skid like we are, it makes it that much more important," Jon Matlack said. With his idle time between starts, he's been sitting on the bench analyzing, trying to figure whether he agrees with each pitch thrown.

He pitches tomorrow on three days' rest. Starting on three days' rest in April sounds like a panic move, but Berra named Matlack before yesterday's loss to set up the rotation for next week's California trip. Now Matlack takes the role of stopper.

"I want so bad to go out and slam the door so hard, beat them so decisively there's no way they can win," Matlack said, "That can turn a team around. I mean breaking bats and having the kind of game a pitcher has only three or four times all year. But how the hell do you know?"

APRIL 18, MONTREAL

What Jon Matlack said he needed to do was "slam the door." It turned out he needed two tries to get the cap off the toothpaste tube.

Today's stopper pitcher woke up with a fever of 102. So the Mets packed Matlack and Jerry Koosman, tomorrow's pitcher, and sent them off to the airport to fly home instead of waiting for the team. Ray Sadecki pitched instead; he lost 8–5. The Mets are 2–8, and the only worse start in their history was in 1962 when they were 1–9 and went on to lose 120.

"We're not jelling, infielder Ken Boswell explained in his best facetious tone. " 'Jelling,' you usually don't hear that word until September. We haven't got the right combination yet. When we get it, we'll call it 'jelling.' That'll be September."

That's what it was last year, anyhow. But last year may not come again for years and years. A hard analysis produces a condition known as gloom and doom. In French that's known as *tristesse et detresse*.

"The only escape this time of year is that you say it's early." Sadecki said. "I hope we don't rock ourselves to sleep saying it's early."

In the category of What Else can Go Wrong?—the Mets went to the airport for the 6:25 flight and there were Matlack and Koosman, after five hours on standby.

APRIL 20, SHEA STADIUM

The Mets had to beat somebody. Fortunately the rain stopped in time for the second game of the series and the Pirates were still there. More fortunately, so was Jerry Koosman, and with him was the first complete winning game by a Met pitcher this year. For seven innings he pitched well and for the last two he was great. He was in the game for the last two because Wayne Garrett hit a home run with a pinch-hitter waiting to replace Koosman.

"All of a sudden I felt super," Koosman said. "Man, I was throwing hard. In the beginning, the first three or four innings, I wasn't confident about my control. But then I knew I had everything. 'God,' I said to myself, 'I really got it.' Hey, I felt so damned good I almost wished the game would go into extra innings. . . . Don't anybody tell Yogi I said that."

APRIL 21, SHEA STADIUM

All Tom Seaver had left was his imperious shield. In five innings the Pirates tore at his confidence and the fans stripped him of dignity. They watched the best pitcher the Mets have ever had take a merciless pounding, and then they booed him.

He kicked a laundry basket, then lingered a long time in the sanctuary of the trainer's room, off limits to the prying questions of the press, before Joe Pignatano told him, "Your public wants to see you." Seaver emerged in a striped robe that looked a lot more cheerful than he did.

"Make it short," Seaver warned. He placed his shaving kit on the shelf of his locker, then accidentally dumped its contents on the floor. It would have been foolishly irreverent to have laughed in the presence of Seaver's grief, so nobody laughed.

The questions that followed were not much different from the ones he heard the last time he pitched or the time before except now he was another game deeper into the season and the evidence of this afternoon was so much more pointed. At one point the Pirates reached Seaver for six consecutive hits—two of them home runs—and eight hits in nine batters. The crowd booed Yogi Berra for sticking with Seaver through the barrage in the fifth and booed again when he was relieved after two more hits in the sixth.

"It's not the first time. It won't be the last," Seaver said. "That's their prerogative. I would have booed, too."

He didn't say it didn't bother him. He has said the sound of a great crowd cheering him gives him the feeling of a natural high. The reverse must be true, too, but Seaver is too much the stoic to admit it.

"I don't like it," said Bud Harrelson, Seaver's closest friend on the team. They even use the same business agent. "I remember they booed him when he won only eighteen games." Harrelson laughed at his expression. "That's the way we talk about Tom: 'Only won eighteen.'"

But that's the way it is. A man doesn't get named Tom Terrific for a 14–12 record. That man isn't paid a salary of $172,000. That man doesn't earn another $100,000 for lending his face to every Sears-Roebuck catalog. When he stumbles, the crowd forgets how much pleasure he's given. Now the statistics on the field are against him. In twenty-five innings, he has an earned-run average of 6.12 and an 0–2 record.

Seaver showered silently, drove to his eighty-year-old home in Greenwich, Conn., and went off to hit golf balls to compose himself.

Seaver is the highest-paid starting pitcher in baseball. Tug McGraw is the highest-paid relief pitcher, and he's not doing any better. He was thrown in for an inning in the 7–0 loss, just in time to give up a home run. But at least he knows what's wrong.

He said he had a pulled muscle in his back that's been bothering him on and off since early in spring training. All spring that problem was brushed off as just a little tenderness that would go away. After today's game Dr. James Parkes gave McGraw a cortisone shot at the base of his left shoulder blade.

"It's nothing worrisome," Dr. Parkes told McGraw, "because it's muscle rather than tendons." X-rays taken before the game showed no bone damage.

"But the other day there was a lump the size of a golf ball," McGraw said. "Today we tried to stretch it out, but it didn't work. Now we know where it is and what it is."

APRIL 22, SAN DIEGO

McGraw was assigned to throw in the bullpen late in the game to see how he felt and, if he felt good, to be ready to relieve. Seaver went to the bullpen to throw fifteen minutes without being assigned. "He looked a lot better," Rube Walker announced. Now everybody is looking for things like that and signs of Seaver's emotional response.

"He's got to be going through a difficult time—emotionally and mechanically," Jon Matlack said. "He's the top pitcher in the whole game. He's the highest paid. It has to be embarrassing and frustrating to him, getting the shit knocked out." Beyond the embarrassment and the frustration, he might be a little frightened, too. "Not frightened," Matlack argued. "He has so much confidence. There's too many little things that could be wrong and could be better any time."

Matlack toweled off from the pre-game workout and went through his normal routine timed for twenty-five minutes before pitching. He figures on ten minutes with a razor-blade device to shave down the callus on the middle finger of his pitching hand so a blister doesn't form underneath and fifteen minutes for a loosening rub by the trainer.

He was afraid he'd be too strong on the mound after his ten-day rest with the flu. But he was glad to exchange the chill and the rain of the Northeast for the California weather of the nine-day trip. Firm dry fields to run on. No chilling winds against overheated back muscles. That must be what the Mets need. And the last time the Mets saw them, the Padres were the worst team in the whole league.

Matlack was weak and the Mets were out of the game in four innings. Where Seaver has been supplying only more questions, Matlack had an explanation for himself. "I was putting everything into it and the ball wasn't going anywhere," he said. He'll need time to build himself up and there seems to be a bit of haste now. "If we don't get pitching, we can't do nothing," Berra said.

APRIL 24, SAN DIEGO

The composure has cracked a bit. It seemed the Mets had been taking the losses in stride, but tonight the loss seemed more like a defeat. They reacted by throwing things in the clubhouse. Not garbage cans or chairs, which would have shown real anger, but soft objects that didn't jar the mourners.

Bob Apodaca peeled off his socks and threw them into a pile. Bud Harrelson threw his long underwear at the floor of his locker. Yogi Berra threw down one shoe. Tug McGraw threw a bit of adhesive tape—with his right hand because he's been told not to throw anything with his left for a few days.

Everything that has been bugging the Mets came together as they lost a 4–3 game to the Padres in the last of the ninth inning. Berra called it the worst of the losses. On paper there have been worse—like opening day was worse—but circumstances are building up ominously and the Mets are acknowledging that for the first time. That's what gloom and doom represent.

George Stone found himself after staggering through the early innings, and Wayne Garrett's two-run homer made it 3–3 in the seventh. The Mets felt the home run was a sign their luck had turned. "I felt good about tonight," Stone said. "We felt we were going to win. Sometimes you can just tell by the atmosphere."

Except a turnaround in that atmosphere feels that much worse. That's what had Apodaca throwing his wet socks and blinking his eyes. Bob Miller came in and got Willie McCovey out to preserve the tie through the eighth inning. Then it became Apodaca's game because McGraw has been ordered not to throw a ball for forty-eight hours. Apodaca wasn't up to the assignment.

He got an out on a fine catch by Cleon Jones then Derrel Thomas doubled and Johnny Grubb was intentionally walked. Then Apodaca couldn't throw a strike to Dave Winfield, who had singled and homered off Stone. The infield converged and patted Apodaca in all the appropriate places to indicate faith.

On the first pitch with the infield drawn in, Nate Colbert, who had homered off Stone for the Padres' first two runs, checked his swing but grounded sharply between first and second. Felix Millan made a diving stop but never had a chance to cut off the winning run at the plate.

"Oh, shit," Apodaca said, whipping himself. He had seen his new baby in the afternoon and now this. "I don't know what's the matter. I can't explain it. Everybody wants to do his part to get us out of the slump and I can't pitch one inning. Just one inning. It really gets you down."

Now the residue of the confidence he built up in spring training seems all gone. Stone is shaken, too. He can't find the breaking pitch that made him a winner last season and earned him a nice raise to $45,000.

"In order for me to be effective, I have to have the breaking pitch," Stone said. "It's demoralizing in a way when you get off to a bad start." The words were intended to describe the feeling of the team, but Stone was talking about himself, too.

APRIL 25, SAN DIEGO

Sometimes Jerry Koosman's logic is bewildering. It's as if he were playing a role out of *Catch-22*. If the situation hasn't made a man crazy, he must be insane. He can make the most remarkable argument for optimism. He went to the mound tonight for a team that had lost ten of eleven games and argued that his greatest problem was that the slope of the mound was too gradual.

Then he pitched nine innings of a 5–2 victory with a fastball he seems to have found packed away with mementoes of 1969 and '70. Koosman is the only Met to win in eighteen days. He's the bloom in the gloom and doom.

He could look at their eleven defeats in the first fifteen games and argue that even if they won a hundred games, they still had to lose sixty-two. "What's the difference if it's now or later?" he said. Of course. Why wait until the last minute?

He was charged with two unearned runs in the first inning and immediately the Mets were behind, 2–1. Another loss was looking them in the face. Then he told the Mets in the dugout, "That's all they're going to get."

And that's all they got. He struck out eleven batters; twelve is the most he's ever struck out in nine innings—back in 1969.

"It's easy to get down when we've been playing like we have," Jerry Grote said. "Koo doesn't get down. He keeps coming at you. That's why you can't quit."

Koosman even said he was "confident" when Berra let him lead off the ninth inning. How can any man be "confident" at the plate with a lifetime average of .086? Yet he singled and started the rally that won the game.

Of course, he was talking about his confidence after the game, but it was in line with his thinking the whole game. He had the Padres so fooled they were taking strikes that cut big chunks of the plate. He broke Willie McCovey's bat with a fastball for the last out.

"And now we've got the good one tomorrow night," Berra said. He meant Seaver opening the series in San Francisco. Berra said it as if he hadn't been watching all season.

Seaver played in a noisy bridge game before the ball game. He even did his parody of the bean scene from "Blazing Saddles." It was as if everything were normal.

APRIL 26, SAN FRANCISCO

One by one the Mets filed to Tom Seaver's locker to shake his hand. Seaver acknowledged each one deliberately by name as if to indicate he understood what they were thinking:

"Thanks, Koo . . . thanks, Bo . . . thanks, Piggy . . . thanks, Stoney . . ."

He beat the Giants, 6–0. He struck out seven, gave up four hits, and didn't walk anybody. It was a nice game, a run-of-the-mill shutout for him, not some special kind of dazzling Tom Seaver gem. "I wasn't consistent the way I'd like to be," he said, "but I was obviously much better than in the other four games."

It looked like the scene I'd drawn in my mind from the Lux Radio Theater version of "Pride of the Yankees." Lou Gehrig, not yet aware of his terminal disease, made a routine play he hadn't been making and his teammates congratulated him.

"Some pitches were extremely bad," said Grote, who was the first to notice, "and some were extremely good. It was still not Seaver. Some pitches had absolutely nothing."

But there was the fastball that exploded past Garry Maddox for Seaver's second strikeout. He did retire sixteen consecutive batters from the fourth inning to the ninth. And he did have the two strikeouts in the last two innings to indicate he had power to the end.

Was it a peak he can still reach from time to time? Or was it an indication he was climbing back? A skeptic might have said, "I'd like to see him do it again." Seaver said, "So would I."

APRIL 27, SAN FRANCISCO

Seaver said his legs hurt this morning from the exertion of pitching nine innings for the first time. "I'm glad they do, but they hurt," he said. In nine innings he threw 102 pitches. The Giant starter last night, John D'Aquisto, threw 102 pitches in $4\frac{1}{3}$ innings.

In the moments before Craig Swan went out to warm up, with all of one inning pitched this season, he walked past Seaver's locker, seeking a bit of reassurance or whatever from the resident guru, who has his status back. Seaver, feeling confident enough for a few words to a rookie, sat in front of his locker and Swan stood in front of him, his jaw clamped firmly.

"Remember this," Seaver said, "throw strikes and keep the ball down. Don't worry about setting up the hitters. Just go back to the fundamentals of pitching."

Swan usually laughs nervously at times of crisis. He was too nervous to laugh this time. "He's a good eater," said Jon Matlack, who sat at the breakfast table with Swan. "Today he couldn't eat breakfast."

Seaver gave Swan good advice, but failed to tell him how to be lucky. Swan didn't pitch poorly but was the loser in an 11–2 game. He gave up six runs, but two were unearned and two others weren't exactly earned either. Dave Schneck, the rookie center fielder, stumbled under one fly ball and moments later knocked another down as Rusty Staub was about to catch it. Perhaps when he made the second mistake he was still thinking about the first, when he stumbled on the AstroTurf. He was wearing the conventional metal spikes and most experienced outfielders wear shoes with stubby rounded cleats on the plastic surface. But nobody on the Met staff informed Schneck.

Swan had to pay the price. He was finished with two out in the fifth. "You can't blame Dave," Swan said generously. He was surprised and pleased he'd been able to throw so many strikes and some good sliders, which they didn't let him throw all spring. He said he was also surprised that good hitters were able to get the good part of the bat on the ball even when he jammed them. Welcome to the big leagues.

APRIL 28, SAN FRANCISCO

It's funny how life turns from one day to the next. Schneck was the goat and a terribly depressed man yesterday. Today he was a hero.

Before the game Seaver crouched in front of Schneck as he sat in front of his locker and said what had to be said. Seaver, the consummate professional, told the rookie it was the time to demonstrate he was a professional. Schneck remembered being told, "If you make a mistake, forget it. If you don't it's going to bother your next at-bat and your next play in the outfield."

Then Schneck went out and hit two two-run home runs and Jon Matlack pitched a 6–0 four-hit shutout in the first game. Harry Parker, Tug McGraw, and Bob Miller combined in the second game and the Mets beat the Giants, 6–4. It was merely the Mets' best day of the season.

Matlack's game was a thing of rare beauty. It took him only eighty-seven pitches to put away the Giants. Only twenty-three were balls. A normal complete game usually requires 100–110 pitches.

He did it with his best head on a day he didn't have "the good pop" on his fastball. He struck out only three batters, but he broke a lot of bats. And all the while he was able to follow the progress of the Boston-Milwaukee basketball playoff game on the scoreboard.

They took the cover off McGraw in the seventh inning of the second game and it was a mixed success, but McGraw thought it was worth raving about. He allowed a run in the seventh and left two runners on base; and two of the three outs came on line drives that stung Cleon Jones' hand in left field and left everybody else breathing deeply. "I told Cleon, 'I'll keep them hitting popups and we'll be all right,'" McGraw said.

He came out after walking the first batter in the eighth, but he slapped his glove against his thigh on the way off to indicate to his wife in the stands—or just to himself—that he felt all right. The plan is to pitch him an inning at a time as often as practical to build up his arm again.

APRIL 29, LOS ANGELES

Mike Marshall is unique. His concept of sports, pitching, relief pitching—almost everything—is different. "He'd tell Bulova how to make a watch," said one of his Dodger teammates. But Marshall looks at his role as a pitcher and as a ball player from a different vantage point. He's completing his doctorate in child development and teaching at Michigan State. And he was a knock-around infielder long before he ever became a star pitcher. It's difficult for a newspaper man to interview him except on Marshall's terms. One of his favorite subjects is the dichotomy between pitchers and baseball players. It requires only a few questions to uncover his resentment.

"You have a team meeting and the outfielders and infielders are telling you what to pitch. There's no way an outfielder has any idea what it's like to be on the mound. It just looks easy," he said. "If a pitcher suggests a way to play defense on a hitter, they say, 'Who the hell is he to talk? He's just a pitcher.' The pitcher probably doesn't know what it's like to field a ground ball in the hole at shortstop and throw a runner out."

Marshall remembers the times with Detroit and Seattle when he was struggling to stick in the big leagues and his concepts were ignored. "You're a pitcher; that means you're stupid," is the response he recalls. A lot of pitchers feel that way.

Marshall has no fear of making teammates angry. He visualizes himself as an island pitching off the mound, which is another island. He sees the pitching staff as a sub-group on the team and each pitcher as another sub-group unto himself. "A common purpose, but in competition with each other," he said.

"I've helped other pitchers, but I've got not one thank-you. They always want to take what they can, but they still want to beat you on the same staff. . . . It's seldom you can talk to another pitcher about how you pitched. They tend to taint things the way they want to see them. . . . In competition, they tend to lose their objectivity. They rationalize to improve their own situation."

Perhaps that's a condition Marshall has lived with. Jim Bouton, once a twenty-game winner, calls this "sibling rivalry." The pitchers squabble among themselves and with the pitching coach, but once an outsider challenges them, they all band together.

With the Mets there isn't quite the same internal squabbling among the pitchers. Perhaps that's because there's enough status for all the Mets' pitchers.

Today was Marshall's fourteenth appearance already this year. He pitched the last three innings and helped the Dodgers to an 8–7 win.

APRIL 30, LOS ANGELES

Is this baseball or is it tag-team wrestling? This time the Mets took a 6–0 lead and had to score two in the top of the ninth and hold off the Dodgers in the last of the ninth to win, 8–7. That left Yogi Berra walking knock-kneed around the clubhouse with his tongue out as if punch-drunk. "Exciting, isn't it?" he said.

There was a lot of laughter in the clubhouse. McGraw hollered, "Hey, Rube, Swan is eating all the hot dogs." And Bob Miller, who pitched the last 1⅔ innings in relief of Jerry Koosman, celebrated his first win as a Met since 1962.

But in the midst of the hilarity, Tom Seaver threw down his shoes with irritation. He showered, dressed, and left the clubhouse quickly while others were still reveling in the victory. He wouldn't explain.

For Miller it was a moment in the spotlight, a "This is Your Life" about the Saturday afternoon in Chicago the day before the 1962 season ended. There were tales worth recalling about Miller's lone win that season after losing his first twelve decisions. It was his first complete game after twenty-one starts.

"That's so damn long ago," Miller said. "I do remember there wasn't any people in the stands and there wasn't any writers in the clubhouse after the game."

The writers were absent because that's the nature of the

newspaper business. Most of the New York papers—and there were a lot more of them then than there are today—stopped covering the Mets on the road early in September to send their men off to cover the race between the Giants and the Dodgers. Since it was a Saturday afternoon, even the Chicago reporters were rushing to meet the early deadlines of Sunday morning papers. They didn't feel the drama of Bob Miller winning his first game after being interviewed after so many losing efforts.

Miller remembered being in a jam in the late innings that day and Casey Stengel going to the mound. "I asked him, 'Let me lose it by myself,'" Miller said. Stengel said something about how other people hadn't helped Miller very much all season, and let Miller attack his own problem. The bases were loaded and Miller escaped with his victory. As a reward, and considering that Miller was only going to sit around on the last day, Stengel told Miller he was free to go home.

But the next day there was a stream of insults for the plate umpire from the Mets' dugout and the umpire threw Miller out of the game. At least he thought he did. "Get him out of here," the umpire directed Stengel.

"Tell him yourself," Stengel said.

"Okay, I will," the umpire said. He began to scan the bench.

"You'd better start hitch-hiking to California," Stengel said, "because he's halfway there by now."

That winter Miller was traded to the Dodgers and began a successful career as a relief pitcher.

Ed Kranepool, who was seventeen at the time, sees a distinct difference in Miller. "He's a lot smarter," Kranepool said. "Now it took him only twenty-something games to win. The last time it took five and a half months."

MAY 1, LOS ANGELES

While waiting to warm up, Seaver sat alone in the clubhouse playing solitaire, snapping the cards off the deck. He was still rankled by the things that upset him last night. He discouraged questions.

"Very perceptive," he said when he was told he had been observed out of the mainstream of celebration. Was he upset by the nature of the game? "Partly," he said. "I don't want to say just what."

Matlack noticed Seaver, too. "He was so hot for so long, I didn't want to ask him why; so I decided, better leave him alone," Matlack said. "He's been hot all day."

What it got down to was that Seaver and some of the other pitchers were offended that Koosman was left in the game through the eighth inning to give up six runs after allowing none in the first five innings. "He was losing something in the sixth and he didn't bounce back," Matlack said. "He should never have been left in to pitch to the tying run."

Matlack is not an outspoken Berra supporter. Few of the pitchers are, and Seaver least of all. I remember asking several players during the pennant-clinching celebration of last year what Berra's contribution was. The general response was, patience and confidence and calmness under fire. Seaver said, "Nothing."

The game Seaver pitched tonight was remarkable. "Pick an adjective," Dodger first baseman Steve Garvey said. Seaver didn't win, but he was absolutely dazzling for twelve innings before Harry Parker lost it in the fourteenth, 2–1. Seaver struck out sixteen and was all anybody ever hoped he would be. In light of this one, the last game he pitched against the Giants looks more significant. This makes it two strong games in a row. "I feel I'm all back," he said. "If I had come here and gotten rocked, I'd have asked what was wrong. I'm in good shape." He spoke as if the score was meaningless. After all it was a victory for Seaver.

McGraw was upset because Parker had pitched the thirteenth and fourteenth innings. Last night the manager held McGraw out of the 8–7 game with the explanation that he was saving him for tonight. Tonight, on the advice of the pitching coach, Berra said he'd decided to give Tug another day off. But nobody told McGraw.

"There's a communications gap," McGraw said.

The closest Rube Walker would come to an explanation was a shrug and a drawled, "Might could have used him, but . . ."

"I thought I could have pitched," McGraw said.

"He always says that," Berra said.

MAY 4, SHEA STADIUM

McGraw has had his rest and today he did a job on the Padres. He pitched two innings in relief of Jon Matlack and struck out four—and the Mets won, 6–3. They won it as Matlack sat in the dugout with a towel wrapped around his neck in the seventh inning, imploring Rusty Staub to hit a three-run home run, which Staub did. Matlack had pitched well, striking out nine in seven innings.

"Not great, but good," Matlack said. "I wanted to get something more than a loss." He was in the dugout because the Mets have this rule that the pitcher must stay in the dugout during the inning he leaves the game. It has something to do with the pitcher being part of the team.

MAY 5, SHEA STADIUM

It's a game of individuals—each man doing his thing as part of the whole. It isn't a game where one man passes the ball to the other and one man's performance influences another's—until it gets to the point where one man passes the ball to the other.

McGraw pitched two good innings yesterday and that was in Jerry Koosman's mind when, with a 4–3 lead in the ninth inning, he complained of pain in the middle finger of his pitching hand. Koosman called it "a circulator" problem.

That's one of the many mystical ills pitchers are subject to. You never hear of a third baseman with circulation problems, but Sandy Koufax missed a half-season with inadequate circulation in his hand. Whitey Ford had surgery to improve the circulation in his pitching arm and a side effect was that he didn't sweat on the left side of his body. Pitchers often develop so much muscle on one side that the muscle mass impairs circulation. Ford's left arm was so overdeveloped that he used to have his shirts tailored with the left sleeve a half-inch longer.

This discomfort was nothing new to Koosman, but he gave into it because he knew McGraw was coming in. "I've pitched with pain before," Koosman said. "This is the first time I ever said anything. I saw Tug warming up. When Yogi came to the mound, the first thing I asked was if Tug was ready. Then I told him my finger hurt. If Tug hadn't been ready, I wouldn't have said anything."

Koosman's and McGraw's status on the pitching staff are such that Koosman can admit his feelings without insulting anybody. Once, in 1962, when Luis Arroyo was tapering off from his brief, brilliant career as a relief pitcher for the Yankees, a reporter asked Jim Bouton how he felt about coming out of a game just short of completing it. Bouton said he looked down and knew nothing until he saw Arroyo. The extra pitchers on the Yankees—notably Jim Coates—raised hell until Bouton apologized. Almost anything Bouton said or did irritated some of the old-guard Yankees.

Anyhow, McGraw came in to give up two hits, walk two, and allow two runs in two-thirds of an inning; and he became the losing pitcher before Bob Miller could get through the inning.

MAY 6, SHEA STADIUM

A rainout, plus unpleasant news. Miller has a sprained ankle. Parker got a cortisone shot in his shoulder. And the longer it lasts, the more the McGraw situation worries people. "You got to be concerned, what the hell," Berra said.

When he said, "He'll snap out of it; he's too good a pitcher not to," it sounded as if Berra were trying to convince himself—or McGraw. The tipoff is that McGraw isn't throwing his screwball and that's the pitch that makes him. It's also the most damaging pitch a man can throw. Think of the way you turn a doorknob. If you're right-handed, you twist it in a clockwise direction. Notice how far and how easily you can rotate your hand. Now rotate your hand as if turning the doorknob counterclockwise. That's how a screwball is thrown. You can feel the stress up your forearm all the way to the shoulder, with the greatest strain at the elbow. The hand doesn't rotate nearly as far in that direction, but a pitcher needs maximum rotation to make the pitch break. Think of making that motion as hard as you can fifteen times in rapid order.

No wonder a screwball pitcher breaks down. Mike Marshall says it doesn't have to be that way. He's a student of kinesiology, the science of muscles in movement, and he says that the arm will adapt to the motion. He pitched in a record ninety-two games last year and is going at a faster rate this season, so maybe he has a point. But nobody else has discovered the secret. Young pitchers are discouraged from throwing the screwball, but it's the pitch that made McGraw a highly-paid pitcher.

One of the secrets of being a relief pitcher is having a freak pitch. Some successful relief pitchers have been power pitchers, like Joe Page and Ryne Duren with the Yankees, Joe Black with the Dodgers, and Dick Radatz with the Red Sox. But that was their freak pitch. They could throw an extraordinary fastball and it really was the only pitch they threw. For the short span of one batter or an inning or two they could stand on the mound and fire. In relief of a tiring starter, the new fastball was overpowering and the batter seldom got a second look to adjust his timing. Sparky Lyle achieves that effect with a very hard slider.

Radatz was so big he was intimidating. Duren also made fear work as his best pitch. He wore eyeglasses that were described as the bottoms of milk bottles and he didn't have nearly the control he wished he had. He reminded batters of that wildness by throwing a warmup pitch to the backstop every time he was called into a game.

I remember watching from the ground-level box seats at Dodger Stadium as Duren, then with the Angels, pitched the ninth inning against the Yankees. Clete Boyer had to dive under a high, inside fastball and he lay in the batter's box as if he were hugging the dirt for protection. It was like the Bill Mauldin cartoon of Willie and Joe under machine-gun fire, one of them saying, "I can't get no lower, my buttons is in the way."

In recent years, almost all the exceptional relief pitchers threw a pitch the hitters saw very rarely. Elroy Face and Lindy McDaniel threw a forkball. Make a fist with one hand and wedge it between the first two fingers of the other hand. That's a forkball. It comes out of that grip with little rotation and drops sharply, like a spitball.

Phil Regan, called "the vulture" in the Koufax-Drysdale years with the Dodgers, threw what hitters swore was a spitter. Ron Perranoski threw a curveball that broke in enormous proportions, both horizontally and vertically. He also threw from a "drag-arm" delivery. His arm came around a count after he took his stride, an instant later than the batter expected it. Stu Miller didn't have a pitch that did any kind of remarkable moving around, except that the ball traveled slower than anything else the hitters saw. He also developed the deceptive knack of snapping his head around before throwing the ball.

Hoyt Wilhelm pitched in more games than any other pitcher. He threw a knuckleball that fluttered and darted so much that not even his catchers could handle it.

Clyde King wasn't a spectacularly effective relief pitcher but he was so devious that he became a pitching coach and later one of the few pitchers to manage in the big leagues. One of his tricks was to twist his cap so he could look at the plate while the runner thought King was looking at first base. He once struck out Whitey Lockman with a wad of bubble gum on the ball. When Roy Campanella caught the third strike, he flung the ball into left field to dislodge the gum.

One of King's best-loved memories is of how he struck out the young Willie Mays in 1951, the first time they faced each other. Leo Durocher, who knew King from the Dodgers, was managing the Giants and coaching at third base. As Mays was going to bat, Leo headed him off. He warned Mays about King's barely-legal quick pitch.

"Before you put that second foot in the box," Durocher advised Mays, "be sure you're ready, then tell the umpire you're ready." Mays turned to tell the umpire he was ready, just in time to see strike one was already there.

"Mr. Leo," Mays shrilled, and Durocher called time to advise Mays again. This time Mays tried to speak to the umpire without taking his eyes off King, but shifted his attention enough for King to sneak over strike two.

Again Durocher called time and illustrated his instructions with an exaggerated pantomime. Mays followed orders properly until he couldn't resist one more look at the umpire. And King had called strike three on the way.

All of those people became relief pitchers because they were a little short of making it as starters. Luis Arroyo had a brief fling as an effective starter with the Cardinals but had his real success when he learned the screwball in Cuban winter ball. The Yankees picked him off the discard pile in Triple A. He wound up with his pitching arm so twisted that it hung relaxed with the palm turned out.

His career as a relief star lasted two seasons. That's the nature of being a relief pitcher. Managers use their hot man until he cools off. When he's hot for an extended period, often he gets very cold for a long time. Larry Sherry was great for the 1959 Dodgers and never again. Frequently a relief pitcher will have alternating good and mediocre seasons, as if a man who pitched that often in one season needed a year to rest. Perranoski was an exception. He gave the Dodgers repeated quality seasons in the 1960s.

McGraw was an exception until last season. Once he found himself for the 1969 season, he had four successive good years. Then there was last year, which was a five-month drought. The plan for this season was to leave the hitters expecting his fine screwball by showing it occasionally but giving them something else to hit. Three of the four strikeouts in the two innings

Yogi Berra, manager

Jerry Koosman

Jon Matlack

Bob Miller

Tom Seaver

George Stone

Bob Apodaca

Ray Sadecki

Tug McGraw

Jerry Cram

Harry Parker

Hank Webb

Craig Swan

Rube Walker, pitching coach

against San Diego yesterday were on fastballs. "But I'm not completely avoiding it," McGraw said. His evidence was that he struck out Nate Colbert with the scroogie.

He sounds defensive. "I'm just getting over an injury," he said, "I wasn't one hundred per cent. . . . The screwball is the pitch that puts the most strain on the place I was sore. I was going to try to throw it less this season. It never hurt me. I was throwing it less. . . . I'm trying to get over this injury."

McGraw has never had arm trouble before. Athletes with confidence—and McGraw is one of them—feel they are indestructible. Pitchers know and understand the rational and irrational fears of other pitchers, yet they like to feel it can't happen to them. It's a protection against the worst outrages of reality. Now here he is with those hidden fears perhaps coming to pass. He really doesn't understand what's happening to him.

MAY 7, SHEA STADIUM

Roger Craig was close to a saint in 1963 when he lost eighteen in a row—he always stood up under questioning—but I haven't seen anybody like him since. Certainly not Seaver, who pitched nine innings today and lost a lead again. The Giants beat him, 4–3, in the first game of a doubleheader. It was Seaver's seventh start and he has one win to show for it. Following protocol, reporters waited in the appointed between-game interview room for an appearance by Seaver. We waited and waited. Matt Winick, the public relations assistant, appeared. He looked shaken. "He doesn't want to come in," Winick said.

"What did he say?" Winick was asked.

"I'd rather not say," Winick said.

"He didn't say much to me, either," Berra said.

Obviously, Seaver's pride has been cut deeply. He had his lead in the second inning when Jerry Grote hit a home run that the publicity staff announced as giving the Mets the league lead in home runs. What wasn't announced was that Steve Ontiveros' homer that tied the score in the fourth and Gary Matthews' three-run homer that won the game in the eighth also tied the Mets for most home runs allowed. And Seaver has allowed the most home runs in the League—nine.

You can make some excuses for Seaver. He had a bit of bad luck again, but he's always been stronger than bad luck. With one out in the eighth there was an infield single on a ball that Felix Millan normally handles at second base. If he had, then Garry Maddox would have been the third out. With two real outs, Seaver walked Ontiveros and thought he had a third strike past Matthews. Seaver dropped to one knee the moment he released the next pitch. Then he flung a handful of dirt at the mound. He didn't need to watch it leave the park.

George Stone was waiting for Seaver in the clubhouse when the game was over. "I just patted him on the back and told him, 'Nice game,'" Stone said. "He kept walking to the trainer's room."

It was hard enough for Stone to put his thoughts out for publication, but then I've never seen him hide from the chore. He told about Seaver after his own painful defeat in the second game. Stone went into the ninth inning with his best game of the season, eight scoreless innings, but the Mets didn't make a run for him and he lost it in the ninth, 3–0. "I been having trouble finding my own self," Stone said.

There were some unfortunate breaks for Stone, too, after pitching such a pretty game—and he hasn't won even one yet. He gave up a leadoff single in the ninth and thought he had an edge when Matthews couldn't sacrifice. Then Stone was charged with a balk and the winning run moved to second. On the next pitch Matthews doubled inside the third base bag and the run was home.

Stone thought the balk might have broken his concentration for the next pitch. It was one more thing to be viewed as an unfortunate break, like the fatal slider Seaver hung to Matthews in the first game.

"We're making too many bad pitches at the wrong time, and, damn it, they're not missing them," Berra said.

Ah, the hanging slider, the breaking ball that defies the intention to break down and, instead, sits up so brightly in the hitter's power arc. That's the home run just waiting to happen.

"I don't think it can happen all year," Stone said. "Sometimes they pop them up." It was the only way to face going home to dinner on a Sunday afternoon.

MAY 8, SHEA STADIUM

There are societies, anthropologists tell us, where there are strong pressures for a son not to outdo his father. Almost all of us remember the uneasiness of beating dad for the first time in ping pong or in half-court basketball or striking him out in stickball. Babe Dahlgren must have felt terribly awkward when he replaced Lou Gehrig at first base. It was awkward for Jon Matlack to hold court among the notebooks and pens around the table in the middle of the clubhouse tonight. It's the place the players sit to autograph the required baseballs. It's the place the bridge players commandeer during rain delays. It's the place a player sits after an outstanding performance when he knows there will be a lot of reporters asking questions.

Seaver sat there after his near-perfect game of 1969. Actually he sat on it, there were so many people who needed to hear what he had to say. He sat there when he struck out nineteen batters in 1970. Four of every five appearances at that table had been made by Seaver it seems. It was fine for anybody else to appear there when Seaver was going good, but sitting there now made Matlack uneasy. He had pitched a four-hitter, striking out twelve Giants in a 4–2 victory. It was his fourth victory of the season and the prospects for him are exciting.

Since Seaver arrived here in 1967, he's been the "Big Guy" of the pitching staff. Last night Seaver walked past the cluster around Matlack in silent observation. Jack Lang of the *Long Island Press* called to Seaver, "The big guy is here." Seaver smiled, nodded and continued on his way. Later he returned and made an exaggerated presentation of his handshake to Matlack. There was no telling if the remark had drawn blood. But Matlack felt it. "I feel everybody is giving him a hard time," Matlack said. "They're more or less forgetting when you couldn't beat the son of a gun."

Matlack has heard Seaver booed his last two times out. That comes after a bad month—seven starts and one win—following an uncertain spring training, following a disappointing last month of last season. At the moment, Matlack is the Tom Seaver of the Met pitching staff, but he still sees Seaver at the head of the pecking order.

"I realize on paper I might look better," Matlack said. "But what's on paper doesn't mean a hell of a lot. He's still number one to me. So he's had seven starts. He's got thirty to go, a whole season . . ."

In the meantime, the hitters continue to say Seaver is not quite the same Seaver, and they rave about Matlack as if they were watching the succession to the throne. It was Matlack's first complete game in the big leagues without a walk, another sign of increasing maturity.

"The pecking order is not going to change, not this year," he protested. "Let's say I've got a chance to be in the position Tom is in now. Tom doesn't have it together yet. He may not be throwing as hard as Tom Seaver can throw. . . . I'm not disputing the fact that I'm getting better."

Seaver has always been eager to recognize Matlack's talent and eager to help him. Seaver sees some of himself in Matlack's desire to improve himself and Matlack admires the consistency Seaver has attained. They have more social contact off the field than any of the pitchers. Matlack feels for Seaver. "I feel something," Matlack said, "I can't feel sympathy. He doesn't want it."

For one thing, in his success, Seaver has not been an especially sympathetic character. But, more than that, there is this feeling of Seaver as a security blanket on the team. None of them is ready to replace it yet.

It might take all season. And if it came to pass that this was the season he supplanted Seaver, would it disturb Matlack? "Hell no," he said.

MAY 10, CHICAGO

What Jerry Koosman had called "a circulator" in his finger turned out to be a broken capillary, but it was just fine today. He pitched all but the last out of a nice 7–2 victory over the Cubs.

It was Bob Miller, not McGraw, who came in to throw one pitch for the last out. Miller's 4.20 is the lowest earned-run average in the bullpen. McGraw's is 7.36; he hurts inside and out. Continuing to be McGraw is more difficult for him all the time.

"Right now I'm at the stage where I know what's wrong so I'm very depressed fighting off bad moods," he said. "I'm trying to act flakey and have a good time. I mean, I know ya gotta believe, but it's hard."

Last year there was no explanation for McGraw's mid-season slump—no ache, no pain, just no effectiveness. It was bewildering. "I almost wished for it sometimes, to wake up and have something wrong with my arm," he said. "Now that I have my wish, I just wish I'd hurry up and get rid of it so I can go out and enjoy playing."

The muscle strain that was a big lump in the left side of his back is now a small lump. He says the pain is somewhat less. But it's still pain. "How do you measure pain?" he asked. "Is it two ouches or 2½ ouches or three ouches?"

"After a while," he said, "you start to wonder a little if you're jaking. You wonder if your teammates think you're jaking. The fans, you wonder what they think. I'm making $90,000 a year and they get on me for it. It's a natural thing to do, to yell, I don't deserve it. You can't go around telling everyone, 'Ouch, ouch, ouch. It hurts because nobody knows how you feel but yourself."

McGraw has been spending some time on the road promoting his book *Screwball*. He does well on radio interviews. "The other day I was asked which I preferred, grass or AstroTurf," McGraw said. "I said I didn't know, I had never smoked AstroTurf. Some of the guys said that was in bad taste." Some of the guys also say McGraw is spending too much time promoting the book.

MAY 11, CHICAGO

Up the stairs enclosed in mesh to keep the fans from abusing the players—and vice versa—climbed Jerry Grote with the baseball in his hand. Craig Swan was waiting to accept it in the clubhouse at the top of the stairs. It was a memento of Swan's first major-league victory.

"I'll keep it. I'll keep it forever," Swan said.

It was hard enough to get. It was his fourth start, including one at the tail end of last season, and he had a measure of bad luck in all of them, including this one.

He had a 1–0 lead after four innings and then there was a forty-minute rain delay. The lead grew to 5–0, and after five innings Berra and Walker decided Swan had had enough work. He had thrown ninety-eight pitches and he had to warm up twice because of the rain. "What the hell, you don't want to take a chance with a kid like that," Berra said. All Swan had to do after that was watch the Cubs cut three runs off his lead with Ray Sadecki pitching in the seventh and eighth and towel the nervous perspiration off his face in the clubhouse as Harry Parker pitched the last $1\frac{2}{3}$ innings.

At 220 pounds, Swan is supposedly in some kind of shape. His body doesn't look lean and hard, but then I can hardly visualize him at 252 when he joined the Mets last September.

On the way to Wrigley Field this morning the team bus passed a McDonald's and a voice from the back yelled, "Stop here, bussy, and let Swan out." The other pitchers needle him about his eating habits all the time. You might think they do it helpfully to remind him that he has to watch his weight, but I think they do it more to get a laugh for their own benefit.

Who knows when Jon Matlack is going to be able to pitch again? He was minding his business, shagging balls in the outfield before the game and felt something pull in the front of his thigh. He was pitching so well after recovering from that nine-day layoff last month, it would be a shame for him to lose his edge. His reaction was, "Why me?" And there is no answer. He said it felt as if he had been struck by a golf ball.

"I've never had muscle trouble before," Matlack said. "I was loose out there. I didn't slip or step in a hole. I didn't even stretch for the ball. I was just gliding under it and *pow*."

MAY 12, CHICAGO

Yogi Berra peeked out of the manager's office into the clubhouse where the Mets celebrated winning the Eastern Division championship last September for a glimpse of Seaver's reaction to another late-inning defeat. That celebration seemed long ago as Tom Seaver sat, uniform shirt off, pants open, his elbow on his knee, studying the floor between his feet. For twenty minutes he absently cleaned the dirt from his spikes and picked at his nails and stared while teammates who bank on him stole furtive looks. When he rose to borrow a cigaret, eyes followed him about the room. Seaver rarely smokes.

The Mets got two runs to tie in the eighth and George Mitterwald got a broken-bat single with one out in the ninth to win it for the Cubs in sudden death, 4–3. Actually, it was sudden death only on the scoreboard because there were several earlier wounds.

The first was a two-run home run off Seaver by Jose Cardenal in the first inning. In 290 innings last season he allowed only twenty-three. With one out and no one on in the last of the ninth he walked Carmen Fanzone and pinch-runner Matt Alexander stole second. Perhaps Alexander got such a good jump because Seaver was concentrating so hard on

Mitterwald at the plate. It's understandable that Seaver should have some tunnel vision at this point.

The condition of their security blanket must have some effect on the minds of the other players. They are closing ranks around him. "He will win," Rusty Staub said.

"I'll take my chances with him," said Ed Kranepool, who has been a part of all of Seaver's seasons here. "By the end of the year he'll have the most victories on the club or be close to it."

But right now, when the Mets need something to keep from falling fatally far behind, Seaver can't help. "I don't think it should affect the team," Kranepool said. "Just because he's not winning doesn't mean we're going to lay down. We're not going to win without him, but I'll take my chances with him no matter how bad he's going."

Of course they're not going to lay down. Of course, as Kranepool said, Seaver's struggle shouldn't affect the team. If they were all computers Seaver's problems wouldn't interfere. But when they all have the realization in the back of their minds "we're not going to win without him," how can it not affect the team? How much does Seaver's gloom rub off on the other players? If he's taking the losses so hard, does it give the whole team a shove toward losing again tomorrow?

Seaver didn't pitch poorly today. He pitched just well enough to lose. He's not a man who can accept consolation from others and there aren't many offering to console him or to advise him. "I always listened to advice," Koosman said. "I might not take it, but I listened to advice. In his mind, Tom thinks he has to find it himself."

Having failed to communicate with Seaver in the clubhouse, Henry Hecht of the New York *Post*, a short, dark young reporter who seldom wears socks, tried again at the airport before the flight to St. Louis. His luck was no better. "I'm trying to be as nice as I can," Seaver explained.

I ask players on other teams how they feel about what Seaver is going through. They all say they understand perfectly, but when I ask them if they feel sorry for him, most of them laugh. "We've been saying," said Bobby Bonds of the Giants, "maybe his wallet is too heavy."

MAY 13, ST. LOUIS

With Matlack unable to take his turn, Berra gave the ball to Bob Apodaca for his first start in the big leagues. Against Bob Gibson, no less. It was worth a celebration. The Mets won, 5–3. Apodaca had his first victory in the big leagues and all it cost him was a little skin on the middle finger of his pitching hand.

"You think about your first win, how it's going to come," Apodaca said, expressing the fantasy of every rookie pitcher and every pitcher in the minor leagues. "Will it be a third of an inning? Will it be a complete game?"

It was something in between, but all anybody could have asked of a man who hadn't pitched in two weeks, had an earned-run average of more than seven and dark visions of being sent to Tidewater at any moment. He pitched five innings, allowed two runs and six hits, and it wasn't the Cardinals who ended his game but a blister on that finger.

People who don't know baseball ridicule baseball players for the injuries that keep them out of action. "This isn't some sport," says former football coach Norm Van Brocklin about his own machismo game, "where you play 8,000 games and run out to second base and call time out because you've got a hangnail."

There is this basic difference. Football, for the most part, is a strength sport. Baseball is a skill sport. Matlack could have played with his muscle pull taped if he were an interior lineman who spent his whole game within an area of a few yards. Apodaca could have stayed in the game if he could have had his hand taped. But since he depends on touch to throw the ball over a thin slice of a seventeen-inch target at a distance of sixty feet, then a blister is a real handicap.

"When you're not throwing enough, your fingers can get soft," Apodaca said. And each time the seams roll off a fingertip, there's friction. "It wasn't really that bad, but Yogi came out and didn't want to take any chances," Apodaca said.

He said he felt strong enough to pitch nine innings. "He was coming out after six anyways," Berra corrected. Harry Parker struggled through the sixth inning, which Apodaca began by walking a batter, but handled the next three innings well.

Despite his success of the night, Apodaca felt uncomfortable as a starting pitcher. He's been trained as a relief pitcher and that's how he sees himself. "I want to get back to the bullpen as soon as I can," he said. "I just feel more comfortable out there."

Tug McGraw threw on three occasions in the bullpen and pronounced that worthy of a celebration of his own. "Wo, ho, you're goddam right I was ready," he announced. Then he whispered, "I've got a big scoop, I may not be ready to get anyone out, but McGraw is ready to take the mound. I'm poppin' it, I tell you. I'm poppin' it. Well, I wasn't poppin' it, but I was throwing okay. I've got a new secret pitch. They'll find out soon enough what it is. They'll be saying, 'That sumbitch, he was so tough before, now he's got a new pitch.'" And the Cardinals' doctor examined Matlack's leg and said he could begin throwing in two days.

MAY 15, ST. LOUIS

When they blow the siren here after a home run by the Cardinals, it's intended as an act of celebration. It isn't meant as an act of cruelty. But the screeching was a harsh underline as Tom Heintzleman was running out his home run and Yogi Berra was walking to the mound to take out McGraw.

Whatever McGraw said the other night about feeling so good indicated nothing. Maybe he was trying to sell himself a bill of goods.

With the Mets on the short end of a 6–0 score in the eighth inning, it seemed like a safe place to try McGraw for the first time in ten days. What happened was brutal.

He walked to the mound with none of the bounce that's always been his style, as if he knew in the bullpen that the bright things he said Monday were just words. He took long pauses between pitches and when he threw there was no zip. "He's not throwing good," Berra acknowledged. "He had nothing."

"I told Yogi he didn't have much," said Duffy Dyer, who caught McGraw's warmups in the bullpen. "But at least he was coming from the right spot with his arm, coming over the top. The other day he wasn't even doing that."

Maybe McGraw felt better because he had dropped his arm down in his delivery. Sidearm often seems more comfortable for sore-armed overhand pitchers.

For a moment it looked as if McGraw were going to get out of the inning, perhaps to meet his fate another time or to be on the road to recovery. After a leadoff single, he got a double play and St. Louis pitcher Lynn McGlothen lifted a foul fly. But left fielder George Theodore and third baseman Wayne Garrett collided and the ball dropped untouched. Then McGlothen singled and Jose Cruz tripled and Heintzleman hit his first major-league home run. And Berra had to go to the mound to get McGraw.

When it was all over, McGraw sat at the table putting together a sandwich of American cheese, well-done roast beef, and salami on white bread. It seems that no matter what happens, ball players are never too disturbed to eat after a game.

McGraw was too upset to talk. "This is the first time I've had no comment since '65," McGraw said. "It's just that I don't know what to say."

Before he left, McGraw had the presence to scribble a note of congratulations and have it sent down the corridor to McGlothen in the St. Louis clubhouse. McGlothen, who came from the Red Sox before this season, had a shutout until one out in the ninth in his first game against the Mets.

It was a trace of the real McGraw. "Just say the note he sent me is a sign of a lot of class," McGlothen said. "It's a nice gesture. I think he's a nice guy. He's always been a nice guy."

He's having some problems now. I hope he works them out." McGraw may have a whole league rooting for him, but nothing seems to help.

MAY 16, ST. LOUIS

McGraw didn't have to wait until the team left after the 6–4 win over the Cardinals. The Mets put him on a plane home in the afternoon and he's supposed to see the doctor tomorrow. It seems unbelieveable underneath all the grief, but the Mets won four of the six games on the trip. "It doesn't seem like we played that well," Harry Parker observed.

Parker pitched well picking up George Stone in the seventh inning and Stone did well enough getting to the seventh. It was the first win for Stone. All he had to show for the season was three defeats and the theft of his car from in front of his apartment near Shea Stadium—the car, a two-door car with one door handle. And when the plane got to LaGuardia, Diana was there to meet him. Life isn't all that bad.

MAY 27, SHEA STADIUM

A request was made for McGraw to be placed on the disabled list. That means he can't pitch for twenty-one days. The doctor says the problem is purely muscular and rest is the treatment. So Berra needs another pitcher. Hank Webb is the only one doing well at Tidewater and he's not a relief pitcher.

What the Mets really want is more of the Seaver who shut out the Expos tonight, 5–0. He struck out thirteen, allowed five hits and didn't walk anybody.

"That's the best Tom Seaver I've seen since I've been managing the Expos," Gene Mauch said. He's a good man with a quote. He can make a keen analysis in colorful terms or he can spread bullshit with a wide brush.

Seaver said he wasn't all that impressed. When Seaver went to the mound, he chose to throw his curveball rather than the fastball and maybe that's what made the Expos look so bad. Jerry Grote thought Seaver threw more good curveballs than he'd ever seen before in one game from him, which is mixed praise. "He seemed to be throwing the wrong pitch for them at the right time," Grote said. "But he didn't have his real super fastball. He's gettin close but he's still not coming quite over the top."

It's funny the way Seaver feels his body doing something different from what Grote sees. In Seaver's last start in Chicago Grote told him he looked like a sidearm pitcher and Seaver said that if he tried to get on top any farther he'd fall on his back.

Seaver is very deep into himself on the mound. Since the Expos had so few runners on base and were behind three runs after the third inning, they didn't have a chance to run on Seaver, but Bud Harrelson observed the depth of Seaver's self-absorption. The scoreboard flashed the wrong number of outs one inning and Harrelson went to the mound to talk to Seaver thinking there were two outs. When he mentioned it, Seaver said, "No, no. That's wrong. One out."

"Another time he might have kidded about it," Harrelson said. "That wasn't his mood. But maybe tonight he should have been serious."

MAY 18, SHEA STADIUM

A group of players formed a quarter circle just inside the door to the manager's office at one end of the Mets' clubhouse. They left just enough room for Yogi Berra to see the big screen of the color television so they could all watch the Preakness.

There's nothing like a little winning streak to enable ball players to be involved in something other than their own problems. Jon Matlack shut out the Expos, 6–0, and got it done in time for the horse race.

Then Matlack was free to observe how well Rusty Staub was swinging and to appreciate his two-run single, which helped give Matlack a four-run lead in the first inning. After that, it was a whole lot easier for Matlack to test the thigh muscles he tore a week ago. He took a one-hitter into the seventh inning.

"I realized when I was warming up that I was going to be all right," Matlack said, but he told Rube Walker he didn't know about stamina. "I told Rube not to let me get in too deep because I didn't have too much reserve." Matlack never got in too deep and had enough left to strike out two batters in the ninth inning.

Tomorrow the Mets can get back to .500 if they sweep the doubleheader.

MAY 19, SHEA STADIUM

Today most of the Mets would have missed the Preakness. They didn't get to .500. They lost both games to Montreal, 7–4 and 5–0, and there was nothing pretty about it.

They had a chance in the first game, but the bullpen let it get out of reach. The bullpen has made fifty appearances and has compiled a record of two wins, eight losses, and four saves. The composite earned-run average is 6.17, which doesn't begin to account for the runs charged to the starter after the relief pitcher has come in.

It remains for a man like Jerry Koosman to act unconcerned, even after being pounded for ten hits in eight innings in the second game. "This happens every year," Koosman said about the relief situation. "But this year it's just lasting a little longer. In the past, most of the attention has been focused on Tug carrying us. This year the other relievers had to hold him up. I'm not saying this is the reason the other relievers aren't doing their best . . ."

Calm as Koosman may be, Apodaca can't be. His earned-run average is 6.88. "It's kinda hard to explain, isn't it?" he said.

He hasn't learned the lessons of the bullpen as well as Bob Miller, who mopped up with a scoreless inning in the second game. With a 3.94 ERA, Miller doesn't remind anybody of what McGraw should be doing, but it's the best the Mets have. Besides, he's been around sixteen years and there's no guarantee that Apodaca will finish this season.

Miller spent the early parts of both games with his legs propped up, reading magazines and newspapers. "The most important part of being a relief pitcher is the ability to relax," he said. "To me a pressure or nervousness is a fear of losing. I'm not afraid of losing. Either you do it, or you don't."

Apodaca still has to learn, but there have been a lot of lessons in losing for the bullpen lately. "It'll snap out," Rube Walker said. It's the only way to think.

MAY 20, SHEA STADIUM

There's a lingering feeling among some of the Mets that certain umpires are giving them a trimming ever since the club reported to the league that they weren't getting back all the extra baseballs given to the umpires. There was a newspaper story about the losses. The Mets kept track and pinned the loss down to one team of umpires, and those are the ones the players feel are making the close calls against them. Of course, it's normal for a team that's losing more than it should to feel there are outside forces working against it.

The illustration tonight was the pitch that got past Jerry Grote's glove and narrowly missed plate umpire Bruce Froemming. Froemming said Grote deliberately let the ball go. That followed a pitch to Billy Williams in the eighth inning that the umpire called a ball. Grote asked where the pitch was and Froemming didn't bother to respond because, "he gives you a sarcastic answer whenever you do answer that question."

Grote and Harry Parker, who pitched a good eight innings and was the loser on an unearned run, said the ball escaped Grote because it wasn't the pitch the catcher called for. Parker wears glasses for reading, but not for pitching, and he said he misread Grote's fingers as calling for a fastball rather than a slider. Froemming said that if that were the case and the pitcher had crossed up the catcher, Grote would have gone immediately to the mound.

Grote said his evidence came before the game when Froemming returned the balls sent to the umpires' room to be officially rubbed up. There was a note, Grote said, that read: "Here's your five dozen balls. Count them."

Despite Grote's nature—"Will Rogers never met Jerry Grote," says Joe Valerio of the New York *Post*—the pitchers regard him very highly as a man to work with. They missed him sorely when he was out half of last season with a broken arm. When he returned, the collective earned-run average was half a run better.

"The average fan has no conception of what he means to our staff," Jerry Koosman says. "He knows as much about me as I do. He knows how to handle every one of us. I was lost without him last year."

It wasn't always that way between Grote and the pitching staff, especially Koosman and Tug McGraw. Grote always had that great arm and short fuse. As hard as the pitchers threw the ball, Grote threw it back harder. It was very unsettling. McGraw recalls being called up from the minor leagues, getting one puffy glove hand and asking Wes Westrum, then the manager, to have someone else catch his next start. "I went out to learn to control myself," McGraw recalls. "Jerry was doing to me what I'd been sent out to learn not to do."

In the charge to the pennant in 1969, Koosman and Jim McAndrew objected to Grote's handling. McAndrew, a sensitive soul, complained that Grote yelled at him. Koosman complained that Grote called for the fastball so he would have a better chance to throw out the baserunners instead of calling for the pitch the situation indicated.

"It was a struggle for me then," Grote says. "Sometimes I didn't know what pitches to call. I was just sticking out fingers. Then maybe three years ago, all of a sudden things fell into place. Then I could sense the difference in myself. I could read a hitter. I understood our pitchers better. I knew exactly what I wanted to do."

The final responsibility for selecting the pitch belongs to the pitcher. If he doesn't believe in the pitch he's about to deliver, it's not likely to be much of a pitch. But the catcher is supposed to be an extension of the manager and the pitching coach. He's required to remember the pregame meetings on the strengths and weaknesses of the hitters even if the pitchers forget. The catcher is supposed to catch the ball in the dirt with a runner on third base and at the same time observe the flaw in the pitcher's delivery that allowed a runner to get to third and caused the pitch to be in the dirt.

Pitchers rarely become managers. They're so isolated by the demands of their art that they rarely get a full view of the demands of the rest of the game. Seven of the current managers are former catchers. None are former pitchers.

The catcher's signal is a recommendation to the pitcher, but if the catcher has enough status on the team, his wish is the pitcher's command. It took Grote a long time to form a good working partnership with Seaver. "It took four or five years before we reached the point where I would call something and Tom would shake it off and I knew exactly what he was looking for."

The pressure on the catcher can be excruciating. Jim Hegan, now a coach with Detroit, enjoyed a long career as a .224 hitter because he was so skilled in handling the fine Cleveland pitching staff of the forties and fifties. Many of those years were spent in second place, chasing the Yankees with the awareness that the wrong pitch called could be the difference in the whole season. Hegan says he often spent long hours after games slumped in a chair at home before he was able to bring himself to the dinner table. He says he wouldn't want his daughter to marry a catcher and have to live with those tensions.

In 1940 the Cincinnati Reds were in the August heat of the pennant race when a late-inning home run broke up a game. Catcher Willard Hershberger brooded about it long after the game. A day later he was still deeply depressed. Then he was found in his hotel room. He committed suicide.

MAY 21, SHEA STADIUM

Tonight George Stone pitched his first complete game since last July. It wasn't very pretty, but it was a win. He scattered twelve hits but won, 10–5. Bob Miller was up in the bullpen three times. If Stone had allowed one more baserunner in the first inning, Bob Apodaca would have been called. But Stone wasn't looking for perfection. He was perfectly happy with what he did with his 131 pitches.

Stone's fan mail says he's throwing too many curveballs. Stone says the problem is concentration. "My mind doesn't focus too good until later in the game the last few times," he said. "It seems to me I'm going to have to make out I'm in the fifth inning when I'm in the first."

Apodaca is now the early man in the bullpen and Miller is the late man. That's a reversal of status.

MAY 22, SHEA STADIUM

Another jolting loss for Seaver. Two more home runs and six runs in five innings. But this time he was around to answer questions after the game. "I'm not crazy about sitting around answering questions," Seaver said. "If I were really down, I wouldn't be here. I had a lousy day. A miserable day."

There appeared to be as much reason for Seaver to be "down" as he was in Chicago or in Shea the times he refused to answer questions. But there has been considerable criticism of Seaver's behavior. Dick Young of the *Daily News* has offered the thought that Seaver's leadership extends to spreading misery and self-pity in the clubhouse, and the players fear Young's criticism. Others have pointed out that the test of a man is how he responds to adversity. Young's comment doesn't exactly add to a man's image and Seaver's image commands a high price on the advertising market. Seaver's business agent, Matt Merola, says he's suggested to Seaver that he was hurting himself with his impatience.

So Seaver held himself up for examination again tonight. The problem is that the questions have all been asked and the answers are all the same. It's just that they're now ten starts into the season—more than a quarter of the way through. His season and the Mets' season have taken on a very depressing tone and the recollection of last season's comeback doesn't penetrate his gloom.

"What's most depressing," Seaver said, "is being very inconsistent. Not just game-to-game, but inning-to-inning. I'm just throwing a tremendous amount of bad pitches with nothing on them. The ball just seemed to be dead."

MAY 23, SHEA STADIUM

Apodaca is shaken. Seaver has status that says he'll start in turn all season unless Shea Stadium fills with water, as originally predicted. Apodaca has to worry when he sends out his laundry. Can Tidewater be far behind? "As much as I enjoyed the style of living in Virginia last year, I don't want to go back," he said. "It would be embarrassing to go back down now. People would say 'he had his chance.'"

He's played last night's ninth inning (in which he gave up a three-run homer in relief of Seaver) over and over again. "A couple of days from now, if I haven't pitched, I'll probably still think about it," he said. "You worry your first year up. It's affected my wife as it has me. She goes through the same pains I do.

"Yogi was kind of mad that I didn't go with my best pitch to Morales," Apodaca said. He had struck out Morales with a curve the previous time up. Berra said he ordered Rick Monday intentionally walked so Apodaca could use the curve on Morales again. Ron Hodges called for it, but Apodaca shook off the signal. Pitchers are obligated to remember what they throw to each hitter, especially a pitcher like Apodaca who isn't overpowering. He has to be a smart pitcher. That was the problem; Apodaca was trying to be a smart pitcher.

Maybe the problem was that Apodaca's fastball was not quite inside enough, not that it was a bad choice. If it had been a good fastball and broke Morales' bat, Apodaca would have been a smart pitcher.

MAY 28, CINCINNATI

George Stone couldn't get out of the fifth inning. In $4\frac{2}{3}$, he was hit for seven runs, six earned. The Reds won, 7–2. But

THE PITCHING STAFF

things are very calm and quiet on the Mets. The Mets have always been dominated by the college football ethic—they rarely grumble in the open.

On the Pirates, it's something else. They're as far down as the Mets in the standings and Jim Rooker says he thinks that's criminal. Rooker is a pitcher and pitchers normally don't seek roles as team leaders. Seaver has the status on the Mets to be a leader with his manner as well as with his pitching—when he's pitching well—but it's a difficult responsibility for a man who plays only once in five days. And Seaver doesn't seek that kind of role.

Rooker said some of the Pirates ought to take their paychecks with their backs turned, the way they're playing. "With the kind of money some guys are getting on this club, it's a shame," Rooker said. That might have been an expression of momentary outrage. At least that's how it sounded.

But yesterday, after the Pirates swept two games from San Diego, Rooker hinted that he spoke his mind as a cool psychological ploy rather than in a moment of anger. "If I have to say this every day, I'll say it every day," he said, "I'll do anything it takes to win." Maybe the Mets could use a little of that too, but it's not in sight.

MAY 29, CINCINNATI

McGraw can't pitch but he's on the trip, for whatever that's worth. He can try to keep in shape by running in the outfield and by shagging flies, and he can try to have a little fun by putting a glove on his throwing hand and taking throws at first base in batting practice. He can try to feel a part of the team.

But the game begins and there's no place for him. McGraw showered and took the elevator to the press box. It's air conditioned and heated and around the fifth inning there are snacks available, but the press box at Riverfront Stadium is sealed from the outside world. There are no sounds of excitement from the fans who come to see the Western Division champions meet the Mets, who beat them in the playoffs. It's like watching giant screen television with the sound off.

It took ten innings before the Mets succumbed. Jon Matlack pitched nine of them and left with a 2–2 tie. Harry Parker got two outs in a Tug McGraw situation and then gave up a sudden death home run to Tony Perez.

"I felt kind of funny being up there when I could have been down there," McGraw said afterward. "Who knows? If I was ready to pitch, that could have been me in Parker's situation.

"When I saw Parker he looked like he was throwing good. I thought we had a chance with him in there. But when Perez homered, I just got up from where I was sitting and just said to myself, 'Well, we lost another one.' It was kind of a sinking feeling. It doesn't do any good to think, 'What if I were there.' If you think like that, it only bothers you that much more."

The circumstance of Perez' entrance and departure brought back unpleasant memories. The last time Parker pitched against the Reds was in the twelfth inning of the fourth game of the playoffs, and Pete Rose homered off him to beat the Mets, 2–1, and sent the series into the fifth game.

Everybody on both sides instantly recalled the occurrence when Parker entered the game. "Oh, boy, did I ever think of that," Johnny Bench, the Reds' catcher said. He even yelled from the dugout, "Hey, Parker, we're gonna get you."

Parker said he wasn't thinking at all about last year's playoffs. "What kind of a pitcher would I be if I was still fretting about something that happened last season?" he said. Parker made two good pitches low and away and then got one high and inside. Perez put it in the left field loge.

Matlack couldn't go beyond nine innings because that pulled thigh muscle gave him trouble running out a hit in the eighth. If he could have run harder, he would have scored on Bud Harrelson's double. If his thigh didn't bother him, he could have stayed in the game. It's that kind of season.

MAY 30, SHEA STADIUM

The Mayor's Trophy Game is an exercise in civic schizophrenia—the Mets against the Yankees in the ballpark both teams call home this season. It was precisely as the fan in right field put it on his sign: "Beat New York."

It used to be a big deal. The Mets wanted very much to win and the Yankees certainly didn't want to lose, no matter what their casual front said. But now both teams are involved in games that count in the standings. All right, so there were 35,894 fans in the ballpark, which is a nice crowd for a mere exhibition game, but the managers on both sides knew what their pitching problems were and this was no time to spend somebody important. So both sides called up minor-leaguers to pitch tonight.

There were two reasons for that. One was, obviously, that it saved wear and tear on the arms already in use. The other was that it was a chance to look at Mike Wegener and Bob Kammeyer against big-league competition. When the Yankees called George Medich up from New Haven to pitch in the game two years ago, they were thinking of keeping him. If he had pitched well, they would have. But he demonstrated he wasn't ready.

That left it up to tonight's two pitchers to draw their own conclusions about what the game meant. "I don't know if they brought me up to be the scapegoat or if this is my big chance," Wegener said, mixing his metaphors.

Wegener is twenty-seven. He spent two full seasons with the Expos and was released last season after two seasons in Triple A. His right arm is permanently crooked. "They tell me I was on the table for six hours," he said. "They took out bone chips, decompressed the elbow and shaved the end of the elbow." He also hadn't started a game in two years.

Kammeyer is twenty-three. He is with the Yankees' Double A team at West Haven and is still listed as a prospect. He's a patient prospect. He has a degree in economics from Stanford and if he decides he's not going to make it as a ball player, he'll go to law school. His wife begins law school this fall, and Kammeyer figures he'll have three more years of baseball to make up his mind.

Wegener is beginning to get into the things a ball player does when he can't play ball any more. He's investigating a real estate license or selling insurance or selling something. He's also interested in getting the few months he needs for the four years that qualify for the pension.

What they both know is that they are outsiders in the clubhouse. They are replacements called to the trenches in combat. The others will look out for their own first. There was no great warmth for them in the clubhouse, no real rooting for them on the field. If one of them stays, one of the boys has to go. They could have been accepted in spring training, but not when the boys have come this far together.

As it turned out, there wasn't much to worry about. Wegener was wild and when Rube Walker went to the mound to tell him to throw strikes, Fernando Gonzalez hit a home run with the bases full. Kammeyer didn't do anything to make Bill Virdon insist on keeping him with the Yankees. They told him to go back and finish a good year at New Haven and be ready for spring training.

"It's hard mentally going to spring training every year and wondering when is it gonna happen, when am I going to make it. It's kind of fatiguing," Kammeyer said. "Tonight, I look at it and I feel discouraged, but I say it's only an exhibition. I haven't thought about just quitting baseball, just giving as much as I can for as long as I can. Oh, boy, it's definitely a struggle. I always wanted to play baseball. It's the American dream for me."

Another thing. Craig Swan has been trying to correct his pitching motion, you remember. Well, he has developed tendinitis in his right shoulder and will miss his next start.

MAY 31, SHEA STADIUM

Tug McGraw tested his arm for the doctor this afternoon the way porcupines make love—carefully. He said it felt good. "No discomfort," he pronounced. But then he's said that before. He simulated his pitching motion without pain and then threw softly on the sidelines, which wasn't much different from the way Jerry Koosman, Bob Apodaca, and Bob Miller pitched in the 7–1 loss to Houston.

"I was a bundle of nerves all day waiting to throw," McGraw said. He said he never thought about velocity, just about the lump below his left shoulder blade. It's smaller, but it's still there.

If he doesn't react poorly to the exertion, he's to throw tomorrow and the next day. "If that works out, I go a day without throwing and then try and throw harder and longer," he said. He's eligible to come off the disabled list in five days.

And if he still can't throw hard—McGraw has thought about that a lot. "I've spent most of my money on booze, women, partying, and fancy material things," he said. "And what was left over from that was probably spent foolishly."

JUNE 3, SHEA STADIUM

There were a couple of signs tonight that the impact of the twenty-nine losses is greater than the fact that there are 112 games left on the schedule. Jon Matlack gave one sign and read the other.

"I think everybody is a little complacent now," Matlack said, "a little too much of the 'It's Early' theory. You can never regain a lost game and I'm worried about this 'It's Early' stuff. We've got better manpower potential then last year and we're not clicking. Where the answers lie, I don't know."

The 5–2 loss to the Reds was naturally disturbing to him. Were the Reds reading his pitches? The Reds say that's so much baloney. "We're not reading him," Pete Rose said. "You got a fastball like he does, you got to use it more often." As good a hitter as Rose is, he's too ingenuous to be devious.

"Matlack's not tipping his pitches," Sparky Anderson, the Reds' manager, said. "But after the second inning, he started almost everybody off with a breaking ball."

That's as revealing as telegraphing pitches, and as damaging. Tomorrow, Matlack said, he'll study the films for telltale flaws.

When Wes Westrum was the manager in the bad years of the Mets, he always suspected somebody was spying from the scoreboard or the bullpen when his pitchers were knocked around—the way Eddie Stanky looked for communists under the bed.

JUNE 4, SHEA STADIUM

Jerry Koosman, pitching on three days' rest, pitched out of jams in the third, fourth, and fifth innings and was exhausted when he got into trouble in the seventh. "That's what you got a bullpen for," Yogi Berra explained.

So he brought in Harry Parker, who gave up the game-tying hit. Ray Sadecki bailed out Parker in the eighth, breezed through the ninth, and gave up three runs in the tenth. Another loser, by a score of 6–3.

The winner for the Reds was Pedro Borbon. It was his fourth win. He has seven saves. That's more than the whole Mets' bullpen. Koosman didn't stay around to talk about it.

JUNE 6, SHEA STADIUM

Now reverse everything. Pedro Borbon was the loser for the Reds tonight and Ray Sadecki was the winner for the Mets. That's what relief pitching is all about. The Mets won it, 4–3, but the Reds had the tying run on third with two out in the last of the ninth and the count on Dave Concepcion was three balls and no strikes. Johnny Bench was on deck. Bob Miller was primed in the bullpen. If Concepcion reached base, which looked likely, Miller would be the man to pitch to Bench.

It wasn't a pretty prospect. "I think I'm going into the game," Miller said.

Then Cincinnati manager Sparky Anderson told Concepcion he was free to swing. Anderson said he'd always give the hit sign in that situation, "no matter who's up and who's on deck."

"Then the fly ball goes up and we all said the same thing

down in the bullpen: 'I can't believe what I just saw,'" Miller said. "Not that Concepcion is a bad hitter, but you got Johnny Big Red Machine on deck."

JUNE 7, HOUSTON

When the manager says: "When we get hitting, we don't get pitching; when we get pitching, we don't get any runs. We'll be all right when we get things straightened out," it's usually the sign of a bad team that will never get straightened out. Tonight Harry Parker pitched a splendid six innings giving up only three hits and one run. And Bob Apodaca allowed one hit and no runs in two innings. And the Mets lost, 1–0.

Tug McGraw was eligible to come off the disabled list today, but he'll stay on a couple more days. "My back feels great, brand new," he said. "In fact, it feels so good I went out and got a haircut."

But he thought another three days off—until Tuesday night in Atlanta—would be prudent. There's some stiffness in his shoulder, he said, because of the long layoff. "I'm throwing close to full speed now," he said. He winked. "Which is like Stu Miller," he said.

Ah, Stu Miller the magician of the slow ball. At least McGraw can still kid himself.

If Buzz Capra had ever stuck around here long enough to get close to the establishment, Tom Seaver might have asked across the clubhouse how Capra did with the Braves tonight. Seaver rarely misses a chance to inquire about Nolan Ryan, especially when the general manager is around.

What Capra did was pitch a three-hitter, another shutout, and extend his shutout string to twenty-five innings. He won his fifth consecutive game.

The Mets didn't have a place for him. It's funny, the Braves didn't have a place for him either. He would have pitched long relief for Atlanta unless someone got hurt or they switched to a five-day rotation. Ron Reed got hurt and Capra got his chance.

Each time he goes out to pitch, he has that much more confidence. On the club that couldn't use Capra, only Jon Matlack is pitching as well.

JUNE 9, HOUSTON

"You have to do everything well to win," Ken Boswell noticed. "You have to pitch, hit, and field. But no club has ever won anything winning every game 8–7. You have to get good pitching. And we got a reputation for having a well-blessed staff."

The Mets didn't win 8–7 tonight. They lost, 11–1. Koosman was shelled in the first five innings for seven hits and seven runs and George Stone was shelled in the last two innings for six hits and four runs. Stoney says his arm is fine, if you believe him.

In between, Craig Swan threw three pitches and left after the third was driven off his foot. His foot was okay, but his arm wasn't, and he's already sat out the last two weeks with a sore arm. That dumps another man's load on the pitching staff, which is a minor consideration compared to what it does to Swan's head.

"My elbow felt all right while I was warming up," he said. "But on my first pitch it hurt. It wasn't as bad as before, but I didn't want to throw with any pain. I don't know what we're going to do."

Some pitchers pitch half their career in pain. Steve Barber once compared the intensity of his pain to the intensity of colors. He said on the bad days his arm felt a bright red. And when it wasn't so bad, it was hot pink. In time he learned to live and pitch with it. Swan hasn't been around that long. He still thinks he should feel good. He was very pale when he talked about it, and his voice was hesitant. "I had arm trouble before," he said, "but none this severe." Berra said he'd call Scheffing in New York tomorrow to discuss whether to bring a pitcher up from somewhere in the farm system and whether Swan would replace McGraw on the disabled list.

McGraw threw again before the game and said he was ready. "I threw screwballs, too," he said. "But I could have come back to pitch even if my screwball wasn't ready. The hitters would be looking for it anyhow."

JUNE 10, ATLANTA

The juxtaposition would have been remarkable. For the off-day the Braves tried to set up a press conference with the two pitchers for tomorrow night's game. It's a promotion of some size for the Braves, and since Henry Aaron has already provided his climax by breaking Babe Ruth's home run record, the Braves can use all the promotion they can get.

They proposed to put Tom Seaver and Buzz Capra side by side for interviews—Capra, runty and unimposing, and Seaver, the strong young man with the regal carriage, last season's Cy Young Award winner. It's the first time the Braves and Mets have met and surely the New York press wanted to ask Capra how come he's pitching so well. His 1.17 earned-run average is the best in the league. And surely the Atlanta press would appreciate a chance to talk to Seaver in the comfort of a non-game situation—to ask how come he's not pitching so well. And what else did Seaver have to do on the afternoon of a day off in Atlanta?

Well, anyhow, Capra was there. Seaver said something about not wanting to horn in on an afternoon when Capra deserved the attention. Whatever, his explanation isn't going to sell any tickets here tomorrow.

Right now Capra is the hottest pitcher in baseball and he finds the fact difficult to absorb. He cost the Braves only $30,000. "When they told me I was wanted for a press conference," Capra said, "I said, 'Who, me? You gotta be kidding.'" It's all bewildering to him. He was one of those guys who keep coming back thinking there is a flicker of hope and keep getting knocked back down. Perhaps there really never was a flicker of hope for him on the Mets.

"In spring training, I could see it," he said. "A ball player knows. I was the eleventh man on a ten-man pitching staff. When I signed my contract, I said to Bob Scheffing that all I wanted was a chance. But no one ever said to me, 'don't worry.' With the Mets, every time I went to the mound I felt this was my last time out there, that if I got pounded, I'd sit on the bench for ten days. There's enough pressure getting the hitters out without having to worry when you're going to pitch again." He had three separate shots at the Mets, twice when they needed him. In his mind it wasn't much of a chance.

Technically, the difference is that the work has improved his fastball and he's throwing it more often. He always had guts, and now his confidence is building. But it will always be a mystery just why a pitcher with a mediocre history is suddenly transformed.

"Sometimes," Capra said, "I say, 'What am I doing?' Whatever it is, I want to keep doing it."

JUNE 11, ATLANTA

The Braves got their crowd—45,296, some of them buying tickets as late as the fifth inning—but Capra never got to see them all. And not all of them got to see Capra.

He got two out in the second inning and his last throw produced a puff of dust—the rosin bag striking the mound. "I just tried too hard," Capra said. "I've been telling myself for three days not to do it. I learned it's tough going against your old club the first time around."

Seaver did somewhat better, but neither starter got the decision, which went to the Braves in the eleventh inning, 5–2. The losing pitcher was Apodaca, the relief pitcher who took Capra's place on the Mets.

Capra could take his failure in stride; he has a cushion in the back of his mind for the first time in his career. For Seaver it was one more frustration. He allowed three runs in eight innings, which isn't bad, but he had a 3–2 lead in the bottom of the seventh when Johnny Oates hit a home run to tie the score. It was Oates' first home run of the season, playing in a ball park where the home runs jump out like popping corn. And Seaver had overpowered him his first time up.

"The homer, it wasn't a good fastball, it wasn't a Tom Seaver fastball," Oates said. "I guess you can say the one I hit was a lame duck."

JUNE 12, ATLANTA

Bob Miller has had a good career—nearly 700 appearances and three World Series. And now he's a parody of how a grizzled old relief pitcher ought to look. Miller wears his trousers long, the elastic of the cuff ringing his leg below the calf rather than bloused at the knee. The belt is slung below a little potbelly. He wears his cap low over his eyes so he has to raise his head disdainfully to see under the bill. And he chews gum slowly and deliberately and with his mouth open. He can't pitch as often as he used to and the Mets need any relief pitcher who can pitch as often as he used to.

Yogi Berra decided Parker had had enough when Henry Aaron cracked a foul homer on a one-ball pitch with one out and runners on first and second in the eighth. Miller took his warmups and attended to his grounds-keeping on the mound. With the spikes of his right sole he carefully made sure the dirt was filled into Parker's hole. Then with his foot he drilled his own hole. Then he strutted stiff-legged around the mound and casually reached up, his body half-turned away from the plate, to take the toss from the catcher as if in slow motion.

With elaborate precision, he put his right thumb under his belt and tugged up at his trousers. In his motion he cocked his leg and peered over his left shoulder as if coyly hiding behind it. Aaron smashed Miller's first pitch on a line into left-center. Dave Schneck raced over, gloved it, and dropped it. Cleon Jones picked it up and threw to third to force a confused Darrell Evans. Then Dave Johnson singled for the winning run.

For his efforts, Parker got his second straight 1–0 loss. He has a 2.33 earned-run average and a 1–5 record. The Mets have used four short relief pitchers the last two days and Tug McGraw wasn't any of them.

JUNE 14, SHEA STADIUM

Being a purist, Mike Marshall thought it was unfortunate Tug McGraw wasn't at his best. Marshall says he enjoys challenges even more than he likes winning and if McGraw were himself, the game would have been a challenge. It was Marshall's thirty-ninth appearance in the Dodgers' sixty-two games. He said he was even excited about coming in to pitch to Rusty Staub. "If you don't get excited about pitching to Rusty Staub, you don't belong out there," Marshall said. Of course, he regularly says he'd be just as excited if he were a full-time teacher and the best hitters were flown into East Lansing each weekend to compete against him. The teacher threw three screwballs for fouls by Staub and a fastball for Staub's third strike.

This, Marshall said, was getting into the most exciting time of the year. "The hitters are ready," he said. "The pitchers have settled into what they can do. They're both at their peaks for the next three months."

But McGraw, who pitched for the first time since May 15, doesn't know if he's settled into what he can do. He knows he hasn't been the real McGraw, except for his sense of humor.

With two out and a man on second, he fielded a ball and trapped a runner, but threw too soon. The imperfect rundown permitted the batter to reach second and enabled him to score what proved to be the winning run on a single. McGraw said he had lost his "perspective of the infield" because he was so preoccupied with his pitching.

Then he reacted too slowly on a topped ball and all he could do was pick up the ball and hold it. "When you eat a ball like that, it's the first noticeable difference between the horsehide and cowhide ball," McGraw said after a single scored the third run. All in all, McGraw pronounced it a satisfactory test. "Everybody is waiting to see how my arm reacts," he said. "I feel I'm all right."

Jon Matlack, who has been the only pitcher who could win regularly, has seen his luck change. His earned-run average is a nifty 2.71 and yet he's 5–3. Dodger Tommy John, the winner, has a 9–1 record with an earned-run average 0.04 better than Matlack's.

John, a cheerful man, did his version of the bravest man in the world, laughing and joking while he froze his arm in the trainer's room after the game. (The Dodger system requires the pitcher—except for Marshall, who makes his own requirements—to soak his arm in ice water after exertion. They think it stops the theorized bleeding in the muscle and restores it more quickly. The Mets don't believe in that.) John, the pitcher with two first names, is of Welsh ancestry. He says his is a common combination of names in Wales. He has a cousin whose name is Thomas Thomas Thomas.

John took a few sips of soda and dumped the remainder of the cup into the ice basin, tinting the water a medicinal brown. "Things go better with Coke," trainer Bill Buhler explained.

With Craig Swan relocated to the disabled list, the Mets bought thirty-three-year-old Jack Aker from Atlanta for the bullpen. It's his sixth team and he wasn't burning up the town in Atlanta.

JUNE 15, SHEA STADIUM

Jerry Koosman pitched a complete game this afternoon to beat the Dodgers, 4–1. It was the Mets' first complete game since June 1. It was Koosman's first win in three weeks, and his first victory over the Dodgers since August of 1969. Koosman pitched that awful 8–7 game against them on April 30, which was about the time he slipped into bad habits. "I got to jerking my head and falling back instead of following through," he said. He's very good on explanations.

JUNE 16, SHEA STADIUM

The cords stood out in Tom Seaver's neck and his face flushed as he gestured and screamed at the plate umpire. He wasn't just yelling, he was screaming. There was a whole season's rage in Seaver and he was venting it at Terry Tata, who was almost an innocent bystander.

That's the state of Seaver's mind. He was striking out at everything that frustrated him—the defense, the offense, the weather and the unloving luck. Tata was the target because he was pointing for the Dodger pitcher to take a walk to first base and for the runner to walk home from third base.

How often does Seaver walk a pitcher with the bases loaded? A little bit of the sky should fall. How often does Seaver lose his temper over the call of a ball or strike? Seaver recited chapter and verse on the other two times in his eight seasons in the big leagues.

But a dreadful frame following six shutout innings, on top of the misery of fourteen previous starts that had blessed him with only three victories, broke Seaver's composure. Seaver stormed off the mound and drew his hand across his knees to indicate where he thought the pitch was. People who had binoculars and could read lips could discern Seaver saying it was the worst call he'd ever seen. Horrible.

"You reach a point where it's not always the umpire you're yelling at," said Bud Harrelson, a veteran Seaver-watcher.

Now everything seems to be against Seaver. There's a certain status a pitcher or a hitter reaches where the umpire gives him the benefit of the doubt. The umpire expects a good pitcher to throw strikes so he calls them; the umpire expects the good hitter not to be called out on strikes so he doesn't call it. And then the tide seems to turn. Now it seems the umpires have shrunk the strike zone when Seaver is pitching. As Richie Ashburn observed about the umpires' treatment of the original Mets, "They fuck you because you're horseshit."

"It's easy to say that," Cleon Jones said. "I don't know if it's true. It seems that way. Always."

A man doesn't have to be entirely paranoid to think that. He just has to want the call his way badly enough and his mind tells him it should have been his. Seaver anticipated an out on a ground ball until he saw John Milner side-saddle it at first base. When it went through for a single, Seaver kicked up a cloud of dirt. That was one of the irritants in the inning. Then there was the intentional walk that put Seaver face to face with the Dodger pitcher.

"I thought the pitch was low, but Seaver was in a better position to see it," Dodger pitcher Andy Messersmith said. "Usually you don't see him get upset like that. When you're having trouble, something like that can break your back. I'm sure that's what he was angry at. He needed that pitch and he knew it."

It was Seaver's last pitch. Bob Miller relieved and promptly gave up a two-run single. The Dodgers had five runs and Seaver didn't wait in the dugout to see the rest of the inning. The Dodgers won, 7–1.

By the time the game was over, Seaver had had time to put on his street clothes and his composure. "When you're going bad, the breaks that go against you seem more glaring," he said. "You notice them more because they have more effect. In reality, the same things happen to you when you're winning, but you're able to overcome them." And Seaver is going bad.

JUNE 20, PHILADELPHIA

Laughs are almost as scarce as wins. The Mets are thankful for both—or either. Tonight they got both from Koosman. He was still on the mound while everybody held his breath and Dave Schneck pressed his back to the paint on the left-field fence and caught the last out of a 2–1 victory over the Phillies. The tying and winning runs were whirling around the bases.

Along the way, Koosman gave a splendid demonstration of the things a power pitcher can learn if his head stays good when his arm goes bad. The Mets had their 2–1 lead in the fifth with two out and the count was full on Billy Grabarkewitz. In a traditional muscle situation, Koosman threw a changeup and Grabarkewitz struck out.

"He knew I was struggling out there, that it was a hot, humid night," Koosman said. "There was only one thing he was waiting for."

Grabarkewitz didn't get it. "He couldn't believe it," Jerry Grote said. "It takes a lot of nerve to throw that pitch in that spot."

It broke a four-game losing streak. Before the game Koosman tried to break the gloom by needling Seaver. "I've been trying to get some dissension going," Koosman said with his little smile. "I ripped Seaver and he ripped me, and then the first thing you know we both started laughing."

Koosman feels the situation acutely. He has four days between starts to contemplate. In this case, all four games since he last won were losers. "I see that championship flag at Shea Stadium and I say, "Christ, we're in the cellar. Are we really National League champs? When we left spring training, I thought this was the best ball club we ever had. Why we're not winning now I don't know.

"You know, sitting on the bench for four games before you pitch can get boring. I hate playing on a boring team. I would like to get something exciting going. Maybe we need a brawl."

JUNE 21, PHILADELPHIA

Seaver had to come out with an injury. He allowed only two hits in five innings—not overpowering, but effective—but couldn't come out for the sixth inning. The bell rang in the bullpen and Joe Pignatano, the coach with the responsibility of seeing that nobody sleeps out there, told Bob Miller he was in the game. Miller said, "Why?"

"It hurts like hell" was Seaver's explanation. It deflated his 3–1 victory and the first two-game winning streak in a month. The doctor diagnosed his problem as a strained sciatic nerve in the left buttock. The doctor told him the strain would heal quickly. He has to rest and take anti-inflammatory drugs. "I hope I won't miss a start," he said.

JUNE 22, PHILADELPHIA

Bob Apodaca pitched three innings and allowed six hits and four runs. He balked in one run. He was the pitcher who looked so composed in spring training while others came undone.

JUNE 23, PHILADELPHIA

A rainy Sunday in Philadelphia can be torment for a man in Apodaca's position. He badly wanted another chance to pitch today. He looks at the past ten weeks of the season and his eyes plead for another chance. Tidewater looks so close.

"I can say this for Yogi, he's given me every opportunity," Apodaca said. "I can only blame myself for the amount of time I've got left up here."

His time looks short. Tug McGraw appears to be throwing well again. Jack Aker has been added to the bullpen. And Craig Swan is due off the disabled list in eleven days. "Someone's going to go down," Apodaca said. "I guess there is some pressure on me, but it's not bothering my pitching any."

With statistics like Apodaca's, a relief pitcher doesn't need anything more to bother him. In thirty-four innings he has allowed forty-two hits and has an earned-run average of 6.17. His explanation is simple enough: "The curve ball hasn't been there, there hasn't been any hop on the fastball, and the sinkerball hasn't been there." And a twenty-four-year-old rookie who remembers that almost everybody told him he'd never make it has to wonder if almost everybody was right about him. "It's really depressing," he said.

The cause is wrapped in the mysteries of a pitcher's mind. Why should a highly-trained man pitch well one day and not the next. How could Apodaca have pitched so well in spring training and not be able to get anybody out now? The contrast makes it that much more painful. "I had such a good spring, I dreamed I'd be the short man with Tug and take some of the heat off him," Apodaca said. "I had a few goals, too. Get six or seven wins, win more than I lost, get double-figures in saves."

Now the season is eleven weeks old and his only save came in the home opener. And his son is three months old today, which adds another dimension to his problem. A pitcher is a pitcher, but there are mouths to feed, too. Apodaca, Rita, his wife of 2½ years, and Robert II, are just beginning to nest in their apartment on Long Island.

"She doesn't come right out and say it, but I know she's nervous," Apodaca said. "She knows I haven't been pitching well. We're finally settled and I don't like the idea of going back down and uprooting everything. I guess you could call that one form of pressure. I guess it all adds up."

What is pressure? For some pitchers the pressure is in the situation or in the big game. For Apodaca, on the brink of blowing his chance of a lifetime, the pressure is constant.

"Every time I go out to the mound, I tell myself I faced that batter in spring training. But subconsciously I'm trying to make the pitch a little finer. When the bell rings in the bullpen I hope it's for me. I tell myself, 'This will be the time.'"

JUNE 24, CHICAGO

The discipline of the game demands that a pitcher go to the mound as if his game were being played in a vacuum. He mustn't dwell on the outrages of yesterday or the last time he pitched. Sometimes that's impossible.

Jon Matlack tried not to think about what is happening to his season. He pitched seven strong innings, allowed only four hits, and left the game behind, 2–1, because two runs scored on an infield out. He hasn't won since May 18.

All the things the Mets have thrived on the last five years have come undone. They make errors and mistakes and there's little relief pitching and less hitting to help them recover. With the season almost half through, Seaver, Koosman, and Matlack have won a total of sixteen games.

"Watching it every night, it gets aggravating," Matlack said. "Until it comes your day to pitch. Then you forget about it and go out and pitch the best you can."

This time Bob Miller added two good innings, which was one of the things they needed to win, 4–2. What the Mets really needed was the ninth-inning double-play grounder that went through the Cubs' second baseman's legs for the tying run, and the subsequent wild throw by the right fielder for the winning run.

JUNE 25, CHICAGO

Koosman has found himself again. Today it was a 5–1 complete game over the Cubs. Now he's 8–4.

JUNE 26, CHICAGO

If it weren't for Seaver, it would have been a fine flight home. The Mets beat the Cubs in twelve innings, 5–4, giving them their first sweep of a series this season, and the bullpen was superb. Miller relieved Harry Parker to get one key out in the sixth. Tug McGraw pitched four innings and looked better with each batter. And Jack Aker pitched the last two for his first win as a Met.

Seaver was scheduled to start but had to postpone that for two days. He said he was "ninety per cent," but still couldn't pitch with the ache in his butt. The load of pitching has been shifted so often the balance is uncertain. Seaver is the main man. Everything begins with him. With him not winning, the burden has to be picked up elsewhere. Now there's some question of when he can take his turn, let alone win.

"Whether people want to admit it or not, there are degrees of pressure inherent in the pitching staff," Seaver said. "If someone isn't pitching well, the pressure has to be absorbed by the rest of the staff. I haven't been pitching well, but the other two [Jerry Koosman and Jon Matlack] have strong personalities. They're not going to let what I'm doing affect them."

Matlack and Koosman can carry their part of the load, but instead of being the second and third horses, they're first and second. With Seaver not winning, his part of the load falls on

George Stone and Harry Parker. That's where the drop-off is greatest.

Both of them have had periodic arm trouble, especially Stone. He's 2–6 with a 5.31 ERA. He was a good pitcher last season. Nobody had a right to expect him to be that good again, but then nobody expected this.

The Mets intensify the burden on the pitchers. They rarely take the pressure off with their hitting. Koosman has been winning. But Matlack has been pitching well but hasn't won in five weeks.

With McGraw's return, the bullpen has picked up more than the addition of one warm body. With the security of having McGraw behind him, each man is a little looser—especially a rookie like Apodaca. Aker, who just got here, sees it most clearly. "When Tug is healthy and going good, he picks everybody up," he said. "The long relievers know they can always bring in Tug to shut the door."

Then the others can assume their proper roles. "I said in spring training that Bob Miller would be our 'Lloyds of London,'" McGraw said. So far he's had to be the Bank of England. McGraw was strangely subdued on a cheerful day. "Maybe I'm tired," he suggested.

Aker doesn't jump up and down like McGraw when he's elated. He's had too many good times and bad times in too many places to have the kind of highs and lows McGraw experiences. Aker's reaction to the trade was a bright smile on his tanned face. "If anything stimulates you, it's a trade," he said. "It picks you up."

The first trade is always a shock. It never stops being a jolt, having to pick up and move in the middle of the season, but the first time is when it really hurts. Aker is thirty-three and has learned the things that make a trade easier to accept. "What I mean," he said, "is that initially when you're traded you feel bad, like you've been a failure. So you enjoy being with a new club because they act like they've been waiting for you."

He pitched seventeen times for the Braves and was depressed by the fact that it was mostly work in lost causes. "Usually when a fellow's been traded, he does better with the new club," he said. The hard side of the argument is that the Braves aren't overloaded with pitching and they wouldn't be likely to let a good man go.

So there was fresh enthusiasm on the flight home from the daylight of Chicago to the families waiting at the airport and a fourteen-game homestand. "It ain't exactly like we won fifteen in a row," Ray Sadecki said, "but when you've been going like us . . ."

The reality of it is that this could be a critical homestand. "If we have a bad homestand, it might finish us off," Duffy Dyer said.

JUNE 29, SHEA STADIUM

After four losses and three no-decisions since he last won, Jon Matlack remembered what it took to win. He pitched a one-hitter and shut out the Cardinals, 4–0. It was the kind of shut-the-door game he talks about. St. Louis pitcher John Curtis got one in the third inning and that was it. When Matlack did get a pitch in the wrong place, there was too much on it for the Cardinals to hurt him.

"Today was one of those days you have once in a great while where everything falls into place," Matlack said. "You make mistakes and they take them or they swing and miss. The biggest thing to me was the stuff I had on the ball. I've got to put everything together to pitch well. The leg muscles, the back muscles all have to go toward the plate. When those things are together my ball explodes at the hitter. It rushes at him the last ten feet."

It always helps to have a run and the Mets gave him two in the first inning. Then he could work on the hitters, throw a curve on a three-and-two pitch and not worry about walking a batter.

Seaver still has pain and is out of the rotation indefinitely.

JUNE 30, SHEA STADIUM

There goes the winning streak. Pow. Two defeats. Three, actually; one was to the umpires.

The first game was lost, 5–2. The Mets thought they were robbed in the second game. They got two runs in the last of the ninth to tie the score and thought Cleon Jones' single to right had won the game. One umpire ruled that Reggie Smith had trapped the ball and the run was in. After furious dispute by the Cardinals, another umpire ruled Smith had made the catch. That decision stood up despite the Mets' frantic arguing. "How come no one gives me a play like that?" Yogi Berra wanted to know.

The next inning Ken Reitz singled off Tug McGraw and Bake McBride followed with a home run. That left McGraw to stew in his locker and the Mets to dwell on the catch the umpires decided Reggie Smith had made. As Tim McCarver suggested in the St. Louis locker room, "Ya gotta believe."

JULY 2, SHEA STADIUM

A fanfare of trumpets, please. Seaver pitched. Another fanfare. He won. After a ten-day layoff, Seaver pitched into the eighth inning and did well. He allowed only three hits before the assembled minds determined that he had pitched enough.

After striking out Bill Robinson to open the eighth, Seaver beckoned Berra to the mound and said he was tired. He had jarred his hip on a pitch to Robinson and was coming down in his motion onto his heel instead of the ball of his foot. "I was doing it consciously to prevent the hip from hurting," he said.

"What's the sense of leaving him in?" Berra said. "If you lose him for six or seven weeks . . ." Jack Aker saved Berra the need to second-guess himself.

Perhaps in normal circumstances Seaver would not have pitched at all. He said his hip had been stiff all night. "It was tight, like a cramp," he said. Afterward, Dr. James Parkes, the team physician, told Seaver he was wise to leave the game when he did.

In the clubhouse, Seaver's dark humor surfaced. "At least," he said, "the season's only half over and I've got five wins already."

JULY 4, SHEA STADIUM

Another nine-inning job and a win for Matlack in the first game. Ray Sadecki got his usual infrequent start and was the loser in the second game. His seven innings and three runs weren't bad. If he weren't so good-natured about everything, the impulse would be to say, "Poor Ray Sadecki."

There's no deliberate attempt to make being a pitcher difficult for Sadecki. It just turns out that way. There are ways to make it easier, but that's not Sadecki's situation. On the Mets, the easiest situation is Seaver's—when he's well. He always knows when he's going to pitch. It's going to be on the fifth day, unless there's no game. If there's a gap in the schedule, he pitches the next game and everybody else moves in the rotation. That creates a comfortable routine of preparation and anticipation for Seaver. It also means taking the toughest opponents as they come.

A manager can ease things along if he wants. Or he can make them so difficult that success is almost impossible. The classic example is when Ralph Houk was managing the Yankees. In his first term, when he had three winners in three years, he had a young left-handed pitcher named Al Downing. Houk was careful that Downing didn't have to pitch in Fenway Park in Boston, which is such an obstacle for left-handed pitchers. And he was careful to protect Downing from lineups overloaded with right-handed hitters. Downing got as much work as possible against the weaker teams until he developed confidence in his ability to win in the big leagues.

The other side of the record is Houk's treatment of Mike

Kekich in the year of the celebrated "wife swap" with Fritz Peterson. Houk said all the right things to indicate an understanding of contemporary life styles. But he didn't much care for Kekich as a pitcher. All his career, Kekich had walked the tightrope between success and failure. He had exciting stuff, but he was a career disappointment.

He had a pretty good season in 1972, suggesting that he might finally have matured. Despite the complications in his life, he had a good spring in 1973. But that whole spring Houk only twice relieved a pitcher during an inning of an exhibition game. Both times it was Kekich.

But once the season began, Houk could find no place to use his fifth starting pitcher, Kekich. For five weeks Houk was unable to find a place to use Kekich to preserve what edge he had in Florida. Not even as a mop-up pitcher.

Then Kekich was announced as the starter in one of the games of the Sunday doubleheader of May 13. Since he had still not pitched in a game, Kekich was slipped into the seventh inning of the Yankee-Mets game on Thursday night, two days before the start. Then he was lifted for a pinch-hitter in the eighth inning.

What good was one inning of work going to do after five weeks of idleness? But nobody could accuse Houk starting Kekich without any preparation at all. And when Kekich did start, it was against the Baltimore Orioles, who had merely won the last three Eastern Division championships. Needless to say, Kekich had his clock cleaned and never recovered his place on the pitching staff.

JULY 5, SHEA STADIUM

Nine innings again by Koosman and a 3–2 win over the Giants. His work with his curveball was wonderful, thanks to Jerry Grote's ability to handle a pitch in the dirt.

JULY 6, SHEA STADIUM

George Stone is suffering with a sore shoulder. He lost a 1–0 lead to two San Francisco runs in the fifth inning and left after pitching to one batter in the sixth. There's a tremor in his voice when he talks about how he tries to eat and comb his hair right-handed to rest his left arm.

He has a Master's degree in physical education and is qualified to teach or coach somewhere at the college level, but that isn't part of his plans yet. He's still a baseball player and that part of his life is in jeopardy. That's what causes the tremor in his voice. He has a 2–6 record now, which is no way to respond to a raise from $25,000 to $45,000.

McGraw relieved after one batter in the sixth and gave up a two-run homer that put the game out of reach. He struck out four of the next six batters he faced, but he did give up that home run. He said he was so mad about it he didn't know the batters he faced after that.

"I've been making so many mistakes and when I do make one, they seem to jump on it," he said. "I'm just going to have to get my confidence back. Maybe I'm afraid to cut loose, but I don't think that's it. "I'm starting to feel positive. I just have to think it's like last year when I struggled and came on eventually." What he was saying was that he had to believe.

The Mets have exactly the same record they had last year after eighty games—thirty-four won and forty-six lost. It was hard to believe then, too.

JULY 7, SHEA STADIUM

After a gap of half the season, Bob Apodaca got his second save. He pitched the last four innings against the Giants and allowed one hit and no runs. With a 5–0 lead it looked easy. The 6–0 final score was even easier. The win went to Seaver, who walked five in his five innings and left with that pain in the butt.

JULY 9, SHEA STADIUM

Matlack pitched six good innings. Unfortunately, he was on the mound for eight innings. He gave up three hits and two runs on his first four pitches of the second inning and three more runs in the sixth when he hung a curve for a home run by Dave Roberts, who was hitting all of .182.

McGraw struck out two in the top of the ninth, but the Mets' rally in the bottom of the ninth fell a run short when Wayne Garrett hit into a double play with the tying and winning runs on base. Yogi Berra's response to an inquiry about his state of mind was: "Goddammit, you tell the stupidest questions."

JULY 12, LOS ANGELES

Bobby Apodaca came home to the West Coast last night, but tonight was his homecoming. It was a nice little celebration. He made his second major-league start when Tom Seaver was scratched, and beat the Dodgers, 5–2. The Dodgers are running away with the Western Division. The Mets are last in the Eastern Division. And the Mets have beat the Dodgers two nights in a row.

Tonight was Poster Night. There were 50,129 fans in Dodger Stadium and Apodaca never pitched before that many people. Among them were sixteen assorted friends and relatives from nearby Paramount. There weren't many others rooting for the Mets.

"I bet everyone was saying, 'Apo-Who?'" he said. Well, maybe some of them remembered that he used to be an infielder at Cerritos College in Norwalk, which also is nearby. What Apodaca did was overcome the butterflies in his stomach and hold the Dodgers to four hits in six scoreless innings before turning the game over to Jack Aker, who got his second save despite giving up the two Dodger runs. It was Apodaca's second win.

"It's really a dream come true for me to make it this far—and I've always been a Dodger fan, too." Apodaca said. It's still hard for Apodaca to realize that he's a big-league pitcher, but he's coming closer. He said his best pitch, his slider, "was on vacation." So he did the job with his fastball and sinker. Being able to adjust and win without his best stuff is a sign of a big-league pitcher.

For the Dodgers the loser was Tommy John, whose thirteen wins are the most in the league. He had his best pitch, his curveball, tonight. He said his curve was so good tonight he wished he could have bottled it up and saved it.

JULY 13, LOS ANGELES

This is the Golden West. The Dodgers have had only one game rained out since Walter O'Malley moved them here in 1958 and replaced Benedict Arnold as the number one traitor in the minds of New Yorkers who grew up in the Dodger glory years of the late 1940s and '50s.

To ball players who've been on the road for a few years, it is just another city. The quiz programs and children's cartoons on daytime television are as popular with some of the players as they are at other stops in the league. The cabdrivers rarely miss the opportunity to rave about the weather when they identify passengers as New Yorkers. Los Angeles has a lot of fine restaurants, but the Dodgers play at night almost all the time and there isn't much chance to get to those restaurants.

That leaves as much time to kill here as in Cincinnati or Philadelphia, which aren't as glamorous. But in those cities the ball clubs stay at hotels that are much more convenient to movies and restaurants. Ball players are traditionally steak-eaters. Other than Seaver, they rarely stray to a new steakhouse or an experiment in eating. When the season is this far along and fatigue is an increasing factor, room service is very popular, even in the most dreary hotels.

A few of the players read. Tom Seaver is very big on the best-seller list, the crossword puzzle of *The New York Times*, and short strolls through the city. "I like to get out of the hotel room," Seaver said. "I'm not a TV-watcher and the phones and the closeness of the room bother me. Even if I feel like reading, I do it outside the hotel room, in the park or on a bench somewhere." Los Angeles has the warmth for bench-sitting, but reading outdoors here can make a man's eyes sting.

What Los Angeles does have to combat the boredom is a number of firms that offer good deals on clothes to ball players making $50,000 and $100,000. And ball players kill a lot of time clothes-shopping. It's mind-boggling to see them go out for an afternoon and return with multiple additions to already vast wardrobes. Although the Mets aren't as deep into clothes as they were a few years ago, there are still players tasting big-league money for the first time and out of the blue-jean leagues for the first time.

Montreal is a favorite shopping city even though there aren't as many good deals offered. The ball clubs stay at the Queen Elizabeth with dozens of fine shops beneath it in Place Ville Marie, the underground city developed to cope with Montreal winters. Atlanta is very big for shoe-buying. Los Angeles has sweaters and suits and jackets, and the Mets are required to wear jackets and ties on the road.

McGraw is a clothes-horse. Matlack is a neat but plain dresser. Seaver is a closet shopper. Most of his conservative wardrobe—his businessman's tweeds and vests make him stand out among the peacocks—comes from Sears, with whom he has a lucrative contract.

JULY 14, LOS ANGELES

The Mets moved out of the cellar tonight as Matlack overwhelmed the Dodgers, 4–1. It was the first complete game by a left-hander against the Dodgers all season. He was throwing that rising fastball, the one he says explodes on the hitter in the last ten feet. "You've got to get over the top of it or you'll pop it into the air," Dodger Steve Garvey said. "You have to give a guy like him a lot of credit." Matlack's record is 8–6 and it hurts to think what it might be if the Mets hit for him.

JULY 16, SAN FRANCISCO

The Mets celebrated their rise from last place with a day off here yesterday. San Francisco is a special city even for players who've been here dozens of times. There's always a little chill in the air but it's still a turn-on city. The restaurants are elegant and many of them are within walking distance of the Sheraton Palace, where the Mets stay.

In the afternoon it's a walking-around city—cross the streets in whichever direction the light is green and something interesting will turn up. Across the bay in Sausalito, too, there are interesting shops and bars and restaurants.

Unfortunately, the Mets have other problems. This morning Harold Weissman, the team publicity man, informed the press that Tug McGraw stayed behind at his home in San Diego to nurse the flu. He was perfectly okay when he left New York. He was beginning to look like himself on the mound, too. Weissman also said that Tom Seaver wouldn't pitch tomorrow, either. The strained sciatic nerve still hasn't healed and he probably won't pitch until after the All-Star Game on July 23.

That brings one of the harsh facts of the season prematurely to mind. Seaver isn't going to make the All-Star team for the first time in his eight years in the big leagues. The injury settled that before the team was picked. But Seaver wouldn't have been picked anyhow. In addition, Craig Swan is still on the disabled list even though he's eligible to come off, and George Stone is on the active list even though his shoulder is too sore for him to pitch.

Yogi Berra let Jerry Koosman slog through a six-run fifth inning by the Giants. That matched the worst inning by the Mets this season. "I couldn't get comfortable on the mound," Koosman said, being as analytical as usual. "I was falling all over the place. I couldn't find my rhythm. I couldn't make any good pitches."

By the fifth inning, Koosman could see the prospects. He gave up a two-run triple that gave the Giants a 2–1 lead and was surprised Berra didn't take him out. But the manager thought he had a better shot by sticking with Koosman and saving one of his warm bodies to back up Bob Apodaca tomorrow.

THE PITCHING STAFF 159

JULY 17, SAN FRANCISCO

Apodaca began hanging his curve in the first inning and was out of the game with one out in the fourth and five runs in. John D'Aquisto allowed the Mets only two hits in 6⅓ innings, and Giants manager Wes Westrum said his twenty-two-year-old pitcher "has a good chance to develop into a consistent winner like Seaver." Of course, when Westrum managed the Mets nine years ago he predicted that Dennis Ribant would be the Mets' first twenty-game winner. In six seasons Ribant won a total of twenty-four games.

Tommy John, the Dodger pitcher leading the league with a 13–3 record, tore ligaments in his elbow and will go on the disabled list. He may not pitch again this season.

JULY 19, SAN DIEGO

John Matlack pitched a five-hitter for his ninth win and his fourth in his last five starts. He's been named for the All-Star Game in Pittsburgh. He and Jerry Grote are the only Mets going.

JULY 21, SAN DIEGO

Willie McCovey hit two Willie McCovey home runs as the Padres beat the Mets, 7–3, and sent the Mets home for the All-Star break in last place. The comforting thought for the Mets is that they are the same 7½ games behind they were after ninety games last year.

Whatever hopes they have for pulling anything out of this season still depend on Tom Seaver, who had won eleven by this point last year compared to six this season, and Tug McGraw, who was floundering as badly last year. There is no real evidence that they will be able to make a difference the rest of the way.

McGraw pitched two innings mopping up today and Berra said, "You have to wait and see." McGraw smiled wanly and said, "It feels pretty good. We have to see how I do in an important situation." Seaver is scheduled to start Friday night, the twenty-sixth, in St. Louis. "I'm hopeful I'll be okay, but I'm not confident," he said. Tom Jones—the English rogue, not the singer—said hope was a hearty breakfast, but a meager supper.

For Craig Swan, the hope will have to be in Virginia. He was optioned to Tidewater today.

JULY 23, PITTSBURGH

Jon Matlack pitched a scoreless inning in the All-Star Game. That's one of the milestones he said in spring training he hadn't reached. Or might never reach. The All-Star Game takes up the three days off that almost all the other players welcome as a break from the grind.

To Matlack, pitching in the All-Star Game for the first time tells a man he's arrived. Especially for a pitcher. The starting eight on each team are voted in by nature of their popularity and reputation among the fans. The pitchers are chosen by the managers of the two teams. Being selected testifies to the respect the league has for Matlack. Wherever his career goes from here, when it's all over he'll be able to look back and say, "I was one of the best in the league."

JULY 24

Returning to the schedule tomorrow will be almost like an opening day. All of the Mets except Matlack and Jerry Grote have had their break to get their heads straight. They can think they're starting fresh again.

The most hopeful factor is that even though the Mets are last, twelve games under .500, the division-leading Phillies are only three games over .500. Like last year, the Mets are 7½ games behind—and last season they did come back to win. In the country of the blind, the one-eyed man is king. Anybody who goes into September with a .500 record can be a contender.

Whether the Mets can get to .500 rests with Seaver. He threw in the bullpen in San Diego on Sunday before the break, played some golf, and threw again Tuesday to Duffy Dyer on the lawn of his home. Seaver has been taking heat treatment on his hip and Tom McKenna, the trainer, said Seaver reported no pain when he threw Sunday.

JULY 25, ST. LOUIS

Since there was no victory to rejoice over, the Mets found an omen to celebrate. As they did last year, the Mets resumed the schedule by losing two games to the Cardinals. "It's just like it was last year," Yogi Berra said with his What-Me-Worry grin. "I don't know if it's fate or who it is."

As they did last year, Jerry Koosman and Jon Matlack started for the Mets, and Bob Gibson and Allen Foster for the Cardinals. "If we had known that," Koosman said, "we could have just given them the two and showed up tomorrow."

And tomorrow Seaver is the Met pitcher—just like last year. "Well, then," Ed Kranepool said, "Seaver will have to go out and win tomorrow night."

JULY 26, ST. LOUIS

Tom Seaver emerged from his nineteen-day cocoon beautifully metamorphosed and pitched a 3–0 four-hitter. The importance can't be overstated. "I needed that one," he said. "We all did."

Seaver took off his jacket, toweled off the sweat of a long, muggy St. Louis night and some emotional stress of his own doing, and changed into a dry shirt. "Hey, big boy," Jon Matlack said, "think you'll be ready again in another three weeks?" Seaver laughed deeply.

Moments before, Yogi Berra sprang from the dugout as the

last out was settling into Ted Martinez' glove at shortstop and ran to the foul line to congratulate Seaver. It was his first complete game since June 1. He walked only one batter and had no pain. And when he might have been tiring, he still had the power to strike out two pinch-hitters in the eighth inning. Even before he strained his sciatic nerve, he hadn't been able to hold his good stuff for nine innings.

Fifteen minutes later general manager Bob Scheffing declared, "That gets us back in the race." That tells you the burden that was riding both on Seaver and on the other players, who had been facing the last sixty-seven games with no security from their security blanket.

Seaver's confidence had been stretched very thin. He was surprised by what he did. "I didn't expect this," he said. "I didn't care about nine innings." He had talked with Rube Walker and then decided to settle for five or six good innings without pain.

Before the game, he had spent the afternoon according to his established routine. He slept late, rested off his feet most of the afternoon, came to the ballpark before the bus. He put on his long underwear to ward off the evil spirits of the night air and played cribbage. It was just as if he were on the path toward twenty games again.

But as it got near the time to warm up, he began to show the tension. He dressed slowly, precisely placing the adhesive-felt pad on his right instep, the area he drags across the mound as he launches into his release. He seemed deeper into himself than normal.

"Sometimes before a game Tom can be like an old woman," said roommate Bud Harrelson, sweating out the possibility of broken ribs himself. "When he gets crochety like that, you just have to leave him alone."

Two and a half hours later Seaver announced he had no pain. "I ran out of gas in the eighth inning," he said. "That was my only problem. I surprised myself at how strong I was."

It wasn't as if anybody had to be told. "He hit good spots," Walker said, "but he also had something to reach back and get." The pitching coach pressed his lips together in admiration.

Sure enough, history is repeating itself. The only sour note is the vacant stare on Tug McGraw's face.

JULY 27, SHEA STADIUM

A good game from Bob Apodaca, his best of the season. The Expos scored an unearned run in the first inning and Apodaca retired the next nineteen in a row, taking himself into the eighth inning of the 8–5 win. He gave his only walk in the eighth and turned the ball over to Jack Aker, who gave up two hits as the Expos scored four runs.

JULY 28, SHEA STADIUM

Three games in a row in July is hardly to be considered a winning streak, except that in the Mets' case this is a winning streak. Tom Seaver won the first game of the streak. Tonight Tug McGraw was the winner in the third, a 4–1 victory over Montreal. It was McGraw's first win of the season and the grin on his face said what it meant to everybody. "This was just the kind of game I needed," he said. It was just what Seaver had said.

Berra called for McGraw when Harry Parker's arm started hurting with the score 4–1 after seven innings. "We got to find out about Tug," Berra said. McGraw's win was three weeks ahead of last season's first and last season is still the standard of comparison.

It looks as if McGraw is close to being himself. "A couple more games and I'll be ready," he said. He is just beginning to feel comfortable with himself on the mound. Perhaps if he were a starter going five or six innings at one stretch he might have worked it out earlier.

"I've felt good the last couple of weeks and the injury is about $99 {}^9\!/_{10}$ over with," he said. "My trouble is that I've been coming in and somebody else has been pitching and I've been watching. Now I feel more like myself."

The pitcher throws the ball sixty feet and six inches—the six inches because of some draftsman's bad penmanship before the turn of the century—and tries to place it accurately around the edges of the seventeen-inch plate. McGraw's problem lately has been that he hasn't been able to feel how much his curve and screwball would break. The screwball has been especially difficult.

Tonight he pitched two perfect innings, but he threw only one screwball. "I didn't have to use it," McGraw explained. "I like to make them think about my curveball because it gives them three pitches to think about. They can't just think fastball and screwball." That sounds like good reasoning for a man who has had pain when he threw his screwball.

Dr. Parkes' report on Parker: "Not serious. Fatigue of the bicep." Hasn't "not serious" been the word on Seaver and McGraw all season?

JULY 29, SHEA STADIUM

George Stone tries. That's all he can do. He grits his teeth against the ache in his shoulder and he tries. He's had the whole season to get over the ache or to learn to live with it, and neither seems possible. He started this afternoon and in three innings the Expos had eight hits.

"The pain is here in the joint," Stone said, holding his shoulder gingerly. The joint is bad news. Pain in the muscle usually heals with time and a man can force himself through that kind of discomfort. But the joints don't heal readily. They need surgery or the kind of rest a pitcher gets between October and March. But it's only July and too early to give up and call it a bad season. It's too soon for a man who had the season Stone did last year to stop struggling.

How Stone hurt his arm is no mystery. "He just throwed," Rube Walker explained. Stone wanted to report to spring training already in shape so his edge of last season wouldn't slip away. So he found a place to throw and someone to catch him. He threw during the winter, took a sore arm to camp, and never told anybody for fear of losing his job.

"The only cure is complete rest," he said, "but I have to try to work it out, under the circumstances. I don't think any of us is throwing like last year except Koosman."

But now the Mets have a four-game winning streak. Bob Miller came on in the third inning to pitch $4\frac{1}{3}$ innings without a run. Jack Aker finished up with two scoreless innings to get the win, 4–3.

"I needed that, I really did," Miller said. That's three times a pitcher has said that in four games. Everybody is feeling the urgency now.

It was the longest Miller has pitched all season. "That's the earliest I've been in a game in a long time," he said. When he left for a pinch hitter in the seventh, he said, "That's the earliest I've been out of the game in a long time."

JULY 30, SHEA STADIUM

The first game featured one of those rare times lately when Matlack didn't have much. The Pirates beat him, 6–0. To conserve the bullpen, George Stone pitched an inning.

Jerry Koosman was the stopper in the second game as the Mets saved a split, 4–3. He pitched nine innings, which is a better way to conserve the bullpen.

Jim Rooker pitched the shutout for the Pirates in the first game and eloquently simplified the whole concept of pitching. "I was just pitching and they hit it right at our guys," Rooker said. "And our guys just caught it." That's eighty per cent of baseball?

JULY 31, SHEA STADIUM

The pretty Seaver bubble popped and the sound that followed was the booing of the fans again. He left with one out in the fifth. The Pirates shelled him for twelve hits, and all eight runs in the 8–3 loss were charged to him. It was a major event for the team and for Seaver personally, even if he didn't stay around for the questioning.

For Seaver it means winning twenty is almost impossible, and winning twenty is very important to him. He has won seven and he can expect thirteen more starts. He didn't look like a pitcher to win thirteen in a row tonight. No pain in his hip and no excuse. "He was just horseshit," Berra said.

Baseball is full of measuring points—100 runs batted in, a .300 batting average, and 20 wins. The twenty is most indicative. It specifies the margin for error.

Seaver has averaged thirty-five starts in his seven seasons. Winning twenty means winning almost all the games he should win and some of those he shouldn't expect to win. By those standards, the difference between winning twenty and winning nineteen is more than just one. Seaver is quick to point out that Jim Bunning won nineteen games for the Phillies twice but never won twenty in this league.

Some pitchers are always expected to win twenty and Seaver is one of them. Few of them are ever expected to win twenty-five. Seaver was one of the few with the speed, control, and stamina to win twenty-five. At least he was until this season. Now the standards for him are questionable. Will he reach those standards before the end of this season? Will he ever reach them again?

The comparison with Robin Roberts is increasingly apt. Seaver is twenty-nine. Roberts began slipping at twenty-nine.

"I can pinpoint the week it happened in 1955," Roberts says. "It was in August and from then on I never threw a baseball the same." Roberts won twenty-three games that season for his sixth consecutive twenty-game season. He was 19–18 the next season with an inflated earned-run average and never came close to twenty again. "I could pitch good games after that," Roberts said, "but I never again had the ability with a man on third base to rear back and overpower a hitter."

There was no medical explanation. He didn't tear anything that could be repaired by surgery. He didn't suddenly chip a bone. "It was just a pitcher's arm," he said. "It quits on you after a while. I didn't know how to make the adjustment."

Roberts pitched 4,688 innings in the big leagues. Only nine men have pitched more. Seaver has pitched 2,075 in his seven-plus seasons. Only three pitchers—Roberts, Warren Spahn and Early Wynn—in the last thirty years have pitched as many as 4,000. Spahn and Wynn lasted more than twenty years and Roberts nineteen.

Seaver's advantage is that he has rarely had to pitch with less than four days' rest. Three days' rest was the vogue when Roberts, Spahn, and Wynn pitched. But Roberts questions how much advantage Seaver really gets from the rest. "I think the extra rest creates some problems," Roberts said. "He may get too involved in pitching a perfect game every time out. The extra rest gives him that great stuff on occasion to make him think he should do it all the time.

"The most important thing on any given day is just to win the game. There's a thin line between winning a game and putting on a show. You've got to be careful there."

Other pitchers have said that Seaver should have learned how to save some of himself on the easy days, instead of striving constantly for perfection. Ed Kranepool says that explains why Seaver poops out in September. Seaver is a perfectionist. He wears it as a badge. But recently he has allowed that he may be a perfectionist to a fault.

"One of the things I've found over the years is that I'm not able to pitch well if I consciously try to tone down what I can physically do that particular day," he said. "Whatever my stuff is, I find I have to use it at its full capacity."

AUGUST 1, SHEA STADIUM

McGraw pitched three pretty good innings after Bob Apodaca again developed a blister. The trouble was that McGraw was asked to pitch a fourth. He relieved with a 4–3 lead in the seventh inning of the first game. But with two out in the tenth, he walked Don Kessinger on four pitches. Bob

Miller then gave up a two-run single and the Cubs won, 7–4.

"McGraw didn't throw those balls to Kessinger at all," Yogi Berra said. "It's hard to figure. He threw some good pitches and some with nothing on them."

McGraw thought he had an explanation. "My body felt good," he said. "My arm is not as strong yet as I'd like it to be. But I was ahead of the hitters until the last inning, when I ran out of gas." That sounds reasonable—unsatisfactory, but reasonable.

Sadecki started and lost the second game, 3–1.

AUGUST 5, PITTSBURGH

This season on top of last season is enough to age a man. Not the kind of age that turns a good wine to a great wine in the bottle, but the kind of age that gets to a bottle of champagne after it's been opened.

Tug McGraw used to be champagne. Whenever he did something special, he would do a dance step on the mound—an Irish jig, perhaps—and strut off the field slapping his glove against his thigh in exultation to his wife or anybody who happened to be watching. And the bubbles tickled the nose of anybody around him.

Tonight he was special during the game. He hit a three-run triple to break up a 4–4 tie with the Pirates. And he pitched three fine innings in relief of Tom Seaver to get credit for the 10–4 victory. He looked like the McGraw of old. But in the locker room he sounded more like an old McGraw. Like Seaver, he'll be thirty this year, and if this is maturity in McGraw, it's a disappointment.

Once, during the period the Mets were urging maturity on McGraw, he spent the early part of spring training filling notebooks with his thoughts on his new state of mind. It was the spring of 1969, the year of the miracle.

At an intrasquad game at Huggins-Stengel Field, the

reporters were seated at a long table at the right-field foul line like a row of overweight targets in a shooting gallery. Moments after the game ended, McGraw came sprinting toward the table where the reporters were gathering up their notes. The gentlemen of the press parted in the middle an instant before McGraw hurdled the table with Olympic form.

"I could see all the maturity stories being torn up," McGraw observed later. And it was all right with him. If the organization didn't care for his effervescence, and if Tom Seaver thought McGraw didn't use all the cards in his deck, players all around the league liked him.

"When I was young, I didn't know what my potential was, so I savored every success to the fullest," McGraw reflected. "I jumped for joy. Now I know what I can do and what's expected of me. We've got a chance to be in the World Series again, the playoffs, and to make something good out of a terrible first half."

Perhaps struggling uphill has left its mark. Certainly there is merely the faintest trace of life in this season. Maybe the experience of his first sore arm has given McGraw a glimpse of the ghost of Christmas future.

"Well," McGraw said. "I'll be thirty at the end of this month. I have a wife and two kids. I'm getting to a different stage. I don't know, maybe I'll get wild again after I've passed thirty. I might have a second childhood."

Seaver was wild. In six innings he walked five and hit Ron Hunt. (Everybody hits Ron Hunt.) And Seaver made a wild pitch.

"He said he felt good," Yogi Berra said.

Why was he so wild? "I don't know," Seaver said. "It's a question I've been asking myself."

AUGUST 6, PITTSBURGH

McGraw should pitch for daytime television. He's a soap

opera. Each day is an installment, shifting from success to dismal disappointment. After each disappointment, he stands up to the questioning. It must be uncomfortable.

The Pirates beat, or rather outlasted the Mets, 9–8. McGraw acknowledged his role as he sat at his locker and stared expressively at the soda machine. It wasn't just McGraw, it was the whole pitching staff. The Mets assembled a rare collection of fourteen hits and blew leads of 4–0, 7–3, and 8–5. "Jeez," Berra said, "we score a lot of runs and then we can't hold them."

Jerry Koosman began encouragingly on one day's rest after pitching an inning in Sunday's rained-out game with Montreal. He pitched six beautiful innings tonight before being victimized by a scratch single, an error, a walk, and a three-run homer by Rennie Stennett with two out in the seventh. Still, he turned a 4–3 lead over to Jack Aker.

The Mets made it 6–3 in the eighth, but Aker gave up a two-run homer to Bob Robertson in the eighth. Three consecutive two-out hits brought in McGraw to defend a one-run lead with the bases full. McGraw got two quick strikes before Manny Sanguillen singled off a fastball to tie the score.

Then it went into the eleventh inning with the score 8–8. Bud Harrelson made an error at shortstop on the first batter and the second bunted to McGraw. The only play was to first base and Jerry Grote yelled for it. But McGraw threw to second. Too late.

Mario Mendoza bunted, and McGraw swiftly fielded it and made the correct play. He threw to third base where Wayne Garrett was anticipating a relay to first for a double play. McGraw's throw sailed high, went off Garrett's straining fingertips and into left field, and the winning run scored.

"I was throwing good to the batters but lousy to the fielders," McGraw said. "I guess I was over-anxious."

McGraw sat on his stool for a long time while most of his teammates dragged themselves to the shower to wash off what they could of three hours and fourteen minutes that had given them nothing but grief. "A mental mistake, a physical mistake and a fucking shower," McGraw said.

AUGUST 7, PITTSBURGH

Three Rivers Stadium sits across the muddy water from Pittsburgh's Golden Triangle. The stadium is the dot of the exclamation point in the city's vast downtown renewal project. Tall shafts of steel and glass rise in what was a blighted area. The stadium, opened in the middle of the 1970 season, pays tribute to history and to Forbes Field, its ancestor in the times when ballparks had individualism. In the Allegheny Club, the section of brick wall over which Bill Mazeroski's home run passed to decide the 1960 World Series has been reassembled brick by brick.

On a mild summer evening, the ball park is a short, pleasant walk across the bridge from the Mets' hotel, but that part of the city is a disappointment to most visiting teams. For one thing, anybody who wants a hamburger after a game goes to sleep still wanting a hamburger or lies awake wishing he hadn't found one. For another, the team the visitors have to play in that ball park is the Pirates, and they carry big sticks.

The Mets worked wonders here in their comeback last year. The Pirates are beating the Mets' brains out here now. Tonight it was 10–1. The Mets and Pirates have been lying back in the pack. Now the Pirates seem ready to make a move. The Mets are still lying back in the pack: their pitching hasn't been able to stop the Pirates' hitting.

"Good pitching always stops good hitting," former Pirate pitcher Bob Veale once said. "And vice versa."

Harry Parker was battered for six runs in four innings, Bob Miller for three in three, and Jack Aker for one run in one inning. One of the big blows was a two-run homer off Miller by Manny Sanguillen, who used to catch Miller here. Miller pitched on the Pirate division champions in 1971 and '72 and is thoroughly familiar with Sanguillen's knack of hitting home runs off everything but the pitches he's expected to hit for home runs.

"You shouldn't hit home runs off hanging curveballs," said

Miller, visiting one of his former teammates. Miller is everybody's former teammate.

"I didn't know it was a curveball," Sanguillen explained. "I thought it was a fastball outside."

At Syracuse, Craig Swan pitched a strong game for Tidewater, which is last in it's division. "He isn't ready yet," Berra said. The Tides have their own pitching problems. Hank Webb has lost the feeling in his pitching hand.

AUGUST 8, PITTSBURGH

There were three bursts of applause and none of them were for the Mets. The first came when the Pirates scored three runs off Jon Matlack to tie the score, 3–3, in the fourth inning. The second came as the teams changed sides for the bottom of the sixth and the scoreboard flashed the message that Richard Nixon had resigned as president. The third and loudest was when Richie Zisk hit Matlack's first pitch with one out in the last of the ninth inning for the home run that beat the Mets, 4–3, sweeping the series.

The Mets got good pitching and still couldn't win. Matlack, under pressure to pick up for Tom Seaver, is showing signs of inexperience. His stuff has been almost uniformly good, but his pitch selection has been questionable. Not long ago he thought the Reds were reading his pitches, but the Reds said Matlack was just too predictable.

"Every time up he had started me off with an inside fastball," said Zisk, who was Matlack's victim the first four times up. "I just decided I was going to sit on this one and hit it out," Zisk said.

Matlack obliged. "I zoned off the spot and just shut everything else out," Zisk said. "If it had been anything but that pitch in that spot, I wouldn't have swung."

Matlack refused comment, which is unlike him. The times are trying to the best of them.

AUGUST 9, SHEA STADIUM

They say Apodaca is a relief pitcher. Apodaca says he's a relief pitcher. But he pitched seven innings as a starter against the Reds tonight, didn't give any runs in the 4–1 win, and now has a 4–1 record as a starter. He's 1–4 in relief, but his heart is still the heart of a relief pitcher. "I think I'd rather stay in the bullpen," he said.

He says he likes the idea of coming to the ballpark every day thinking he might get in the game. His confidence is growing, thanks to what he's done as a starter.

"He's pitched good," Yogi Berra said. "He certainly ain't pitched bad."

For Apodaca it was another of life's little triumphs. "How many guys can say they beat the Cincinnati Reds?" he said. "Not too many guys from my home town could say that." He survived a rain delay of an hour and nineteen minutes but he left the game again with a blister. "It's a mystery," he said. "Maybe I'm not cutting my nail right."

The Reds' run was a Johnny Bench homer off McGraw, who pitched the last two innings.

George Stone's season may be over. He was put on the disabled list with the ache in his shoulder, still identified as a muscle strain. His earned-run average is 5.03. He has won two and lost seven.

AUGUST 10, SHEA STADIUM

The turn of Tom Seaver's mind is indicated in the line in the box score that says: "SB—Morgan 2, Bench, Concepcion 2, Griffey, Geronimo." The Reds walked off with seven bases and a 5–3 decision. They could have stolen his cup. He pitched seven innings and held the Reds to three runs, but he let a 2–1 lead slip away. He left the game with the Reds leading, 3–2, the lead run the result of the seventh stolen base.

174 THE PITCHING STAFF

That's not supposed to happen with Seaver pitching. He's the man coaches tell their pitchers to study. Seaver prides himself on being the complete pitcher—fielding and holding runners on base included. He wrote a book with a section on not letting the runners get a jump.

But this season hasn't left room in his mind for attention to the runners. "Maybe he was worried about the batters too much," said Duffy Dyer, the catcher. "Usually he gives the catcher a good chance of catching the runners." Of the twenty-two runners who have tried to steal with Seaver on the mound, only six have been caught.

Jerry Cram has been elevated from Tidewater to replace George Stone among the active bodies on the pitching list. Cram is twenty-six and he hasn't made it yet.

AUGUST 11, SHEA STADIUM

Jerry Cram had hardly unpacked his equipment bag and he was in the game. He pitched $1\frac{1}{3}$ innings and the Reds didn't score. He got into the game in the sixth inning because Jerry Koosman was rocked for five runs in five innings and Jack Aker for four more in $\frac{2}{3}$ of an inning.

The loss was Koosman's eighth. He's won eleven and they're coming hard now. Winning twenty will be difficult.

AUGUST 12, SHEA STADIUM

There were two out in the top of the ninth and Harry Parker had a 3–1 lead. The Dodgers had two runners on base and Parker looked into the Met dugout. Parker was acquainted with the situation. He had started twenty-six times in the major leagues and had been relieved twenty-six times. Tug McGraw was throwing in the bullpen. Parker saw him. Parker is not the type who would refuse to see the implications. "I thought Rube might make a trip out," Parker said.

But Rube Walker never budged. "It was sort of a vote of

confidence," Parker said. It was at least that. Parker was permitted to pitch to Steve Yeager and struck him out on three pitches. Parker had his complete game against the best team in the league.

AUGUST 13, SHEA STADIUM

The burden that rests on the pitching staff is abundantly clear. When the pitching is good enough, they can beat the best in the league, as they demonstrated again tonight. The hitters gave Jon Matlack three runs, which is about all he can expect. A pitcher on the Mets learns that as a fact of life. Matlack gave the Dodgers no runs. The combination moved Jerry Grote to say, "We had everything going tonight."

At their best, the Mets are a pitcher with just enough runs to work with. Sometimes one run has to be enough. The pitchers don't grumble openly about that, but they concede a pitcher here rarely has an easy game. They don't go to the mound telling themselves they have to pitch a shutout to win, which is too much pressure to bear, but they all understand that there's every chance in the world that a shutout may be necessary.

"Give them pitching, or give them up," Joe Gergen of *Newsday* said.

Matlack pitched a pretty four-hitter, beginning with the striking out of three of the first four Dodgers. "I thought I could throw a strike any time I really wanted to," Matlack said. It was one of those magic moments for a pitcher when everything is just right. His rhythm is perfect and he flows through his motion. He thinks the ball into the catcher's mitt. "It's a pleasure to catch anybody on a night when they're throwing like that," Grote said.

Now that the Mets have done it to the Dodgers twice in a row with extraordinary pitching, they are stirring the ashes of last season. It was just about this time last year that things began to fall into place.

The shutout was Matlack's fifth. He leads the league in shutouts and is among the leaders in frustration. He has those five shutouts and a total of eleven wins. He's lost nine.

Batting practice tonight was thrown by a sixteen-year-old Canadian, Ray Hannan, recently signed by the Mets. He's already six-feet, two-inches tall. "They sure grow 'em big in Canada," Yogi Berra observed.

AUGUST 14, SHEA STADIUM

Tug McGraw sat in his corner of the clubhouse and said what Mets fans have said in the face of all reality from the beginning. "Let's go Mets!" Maybe they do have a chance.

This afternoon they beat the Dodgers again, 3–2. This time they beat Mike Marshall, who has taken McGraw's place as the best relief pitcher in baseball. They did it in their most essential manner. They did it with Seaver and McGraw and two runs in the last of the ninth. Seaver handed the short end of a 2–1 score to McGraw after seven innings and the crowd booed the Mets for not scoring in the eighth inning with runners at first and third with none out. "Usually, when you get that shot and don't score," Yogi Berra explained, "you go pssss."

But McGraw got the Dodgers out in the top of the ninth and the world's greatest relief pitcher gave the Mets a break by walking Ken Boswell to open the last of the ninth. Either Marshall gave them the break or plate umpire Billy Williams did. He's one of the umpires on the team the Mets said wasn't returning all the baseballs. This time Marshall was upset by Williams. "The umpire must have had the sun in his eyes," Marshall said. The pitches, he claimed, "were in the center of the world."

Then Berra let McGraw bat "because he's a good bunter," and because he didn't have many players left. McGraw bunted two pitches foul and one fair to advance the runner to second. Ron Hodges doubled off the center fielder's glove to tie the score and Rusty Staub hit a drive over the drawn-in outfield to win it.

The Mets are now fifth, eight games behind. Most of them

still fear the Pirates most and Pittsburgh is only six games ahead, in third place. The Pirates have lost as many games as they've won, which is the way the Eastern Division is again. Last season it was known as the National Least.

They have won three in a row. Now if they can have a good road trip, maybe build a streak, they can get back into the race. "If our pitching holds up, who knows?" Berra said. "It happened last year, remember?"

Seaver did well today in allowing the Dodgers only two runs despite eight hits and two walks in seven innings. "I was fairly consistent," he said. "That can be good enough." The great perfectionist is now happy to survive.

Early in the game he abandoned the fastball, which has abandoned him, and concentrated on breaking stuff. That's the pattern he has fallen into—look for the best and be prepared for something less. "It was mediocre pitching," he said.

His record is seven up and seven down and the Mets' place in the standings grinds painfully down to that. "It doesn't bother me that I wasn't the winning pitcher today," he said. "What bothers me is that we could be in first if I'd been pitching the way I should all year. I don't think there's any doubt about that."

AUGUST 15, NORFOLK, VA.

Just what the Mets needed after 114 games was another game on a day off—an exhibition game. A visit to the Tidewater farm put the state of the whole organization into focus.

The Mets had Jerry Cram pitch against them for Tidewater and they borrowed Randy Tate from their Anderson, S. C., farm to pitch for them. Tate pitched two-hit ball for the Mets for seven innings and Cram was the loser.

Tate is twenty-one years old and impressive. "Looks like we may have found another pitcher for next year," Berra said.

But what about this year? Craig Swan hasn't completed a

game here, but he says he's throwing without pain for the first time. He said he hid his pain as long as he could because he didn't want to lose his chance with the Mets. He's fat. Tommy Moore is asking about the possibility of expansion making more big-league jobs next year. John Glass was sent home after a month. He was told if his arm felt good to contact the team about another chance in spring training.

There's a kind of gloom about the Yankees. They are at the brink of an emotional decision about Mel Stottlemyre. For nine years he threw his sinker and the batters hit grounders. He missed only two turns in all that time. He always went out and did his job. On bad teams he was a gleaming jewel. Now at thirty-two he may be at the end of his career. He's been able to pitch only once in two months. Thirty-two is no age for a man to be ending his career, but Stottlemyre's shoulder isn't responding to treatment.

Stottlemyre talks bravely about it. "I don't feel old," he said. "If this was five, six years ago, no one would have thought anything about it. Now, some people may think I won't come back. Who knows? I can't say."

His hope is that he hasn't pitched much this season—113 innings, after averaging 270 for nine years. Maybe it will turn out to be the year of rest his arm needs. "I think every pitcher has that thought in the back of his mind. Any time his arm hurts, he always wonders how he'll come back," Stottlemyre said. "I thought I was through three or four times before in different springs with the same stiffness. But it was only a thought."

Now it's a thought that's with him all the time. He's the last active Yankee to play in their great dynasty. When they won in 1964, Stottlemyre never thought it would be his last winner. Since then he's said if he was ever on a winner again, it would mean so much more to him.

Now the Yankees are making a good run at a championship and Stottlemyre can't be a part of it. The toll of getting this far has been too much. Too much mileage has worn out his right arm. Now he's cheated of the excitement. "I've been awfully lucky," he said. "I never had a serious arm injury until this. . . . I'm part of the team, yet I'm not 'cause I'm not contributing. I've never been through that before."

Seaver said he was disturbed by reports that Stottlemyre might never pitch again. Why, Seaver was asked? "Because he's a pitcher," he replied.

AUGUST 16, CINCINNATI

The Mets were able to beat the Reds, 2–1. Now they have a four-game streak built on the stuff the Mets build their dreams on. They've allowed only four runs in those four games.

McGraw finished up, working out of a tight situation. When he's on the mound, there's always a parade of thoughts and recollections and emotions marching through his head. A relief pitcher should be a kind of Frankenstein monster assembled for the job. He should have a rubber arm, a computerized memory and a chunk of cement where the emotions go.

Now the Mets can think of what they might do. "We still have a piano on our back," McGraw said. "We're still eleven games under .500. But we're doing some things." One of the things McGraw was doing was smiling. He hasn't been doing much of that of his own accord. "Maybe I have been different lately," he mused. "I'm just trying to get myself in gear. I'm trying to forget how good or how bad I feel. I have to go out and take over a game. Maybe I don't feel as good as I thought. Maybe I feel better. I have to get people out. The rest is all chatter."

AUGUST 18, CINCINNATI

A crack finally appeared in the polished wall of silent suffering. A season of Jon Matlack's frustration spilled out. In a time of crisis, he found the Mets to be a crashing disappointment. No more "You got to believe." With his eyes clear and blue, and ice in his voice, Matlack stood in front of his locker and indicted everybody. He included the players sitting in front of their lockers eating hamburgers covered with red sauce, Yogi Berra on the first year of a three-year contract, Bob Scheffing in his last year as general manager before retirement, and M. Donald Grant, the chairman of the board who is accountable for employing both Berra and Scheffing. Matlack was talking about leadership, expressing a conclusion he no longer wanted to hold to himself after the 6–5 loss to the Reds. It was the Mets' sixty-fifth loss and one more Matlack thought they should have won. The rising thoughts of a drive at the championship are realistically very dim now.

"The maximum potential is not being obtained from the guys in this room," Matlack said. "I'm not saying anybody is dogging it, but we're not playing as good as we're capable of."

That quickly defined a leadership gap. "Some guys are capable and don't need anything," Matlack said. "Some guys are capable and need a pat on the back. Some guys are capable and need a kick in the ass.

"I don't know where the pat or kick should come from—the manager, the players themselves, or the general manager. I know it's not coming. We're not a machine; we're not programmed to do things every time. It really helps to have that constructive criticism. Maybe it helps to have somebody tear you down from time to time."

It is a team without a strong driving figure. The manager is easy-going and embarrassed to silence by his own inarticulateness. That leadership could be provided by a player like Pete Rose, who threw himself into a headlong slide to stretch the single that tied the score, 3–3, into a double. On the scoreboard, Rose's hustle opened the door for an intentional walk and a three-run homer by Dave Concepcion. But its effect is felt every day in the clubhouse. A player like Frank Robinson can lead with the things he says as well as what he does. But the Mets have nobody like either.

"I don't think there's anybody here with the driving ambition to be a Pete Rose, a team leader," Matlack said. Cleon Jones and Rusty Staub have the status, but Jones' own ambitions are too mistrusted and he rarely speaks out, and Staub is too deep into himself.

Pitchers rarely emerge as leaders because they don't play every day, but Bob Gibson is a leader with the Cardinals because of his presence. Seaver has the tools, but he's rarely used them and now he's more withdrawn than ever because of his own difficulties.

Matlack may emerge as a leader eventually. "If I were in a position of more seniority or experience, I would try to lead more," Matlack said. "There have been instances where I could have spoken out, but I don't think that's my place. I'm relatively a baby."

Matlack had become irritable at breakfast when George Stone, reading the Sunday morning statistics, found the Mets had scored fewer runs than any team in the league and were eleventh in batting. Matlack said, "Don't tell me that on the day I got to pitch."

In the silence of the bus ride to the airport Matlack and Seaver sat together talking very softly. Matlack spoke for a long time. Seaver nodded and shook his head. He told Matlack what he said was precisely right—but he shouldn't have said it.

From Pete Rose there was a brilliant moment of anti-cliché baseball analysis of how the Reds were cutting the Dodgers' lead. "I'd rather be in first place with the momentum against you than in second with the momentum going for you," he said. Rose also said, "I'm glad that son of a bitch Matlack is gone. He's got to be the best left-hander in the league." Matlack, "the best left-hander in the league," leads the league with five shutouts and has an 11–10 record.

AUGUST 19, HOUSTON

The official reaction to Jon Matlack's comments was a red line of bluster over the phone lines from the offices in Shea Stadium to the Shamrock Hilton. Somebody got to the office early, saw early editions of the afternoon papers, and made a telephone call to Bob Scheffing.

It was an hour earlier where the general manager was sleeping. When the stories were recounted to him they were misinterpreted—as usual. The typical Met front-office reaction: strike out at the people who report conflict as if they had caused it.

The first misinterpretation Scheffing heard from the home office was that Matlack said he wanted to be traded. Matlack doesn't want to be traded. He has a lovely home overlooking the reservoir in Katonah, New York, and he likes living near where he works. He likes New York. He didn't say he wanted to be traded. And nobody wrote that he wanted to be traded.

What Matlack said was that he's been asked at banquet appearances, if he were traded, where would he like to go? He's answered that he'd prefer to go to the Reds. "They're my kind of ball club," Matlack said in his speech. "I have a lot of respect for Sparky Anderson. They have thirty men on the roster who can help."

What he was saying was that he'd like to stay with the Mets and have the ball club more like the Reds. All season the pitchers have suffered in silence like good soldiers. There has been no backbiting. But now there is a puff of criticism and the overreaction begins.

When the team got to the Astrodome, Matlack was summoned to the manager's office, where Berra and Scheffing were waiting. The yellow door was snapped shut. Matlack was asked if he asked to be traded. And Matlack, who hadn't read the papers, said he'd said no such thing. "I told them I'm happy here," Matlack said. "I said those things because I felt them. And I still do."

"I think he's wrong," Scheffing said waspishly after PR man Harold Weissman convinced him that it was his responsibility to speak to the press at such a moment. "I think we've got good leadership," Scheffing snapped

Matlack spent the afternoon refusing to say he'd been misquoted, standing by his comments with a nervous smile. He had put himself in the middle of controversy and few ball players relish that, whether they believe they're right or not.

In the clubhouse, while the interrogation was going on behind the manager's door, players came to Matlack's support. "I agree," Tom Seaver said. "But I don't want my personal feelings in the press."

"They may say to me, 'Why don't you shut up and do your job.' That's fine. I'm just trying to support Jon," Bud Harrelson said. "I don't think Jon stuck his foot in his mouth."

The front office has been stung by the sudden outburst. "If someone can accept credit for winning and success," said Ed Kranepool, who has been around since the first season with the Mets, "they can accept some of the blame, too. If they feel we don't need help, the fans and the press have to judge their baseball sense."

Kranepool has his own opinion of how Berra and Scheffing have utilized personnel this year. Kranepool had already seen tonight's lineup, which had Ken Boswell in right field and Kranepool nowhere. "I can't get in the lineup and I'm the leading hitter," he said. "How do you think I feel with an infielder in right field?"

Suddenly Matlack has brought everybody's disappointment to a head. "I think what he said was valid," said Harrelson. "I don't need to be fired up by Yogi. Some guys do. We're not getting it. Yogi is just not that kind of personality."

Berra is a likeable man. He makes no pretenses. He is committed to his wife and three sons. He kids that the youngest looks like Billy Martin. In the heat of the World Series last year he was full of thoughts on his middle son, Tim, playing football for the University of Massachusetts. Berra thrives on thoughts of Tim going to camp with the Baltimore Colts as a receiver. Larry, the oldest, caught in the Met organization until he hurt his knee.

The Yankees made Berra manager in 1964 and Ralph Houk, the general manager, dumped him as soon as he could even though Berra got the Yankees to the seventh game of the World Series. Berra signed on with the Mets in 1965 in a public-relations coup and was there as first-base coach and newly-elected member of the Hall of Fame when Gil Hodges died in 1972.

The players, for the most part, like Berra. Many of them think it was a misjudgment to make him manager in the first place. "The Peter principle," Tug McGraw says.

The feeling now, with the Mets 10½ games behind, is: Why doesn't somebody do something? "And nobody does," Harrelson said.

By doing something, Harrelson refers to the time he broke his hand and stayed on the active list when all he could do was run, and to the extended period when Tug McGraw couldn't throw but wasn't replaced. Now Harrelson sees St. Louis picking up veteran pitcher Claude Osteen and Montreal adding outfielder Jim Northrup while the Mets go with sore-armed pitchers and two gimpy outfielders.

Scheffing says Osteen and Northrup passed through the complicated waiver process back in June and the Mets were in no position to get them when they were available last week. In June, Scheffing was still depending on pitching carrying the Mets. When Detroit asked for young players for Northrup, Scheffing couldn't give them. Tidewater, the top farm team, is last in the International League.

The players haven't overlooked that fact. "How do the players know our prospects? They only saw Tidewater," Scheffing defended. The Victoria team is headed for its second straight Texas League pennant, but the team that won last year is basically the team at Tidewater now.

"I'm not getting into an argument with players," Scheffing said with disdain. He's been in professional baseball since 1935. "Their job is to play ball. We'll take care of the prospects. I don't want to blame the players. . . . If Seaver and McGraw . . ." He didn't have to finish what he was saying.

Harrelson did. "We need help," he said. "When do we get it? I guess it gets back to Don Grant. He's the man at the top, isn't he?"

They still have to go out and play the game. The last six

weeks of the season may be torture. Tonight was one more demonstration of the ancient delight of death by a thousand cuts. The chief sufferer was Seaver again. The clatter of his protective cup on the shelf of his locker broke the silence of the clubhouse. He pitched about as well as he can pitch and he still lost, 2–1, in eleven innings.

AUGUST 20, HOUSTON

Today the corporate indignation fell on Harrelson. He says he isn't frightened. The Mets don't have another first-line shortstop in sight.

The one who is frightened is Bob Apodaca, who hasn't rocked a boat yet. What he has is that blister again, a split in the skin on the middle finger of his right hand, just when he felt he had survived a rookie's worst traumas.

People get blisters digging in the garden or painting the playroom. Apodaca got his striking out Doug Rader in the fourth inning and had to come out of the game. It was the first time he had pitched since he got a blister on his finger two weeks ago.

Sounds trivial in a world of tendonitis and bone chips. But if Apodaca has a chronic blister, he has a problem. "They can transplant hearts, but they don't know how to cure a blister problem," he said.

It seems like a big issue about a little tissue except that Apodaca holds the ball with his first two fingers along the seams. The friction causes a rotation that causes the ball to sink, which is how Apodaca gets hitters out. Friction also causes blisters. Now the pitching coach is telling him he has to try to pitch with his fingertips on the smooth leather, which is positively frightening to him. "Whenever I've tried that, the ball goes straight," Apodaca said. The hitters start to grin at a straight fastball even before they swing.

Apodaca had just begun to feel he belonged. As of June 22 he had an inflated earned-run average of 5.82 and a deflated self-esteem. "I couldn't throw an inning without giving up a run," he said. "I got to the point where I was even scared to go out to the mound. I thought if I didn't get the ball in exactly the right place, they'd hammer it. Then I got my tits ripped in Philadelphia and turned to myself and said, 'If you go out there scared, you're going to wind up at Visalia.'"

Visalia in the California League is as far down as Apodaca could go. So he decided to have the courage of the freshman who goes to his second college final and decides he has nothing more to lose. Since then Apodaca's ERA is 2.57. "If I block out the first part of the year, which was a nightmare, I've had a pretty good first year," he said.

Now this. He did what he was told to prevent another blister. He sprayed the finger with medication and he filed the callus down and then let the callus build up. For three innings it worked. In the fourth inning, he struck out Rader and the callus split. Apodaca is pondering such extreme treatments as the pickle brine Nolan Ryan tried for his blister problem five years ago, even though he hated the smell of it. There might even be some brine left in the trainer's kit.

"I had felt I was getting myself together and now look," Apodaca said. Now he's conceding he has to try to hold the ball some unfamiliar way. "It's scary," he said.

Even Jack Aker, who's been pitching fifteen years, has no suggestion. "They don't have a cure for the common cold, either," he said.

The Astros won the game, 6–2.

AUGUST 21, HOUSTON

With the pressure almost off now, the Mets hit for twelve hits and ten runs, four of them batted in by Rusty Staub, and made Koosman the winner. He's won twelve and lost eight, which is impressive with this team. "He's been the best," Berra said. "We've lost five games for him when the relief pitchers didn't hold them."

Koosman said he pitched better last year. Last year he had

three shutouts. "I have none this year," he said. "I've been just a fraction worse.

"It's been just luck," he said stoically. "A lot of bad breaks that let runs score."

Quietly, Jack Aker summoned Jack Lang of the *Long Island Press* to his locker in the clubhouse. Lang, the Met correspondent for the *Sporting News*, had written that the Mets were scraping "the bottom of the barrel" when they scraped the bottom of the barrel to get Aker from Atlanta. Aker was insulted.

AUGUST 22, ATLANTA

There are psychologists waiting at every turn. The one here sells shoes. Bruce Friedman runs what he calls the largest shoe store in America here and there's no reason to doubt him. He's a transplanted New Yorker who came to Atlanta with his father a number of years ago, and their store behind the neighborhood shoe repair shop grew and grew.

He carries scads of major manufacturers' expensive shoes with minute flaws and sells them at fractions of their original prices. He can tell you your size with just a look and can remember what you bought the last time. The walls of the showrooms are covered with autographed photos of athletes—baseball, basketball, football, and hockey—who pass through Atlanta. They get additional discounts. "I hate to go there," Yogi Berra says, "because I already got so many shoes and I hate to pass them up."

But the visiting team in town today is the Mets. They have a day off, but the shoe store is quiet.

"You can tell the Mets are going bad," Friedman said. "I haven't seen the Mets. On a normal afternoon they'd all be here. Usually I can expect Tug in to buy eight or nine pairs. Going like he is, I guess he doesn't want to talk to anybody."

"How come guys will still go out and drink?" McGraw said.

AUGUST 23, ATLANTA

The visiting clubhouse here is larger than most. The lockers are wider. When the silence is deep, the room feels like a morgue. When the spacious lockers are unoccupied, they seem like so many empty drawers waiting to be filled.

The Mets responded to a dreadful doubleheader loss by making themselves absent. That left the manager, the coaches, the pitchers who didn't work in either game, and the batboys trying to be invisible as they worked in the gloom. Berra mumbled when answers to questions were unpleasant in the manner he has refined to a high art. He ate an overstuffed hamburger and when a question was asked he would take a bite and answer something that sounded like "Mbglmpf." And then he would clarify, "Ummnuh." And who could dispute him? At a time like this, all questions have unpleasant answers. That's why the room was so empty.

The Mets lost the first game, 4–3, in ten innings.

"I know they're very down a little," analyzed Buzz Capra in the Braves' clubhouse. "I feel sorry for them in a way," he said.

Not everybody feels sorry in any way for the Mets' straits. "Are they still saying 'We can do it?'" inquired Davey Johnson.

In the tenth inning of the first game, McGraw gave up a leadoff single and a sacrifice, got a strikeout, issued an intentional walk and a single. Game over. It was the third time this week the losing hit followed an intentional walk.

In the second inning of the second game, Atlanta pitcher Lew Krausse hit a long fly to left field. Ken Boswell was stationed there for the first time this season. He got to the fence, leaped, reached over and got the ball in his glove. On the descent, it appeared his arm hit the top of the fence, and the ball dropped over for a two-run homer. The Mets were in no condition to recover.

Boswell normally plays with no fence at his back. He normally plays with a sense of humor, too. "Are you trying to say I fucked up?" he demanded. "Where the hell do you expect me to be when a pitcher hits a ball that far? It was a dumb fucking question." Nobody accused Boswell of fouling up. The end is coming painfully and without dignity.

After that play Matlack left the ballpark to keep an appointment in Underground Atlanta with a friend from high school and her husband. "She looks 18," Matlack said. "We did some kind of reminiscing." He has already begun his readjustment a step ahead of Boswell.

AUGUST 24, ATLANTA

The last two balloons of the night drifted over center field, orange and yellow with smile faces taunting the Mets as they marched off the field. They looked like the last balloons of the season, too. The Mets lost another one in ten innings, 4–3.

It began as another night of floundering for Seaver. The Mets scored twice in the first inning and Ralph Garr hit Seaver's first pitch of the night high and far. Garr stood at the plate until the ball disappeared, then sprinted around the bases.

After that, it got worse. The Braves scored again in the first, once in the second, and filled the bases in the third. Seaver took off his cap and wiped his forehead with his upper sleeve after each hit.

"I warmed up and felt like I had the best stuff I've had all year," he said. "I felt like I was going to pitch a shutout. I never believe myself in the bullpen, but I was popping the ball downstairs. The first pitch I tried low and away. I threw it right here, chest high." Seaver held his flattened hand chest high and away from his body. "He still knows what he wants to do with the ball, but he can't get it there," Garr said.

Then, amazingly, Seaver found himself. He got the last out of the third and allowed only one more hit in the next four innings. Where it took him sixty-three pitches to get through the first three innings, he threw forty-seven in the next four and left with a tie.

Jerry Cram got double plays in the eighth and ninth innings

190 THE PITCHING STAFF

and Bob Miller went out for the tenth. He pitches older all the time now. He filled the bases with an intentional walk, got the second out, threw one strike to Norm Miller and four balls to walk in the winning run. Bob Miller pushed his cap back on his head and walked very slowly off the mound.

McGraw never got up to throw in the bullpen. Berra said he might have used McGraw if the game went on but didn't want to use him a second day in a row. "After last night, I don't think he likes to use me one day in a row," McGraw said.

AUGUST 25, ATLANTA

It was classic Atlanta—the heat shimmering off the ground in waves from the first look at the light of day from a hotel window. It was the day for Ray Sadecki to see Rube Walker mop his face on the bench and say, "Hot out there, coach?"

And it was the day for Walker to say to Sadecki, "Naw, I saw a dog chasing a cat this morning."

"What happened?" Sadecki dutifully responded.

"They was both walking," Walker said.

Bob Miller straggled out of the dark tunnel into the blinding shade of the dugout, tipped his cap over his hangover and sprawled across the bench. He was recalling as little as possible of his role in last night's game. "It's gone now," he said. "It took a long time last night."

Seaver pounded a bat on the bench behind Miller. He closed his eyes and winced. "It doesn't bother me a bit," Miller said.

"Don't anyone drop a towel," Jon Matlack said.

Seaver and McGraw stomped in cadence into the clubhouse, clutching their gloves at their chests as in left-shoulder arms, and singing "We are the men of the Mets."

What was needed on the field with the Mets in extremis was a cliché coming true. They needed something like sending Sadecki out to start against the Braves because there was absolutely nobody else and asking him to pitch a shutout. Absurd.

The Mets beat the Braves for the first time in nine tries this season. Sadecki pitched a 1–0 five-hitter and knocked in the winning run. He got it done in four minutes less than two hours, which was important because, as Seaver urged the players dressing in the clubhouse, "Lets go, some of these people are horny."

Nevertheless, there were a lot of people happy for Sadecki, working out of the most awkward position on the pitching staff. He's either a part-time starting pitcher or a part-time relief pitcher, depending on the crisis at hand, and full-time good-humor man.

"I'm the only man on the club who doesn't like him," said Jerry Koosman, the willing butt of Sadecki's Polish jokes. Remember, Koosman isn't Polish, Sadecki is. "I'm the dummy," Koosman said. "Him and I like to laugh."

Sadecki is thirty-three and understands a lot about life. When Ted Martinez recently grumbled, "They ought to pay us," about some requests for his autograph, Sadecki countered, "They do, Teddy." Sadecki has adjusted well to his indefinable role, trying to piece together some kind of routine to his life. He knows when and how much to run to keep himself in shape when he hasn't pitched in two weeks and how to save something in case he's called upon to relieve in the first inning and pitch the next eight.

As difficult as it is physically, it's more difficult mentally, which all the pitchers appreciate. "At this stage of my career, it's tough," Sadecki said. "You question yourself a lot. It's like that for any utility player; it's my job to be a utility pitcher."

His one sense of stability, he says, is that he's not afraid of being traded. "What you going to get for me?" he said.

And when the moment was fraught with peril in the last of the ninth, when the Mets faced another wrenching loss and a thousand miles of high-level gloom, he had the last laugh. He made the next-to-last laugh.

There were two outs and Bad Henry Aaron was walking to the plate as a pinch-hitter. And portly Rube Walker was dog-trotting (walking, actually, in the heat) to the mound.

Sadecki wiped his forehead on his sleeve. He asked Walker, "Where did they get this guy? Do you know anything about him?"

Walker said, "No. But you're not going to let him beat us, are you?"

The Mets shifted into their prevent defense with second baseman Felix Millan becoming a fourth outfielder to protect against a double. Sadecki held Aaron to a single, which wasn't half bad, then struck out Leo (Bananas) Foster to end the game. It was Sadecki's first complete game in 369 days and his first shutout, he recalled, in an awfully long time.

The reality of the situation is that the Mets are still sixteen games under .500. They haven't been that far down since the end of the 1968 season, when they finished ninth.

"The biggest disappointment is the pitching," Berra said. "More than the injuries. But you ain't going to break up a pitching staff because of one bad year."

AUGUST 26, SHEA STADIUM

Right about now somebody from the commissioner's office ought to ring a bell that officially designates the beginning of the stretch run. If not somebody from the commissioner's office, then maybe somebody from Blue Cross. This is the time pitchers go to the mound and tell themselves, if they can get through the next five weeks, they have all winter to rest and maybe count their World Series shares. And this is the time, they know, that pitchers break down.

It happens all season, beginning in spring training, but this is the time they're most susceptible. Pitching is now most influential because so much of it has already worn out. Except for doubleheaders, the Pirates and Cardinals in the National League East and the Red Sox, Yankees, and Orioles in the American League East will drop the fifth man from their rotations and go with their best four. When it comes right down to it, the best of those will pitch on two days' rest, if need be.

They don't dare dwell on the hazards. Pitchers who fail in September are often said to have a tightening in the throat rather than in the arm.

It's not a natural use of the arm in the first place. "If your arms were intended to work the way we use them, they'd be hinged at your waist and stick up instead of hanging downward," says Bob Gibson. He can't straighten his pitching elbow any more.

What pitchers live with is the thought of Bobby Shantz, who couldn't go to sleep without salve and a heating pad on his shoulder in the last years of his career. His arm was so bad he had to begin warming up at six o'clock to pitch at eight. He had to hang from the dugout roof or hold a weighted ball in his pitching hand between innings to keep the muscles from contracting.

"The trouble is that you don't realize what your limits are until you've reached them," Gibson says. He's passed 300 innings only twice in his fifteen big-league seasons. Seaver may never pitch as many as 300 innings. Both are very big on four days' rest.

Just what happens inside a pitcher's arm is still theory; no one has yet removed a pitcher's arm for study after he's come off the mound. Theory says there's microscopic bleeding in the muscles.

Yankee pitcher George Medich, a third-year medical student, is one of the rare people who has examined the condition from both sides. He says he paid particular attention to the arm in anatomy class. He says it's "volume overload because of the extreme G-load" that breaks the tiny blood vessels. Normally they mend between starts. "Twenty-four hours make a big difference," Ray Sadecki says. "You pitch nine innings and the next day you can't throw. On the second day you can throw a little. And by the third you can pop the ball. Sometimes you think about it in terms of hours, like pitching a day game instead of a night game on the fourth day."

By this point of the season, when Jerry Koosman has pitched 216 innings, the whole body is involved in hurting the arm. The best pitchers evolve deliveries that distribute stress through the whole body. But by now a pitcher who's been on the mound 216 innings has been rapped on the shins by ground balls a number of times or has twisted an ankle or picked up a spike wound covering first base. He can't pitch as smoothly and the stress shifts back to his arm.

Or maybe the muscles are merely tired. "If my shoulder is stiff, I'll be a little leery of a lot of breaking pitches," Mel Stottlemyre explains. "When I do throw it, I'll know my shoulder is not 100 per cent and it won't be a good curve. Then I'll know my fastball will have to be a better fastball than usual." Then he may be asking for more than his muscles can stand. Maybe that's how Stottleymyre hurt his shoulder.

Perhaps the damage was accumulating for years, maybe since Little League, which a number of team physicians regard as a tool of the devil. "I wish public opinion wouldn't let a boy pitch more than a couple of innings until he was over sixteen," says Peter LaMotte, the Mets' physician for several years.

The demand on a pitcher is to deliver every pitch with precisely the same motion, which focuses the wear on the same points. By the time Gary Nolan reached the big leagues at the age of seventeen, he'd already had nine years of wear. Last season, which began while he was still twenty-four, he was able to pitch in only two games. He didn't pitch in a major-league game this season.

One cause of breakdown LaMotte cites is something called Woolf's law, which apparently takes precedence over anything that evolved from Abner Doubleday. Simplified, it states that the body reacts to continuous stress with a thickening of the bones. "It means one bone doesn't fit properly into the other any more," LaMotte says. The effect is that some bits of the joint chip away and leave loose particles. Also, the shoulder isn't a secure ball-and-socket joint. It's held together by muscles, tendons, and ligaments. If the muscle is fatigued, it's not able to protect the joint. If the muscle is especially developed, sometimes a tear develops in the cuff, which is believed to be Stottlemyre's problem.

And sometimes the force exerted by the muscle is greater than the bone can take. The Mets had a pitcher in the minor leagues a few years ago who threw so hard he suffered a spiral fracture of the humerus and never pitched again.

But if the race grinds down to the last few days, most pitchers are willing to take the risk. The classic example is the Phillies' notable flop of 1964. While they were blowing a lead of six games with eleven to play, Gene Mauch, then a very young manager, started Jim Bunning and Chris Short three times each on two days' rest over the last three weeks. Neither pitcher won any of those games.

Sometimes cortisone shots enable a man to pitch when his muscles scream for him to rest. Denny McLain won two Cy Young Awards with the help of cortisone. He won thirty-one games at the age of twenty-four and was gone at twenty-nine. "The future is of no concern to the manager or the general manager," McLain says. "In that situation they expect you to do whatever you have to do. Do you think they were concerned with me burning myself out? I don't think so. There was somebody to take my place and there'll be somebody to take his. That's the way it should be."

Koosman pitched his eleventh complete game to win, 5–4, over Houston.

AUGUST 27, SHEA STADIUM

When McGraw got a starting assignment on July 30 of last season, the intent was to give him enough innings to straighten himself out. Tonight the reasoning wasn't exactly clear.

"Maybe Parker will be better down there in the bullpen," Berra explained before the game. Explained what? Will Parker pitch better in relief than as a starter? Will Parker pitch better in relief than McGraw has? Or both of the above? "And

Apodaca can't pitch with a blister. And who have I got to pitch?" Berra continued.

McGraw pitched six innings, allowed one run, and was the winning pitcher over the Astros, 4–2. And Parker pitched three innings with one run for the save. It was Parker's second save and that tied him for the lead on the Mets. The team has amassed a total of nine saves. McGraw alone had twenty-five last season and the Mets had forty, which says something about the standings.

For McGraw, at least it was his fifth win. It was his first as a starter since May of 1969, before the world learned he was a great relief pitcher. "I've got to make two drives," he said. "A salary drive and a don't-trade-me drive."

He said the change in routines from relieving to starting didn't affect him. "When you're a left-hander," he said, "there's no such thing as a routine."

Left-handed pitchers have always been told that they were expected to be eccentric. Bob Miller has a home next to McGraw's in Poway, Calif., outside of San Diego. Miller says one day he was driving out onto the street and looked toward a new home under construction on the other side. He noticed how oddly the men were working on the roof. He said they would look up, quickly look down and drive a nail, and look up again. Miller says he looked back and saw McGraw standing on the hill beside his house, driving golf balls over the new house. McGraw nods at mention of the story.

The other contribution of the pitching staff tonight was that Jack Aker went on the disabled list with a bad back. The man who replaced him was Benny Ayala, the spring phenom who didn't make it. Ayala became the fortieth man to hit a home run in his first at-bat in the big leagues.

AUGUST 28, SHEA STADIUM

Jon Matlack pitched a nifty game: eight innings, five hits, seven strikeouts, no walks, and one earned run. The problem was that Houston was ahead, 2–0, when Matlack went out for a pinch-hitter in the eighth. The Mets scored two in the bottom of the ninth, just in time for Jerry Cram to get his first decision in the big leagues when Cliff Johnson hit a pinch home run off him in the tenth.

AUGUST 29, SHEA STADIUM

A shutout from Tom Seaver, 7–0, over Houston. For those who've counted, it was his first win since July 26. "It's been a struggle," he said. If he sighed, no one heard him.

AUGUST 30, SHEA STADIUM

Casey Stengel says if you watch baseball closely, every day you'll see something you never saw before. Like the time in the World Series the plate umpire hit big Boog Powell over the head with an inflated chest protector in order to kill a bee.

And not everything happens to the Mets. Atlanta pitcher Max Leon, in relief of Buzz Capra, was trying to intentionally walk Wayne Garrett in the bottom of the eighth with the Mets leading, 3–2, and a runner on third. On his third toss, Leon threw a gentle lob over the head of the catcher to the backstop and the Mets got another run.

"Matlack told me he had never seen that before," Berra, the old catcher, said. "I told him, 'Stick around, you'll see a lot of things.'

"I always told the pitcher not to lob the ball. They lob it and think nothing of it and throw it away."

It wasn't quite the same as the time a San Francisco pitcher was in trouble at Philadelphia and put his head down as the catcher was throwing the ball back to the mound. The ball went into center field and the winning run scored. In the clubhouse after the game, Alvin Dark, the manager, heaved a metal stool, caught a sharp edge, and lost the tip of his pinky finger.

The winning pitcher was Ray Sadecki. Another complete game.

Tug McGraw turned thirty today.

AUGUST 31, SHEA STADIUM

Bob Apodaca won his first game in relief and apologized to Jerry Koosman for it. That blister had kept "Daca" from pitching for eleven days until he relieved Koosman with a 4–3 lead in the seventh. A bounced single tied the score and an infield out put the Braves ahead. Rusty Staub's two-run homer turned the score, 6–5, for Apodaca.

"I really felt bad," Apodaca said and undoubtedly he did. "I wanted to save the game for Koo," he said. "All I did was make them hit the ball on the ground like I'm supposed to and they score two runs."

McGraw will start again tomorrow and Henry Aaron is expected to play for the Braves. In April, McGraw said he might like a place in posterity as the pitcher who gave up the home run with which Aaron broke Babe Ruth's home run record. That distinction went to Al Downing. Now there's a strong possibility that Aaron's next home run will be his last.

That would put McGraw's name on some stone tablet in the great beyond, too. "I didn't even think about Aaron until you just reminded me," McGraw said. "Damn you, now I'm thinking."

After careful consideration, McGraw decided. "I hope I strike him out four times." McGraw has his own case to consider at this time.

Last night McGraw's friends gave him a birthday party. He received a silver-plated yo-yo and a birthday cake inscribed: "Youth is like Irish whiskey. It doesn't last long."

SEPTEMBER 1, SHEA STADIUM/CHICAGO

Just what McGraw needed: another excuse for a party. He didn't give Aaron his last home run. McGraw pitched his first shutout in the big leagues. McGraw doesn't need much of an excuse for a party. He's not a particularly big drinker, but he does like to talk about it. He didn't even need a drink to feel high after the game. He left his luggage in the car at the airport and it missed the team's flight to Chicago.

Then he went out to celebrate his shutout at a Japanese steakhouse with Matlack, Staub, Grote, and Harrelson. "You'd be surprised how good Irish whiskey goes with Japanese food," McGraw said.

Underneath the happy talk, McGraw has mixed emotions. "The best thing about starting is convincing myself and everyone else my arm is sound," he said.

The trouble with that is that some of the people convinced may now think McGraw is worth getting in a trade. "You have to have a left-hander in the bullpen," Berra said, mixing his cause and effect. "A lot of clubs are looking for one."

McGraw hopes desperately that he isn't traded. "If I got traded," he said. "I wouldn't even know how to put another uniform on."

George Stone went home to Reston, La., with instructions not to throw a ball until spring training. Nobody can tell Stone what he should think.

SEPTEMBER 2, CHICAGO

McGraw's luggage arrived this morning. Phyllis sent it out with the airline. Then the game with the Cubs was rained out and rescheduled as part of a doubleheader here tomorrow. A doubleheader can't run that late because there are no lights.

That's just as Ernie Banks says it ought to be in "beautiful" Wrigley Field. "God's own sunshine," Banks calls it. "Beautiful day for a ball game, let's play two." He says that whatever the weather. Nobody dislikes Ernie Banks. He's a roving batting instructor for the Cubs after being "Mr. Cub" for nineteen years. He hit 512 home runs and it's one of the inequities of the game that he never played on a pennant-winner. He was close in 1969, before the Cubs were caught in the

Mets' great rush to destiny. That Banks never made it to a World Series is not a sadness to everybody, not even to everybody who likes him. It's merely baseball.

"I thought about that one time," said Bill White, with the Cardinals then. "Then I never thought about it again."

Hank Webb reported from Tidewater and threw briefly to Rube Walker in the rain after the game was called. He threw five pitches past Walker, who hadn't been looking for the workout.

At Pittsburgh there were angry words between the Pirates, who are in first place, and the Phillies, who are third and think they have a chance at first. The Pirates bumped their lead over St. Louis to $2\frac{1}{2}$ games by beating the Phillies twice while the Cardinals were rained out. In the process, Dave Cash of the Phillies was hit on the helmet by a pitch from Bruce Kison. Cash wanted retribution. "We're going to get even, and if nobody else on this team will throw the ball, I will," he said.

Cash was issuing a challenge to his own pitchers. It's the responsibility of the pitcher to protect his own batters. An eye for an eye. Otherwise, his teammates think he's lacking in masculinity. Of course, it's always done in retaliation. Hardly ever has a pitcher said he threw at a batter on purpose, or has a manager admitted he ordered a pitcher to throw at a batter without provocation.

From time to time a pitcher will tip the balance between being sent out or making the club by pleasing the manager with his guts. He'll throw at a batter. Often an aging pitcher traded to a new club feels it imperative that he demonstrate his courage immediately. And often a young pitcher will be intimidated by the situation.

The Mets were always displeased by Jim McAndrew's reluctance to return fire. Of course, if McAndrew had been a better pitcher it wouldn't have mattered so much. The best pitchers don't have to live that way. Jim Palmer, who throws lightning, won twenty-two games last year and hit only three batters. Seaver won nineteen and hit only four. Sandy Koufax rarely hit a batter. Of course, the hitters were upset about hitting against Koufax' stuff in the first place.

The inherent purpose of making a batter duck is to frighten him into backing off the plate and conceding the outside edge to the pitcher. Some pitchers don't have to do that on purpose. They are conveniently wild.

For years managers and coaches were convinced that black and Latin players were afraid of being hit. "Knock him down the first time up and he doesn't want to play the rest of the day," was the standard line. Willie Mays was knocked down often and so was Frank Robinson, and you'll notice how much it hurt their careers. The truth of it is that all hitters have to discipline themselves to stand in against a pitcher who pitches up and in.

Phillie relief pitcher Eddie Watt suggested that Cash wouldn't have to take things into his own hands. "The next time I throw a baseball in this park, I will be trying to kill somebody, and that somebody will be a member of the Pittsburgh Pirates," Watt said.

SEPTEMBER 3, CHICAGO

The Mets can so win a doubleheader. Jon Matlack pitched a four-hitter for his sixth shutout to win the first game, 2–0. Tom Seaver struggled into the seventh and got help from Harry Parker to win the second, 11–4.

The Pirates beat the Phillies again. Eddie Watt did not pitch. Nobody was killed. No batters were hit.

SEPTEMBER 4, CHICAGO

Ray Sadecki won his third straight. He pitched six and a third and Bob Apodaca finished up for the save as the Mets beat the Cubs, 4–2. It was the second save in a row for the bullpen.

Quietly, the Mets have won seven in a row and ten of their last eleven. "We're doing everything right, that's the only difference," Yogi Berra said. They're nine games under .500. It's too little and too late.

"We have to be realistic about our chances," Sadecki said, "but the streak is fun. It's just more enjoyable to come to the park every day now to see if we can make it longer."

If they had done this earlier . . . well, that's a thought for another time. Perhaps at the trading table.

SEPTEMBER 5, ST. LOUIS

The newspapers and radio broadcasts come and go every morning and none of them mention Bob Miller. They don't say he pitched yesterday for the Mets and they don't say he's been traded.

He hasn't been in a game in a week and the Mets have no serious use for him this season. Probably not for next season, either. But maybe somebody can use a relief pitcher for the last three weeks. Mike Marshall pitched in his ninety-first game for the Dodgers tonight and picked up his twentieth save. None of the other contenders in either league has a relief pitcher like that. Maybe even the Dodgers could use some experienced help for Marshall.

Miller certainly is experienced. When the Mets picked him up last September 23, the purpose was to take the load off Tug McGraw for the last ten days. The price was right.

Somebody always wants Miller—or somebody always wants to get rid of him, depending on the state of the pennant race. It's his second time around with the Mets, his twelfth stop on ten different teams. That's a record. Beginning in 1957, Miller appeared in thirty-five different major-league ball parks—five in New York—which is probably another record. The longest entry in "Who's Who in Baseball" is under his name.

Someday Miller's grandchildren will ask about a famous

player and Grandpa Bob will say, "Well, sonny, I played with him." He'll say it about almost any player, including Stan Musial, Maury Wills, Sandy Koufax, Harmon Killebrew, Ernie Banks, Billy Williams, Willie Stargell, Al Kaline, Mickey Lolich, and Willie Mays.

He has pitched some big games. He started the first game of a doubleheader on the last day of the 1966 season, when the Dodgers needed to win one to clinch the pennant. Miller lost on his own wild throw and was crestfallen. He remembers Koufax patting him on the shoulder and saying, "Don't worry, I'll get it." Koufax won the second game.

For Minnesota, Miller won the game that put the Twins in first place in 1969 and the game that clinched the division championship. He started and lost the last game of the playoff to Baltimore.

But he'll be thirty-six in February and the Mets are losing interest. Miller has pitched in more games than any of them—fifty-three. He hasn't been very good and he hasn't been very bad, but he's been willing and ready, and that's something.

He's had his experiences. When he was a top relief pitcher with the Dodgers, Buzzie Bavasi once mailed him a contract calling for a sixty per cent cut, which was more than the maximum. When Miller phoned, Bavasi said he had an office pool on what time Miller would call. Face to face, Bavasi would put three pieces of paper on the desk in front of Miller, another favorite foil, and tell him to pick one for next year's salary. Miller picked one. Bavasi crumpled the others and threw them away. "I'm glad you didn't pick the other ones," Bavasi said.

"They were probably all the same," Miller said. "We never knew."

With the roisterous Pirates, he saw broadcaster Bob Prince dive from a third-floor window into the swimming pool of the Chase-Park Plaza Hotel in St. Louis. Fully clothed.

He flew from Chicago to Oakland with the White Sox and then was told to fly back to Chicago to join the Cubs. He was in the Tiger clubhouse when coach Joe Schultz asked,

"What're you putting that uniform on for?" Miller replied "We have a game tonight." Schultz said, "You got one someplace else." Miller's wife, Susie, joined him from California in Cleveland one June 14 and bought drapes for their apartment. On June 15 he was traded to the White Sox.

Trade talk hardly scares him. The last time he looked, his uniform still said "Mets." "But it's still early," Miller said. "I haven't read the papers yet."

Jerry Koosman pitched seven creditable innings, giving up only two runs, and lost to the Cardinals, 3–0. It was the end of the Mets seven-game winning streak.

Craig Swan and Randy Sterling were recalled from Tidewater. Swan had a 1–3 record and a fat 5.28 earned-run average and Sterling was 12–11 and 3.39. John Strohmayer was also recalled with 2–4 and 3.45 but that was simply a nice gesture. Strohmayer needs two days in the majors to qualify for the pension.

SEPTEMBER 7, ST. LOUIS

Dick Stello is an umpire. Jon Matlack was not happy with Stello's work tonight. "Why don't you ask Mr. Stello where those pitches were," Matlack said. "He blew a two-two change to Simmons. And then he blows two pitches to Brock. In my book, those pitches were strikes."

For the record book, the Cardinals beat Matlack, 2–1. Or, as Lou Brock put it, "It doesn't really matter too much what Matlack thinks, does it?"

For 8⅔ innings the Cards hit only one ball hard. That was Ted Simmons' double in the fourth that tied the game at 1–1. Matlack was in full stride into the ninth inning when Stello ruled Matlack's changeup to Simmons wasn't a strikeout pitch. Simmons walked. Matlack got an out. Then a bloop double dropped in front of gimpy Rusty Staub. Mike Tyson got an intentional walk and Matlack got the second out. Matlack got ahead of Brock, one ball and two strikes, and then found conflict with the umpire again. "Both pitches were low and outside," said Brock.

"They both looked like strikes on the corner to me," Matlack said. With the bases full, Matlack didn't have much choice in pitches. "Not in that situation," he said. "You've got to go with the fastball." Brock was prepared. He singled to left and Matlack had a 12–11 record.

"Yeah, Matlack's tough," Gibson said. "He's up there with the best in the league, but he's just like the rest of us, too. He goes out there once in a while and gets the shit beat out of him." Gibson pitched the complete game for the Cards. He'll be thirty-nine in two months. He can still overpower hitters occasionally, but he has a 9–12 record and he's never had a season under .500.

SEPTEMBER 8, ST. LOUIS

Tom Seaver looks as if he's making an adjustment. He struck out only three, but he pitched nine innings and beat the Cards, 5–3. Instead of losing and falling back to .500, he raised his record to 10–8.

Two quick stories about pitchers:

Harvey Haddix pitched the longest perfect game in history in 1959 and lost. He was perfect until two out in the thirteenth inning for Pittsburgh against the Milwaukee Braves and lost, 1–0, when Don Hoak made an error and Joe Adcock hit a ball over the fence. Because of base-running confusion only one run was permitted and the hit was scored as a double.

Anyhow, Haddix received scores of letters of condolence. He and his wife were culling them when his wife grumbled at one and tossed it on the floor. Haddix insisted on seeing it.

That one hangs framed in his den. He figures the letter came from students at Texas Tech since the letter was postmarked Lubbock, Tex. It said simply, "Dear Harv, Tough shit." Haddix says the letter was exactly right.

When Bob Shaw was a young pitcher with Detroit in 1958, he was constantly preening himself and pontificating on one thing or another. His roommate was Italian-born Reno Bertoia. One day Shaw so disturbed Bertoia with his theorizing that Bertoia said, "Shaw if you don't shut up, I'll—I'll break every mirror in the room."

A footnote to history: Shaw was a pitcher on the Mets in 1966 and 1967 and Haddix was the pitching coach.

SEPTEMBER 9, SHEA STADIUM

Ray Sadecki won his fourth straight today, a nine-inning 7–1 job over the Expos. It was his eighth start of the season and the first time he has pitched four times in a row in rotation. He's the third Met to win four in a row, but the other two—Jerry Koosman and Tom Seaver—have been trying all season.

The winning streak doesn't fool Sadecki about his status as a pitcher. He had his twenty-game season in 1964. "It's fun now while it's happening," he said. "It's an old cliché, but it's the truth. You got to pitch well to pitch often and pitch often to pitch well. The question is which comes first?" The effect of Sadecki's flurry is that it may revise his "What're you going to get for me?" trade status.

SEPTEMBER 10, SHEA STADIUM

No winning streak for Tug McGraw as a starter, but seven strikeouts and four runs in eight innings isn't exactly discouraging for a pitcher who spent almost the whole season in drydock. Bob Apodaca pitched the ninth and gave up the other two runs in the 6–4 loss to Montreal.

Craig Swan will not spend the winter with such encouraging thoughts. He'll spend a lot of it with his pitching arm in a cast. He has a stress fracture, an injury caused not by a severe blow but by constant repetitive stress.

Swan was told not to pick up a ball until spring training. The first time he tries to throw will scare the daylights out of him. There is nothing Dr. Parkes can prescribe for that.

SEPTEMBER 11, SHEA STADIUM

Forsch, Garman, Hrabosky, Folkers, Bare, Osteen, Siebert, Koosman, Parker, Miller, Apodaca, Cram, Webb. They all pitched tonight; the game went twenty-five innings. It was the most innings ever played in a night game (the record for any game is twenty-six innings). It took more time than any previous night game—seven hours and four minutes. The longest game on record took only nineteen minutes more.

And when it ended at 2:37 tonight—er, this morning—there were few places open to eat, even in New York. "The only thing I regret," Tug McGraw said, "is that all the eating places are closed and I'll have to go home and make myself a bologna sandwich."

It looked as if it would be a routine nine-inning game with Jerry Koosman nailing down a 3–1 decision. With two out, he made Ken Reitz look foolish on a changeup. Then Reitz guessed right on a fastball and tied the score with a two-run homer.

And then nobody scored for fifteen innings, including eight shutout innings pitched by Jerry Cram and nine by Claude Osteen. Players made jokes at the foolishness of it all. The Cardinals, in the thick of the race, were spending a whole pitching staff trying to win one game. The Mets, out of the race, were staying up all night trying to avoid losing another.

When St. Louis manager Red Schoendienst called for a bunt in the twentieth inning, Alan Foster, a starting pitcher, broke up the dugout by telling Schoendienst: "We've been playing for one run for five hours; let's play for the big inning. Let him hit away."

When Brock Pemberton became the fiftieth and last player to enter the game (a record) and got a pinch single for his first major-league hit, the Met bench called for the ball for his souvenir. "Don't give it to him," Tom Seaver yelled. "It's the last ball we've got."

The deciding run came when the game appeared certain to match the twenty-six inning record. Bake McBride beat out an infield single to greet Hank Webb, the sixth Met pitcher. Webb then caught McBride frozen ten feet off first base. But Webb's pickoff throw sailed far past John Milner at first base. McBride kept running and scored when catcher Ron Hodges couldn't hold the throw in the collision at the plate. The Mets, who hadn't scored since the bottom of the fifth inning, didn't score in the bottom of the twenty-fifth, either.

For the record, Met pitchers threw 331 pitches. The Cardinals keep count only for starters, but the grand total had to be around 700.

Ed Sudol, the plate umpire, called them all. He was the plate umpire in the twenty-three-inning Met game in 1964, the one that set the elapsed-time record. He was the plate umpire in the Mets' twenty-four-inning game at Houston in 1964, the longest 1–0 game ever. "Why," he said, "do these things always happen with the Mets?"

SEPTEMBER 12, SHEA STADIUM

"At 5 o'clock this morning, I counted forty guys in the Stage Delicatessen," Joe Torre of the Cards said. "It looked like a team meeting."

"I slept until 2:45 this afternoon," Ken Boswell said. "I can't understand it. When I got here today, most guys were in early."

Jon Matlack was the one who looked tired on the field. He allowed six runs in the sixth inning, though three were unearned.

Bob Gibson, who left with a pulled groin muscle after pitching five innings, was the winning pitcher in the 12–5 decision. "Now don't go asking me how I feel when I win a game like that," Gibson challenged. "All right, if you must know, I feel great."

THE PITCHING STAFF 209

After all his success, Gibson still has his goals. He wants more. "I know I don't have much time left," he said. "I just love the idea of another World Series."

The Cardinals say "God forbid" to the thought of Gibson missing a turn. He's still the leader. He promised he would still be a factor over the last nineteen games.

SEPTEMBER 14, SHEA STADIUM

Ray Sadecki tried for his fifth straight victory and got as far as one out in the second inning. The Cubs beat the Mets, 12–0, the Mets' worst losing margin of the season. But don't blame Sadecki alone. He had help. Bob Miller came in and walked a man intentionally, filling the bases, and another unintentionally, forcing in a run. Harry Parker gave up four runs and Jerry Cram two. And John Strohmayer, who has the two days necessary to qualify for his pension, pitched a scoreless inning.

There's not much for the Mets to get excited about except trying to make the season's statistics look as good as possible for contract negotiations. That's what they mean by the "salary drive."

SEPTEMBER 15, SHEA STADIUM

There's an air of fatalism about Tug McGraw. It's a pre-nostalgia. When he thinks about the future, his mind takes him back to the past. He's the senior member of the pitching staff. Only Ed Kranepool has been on the Mets longer. McGraw's whole working life has been in New York. He came out of Casey Stengel's instructional school with Jim Bethke, Danny Napoleon, and Ron Swoboda. They are all gone now. McGraw got a certificate for being the first occupant of his room in the Sheraton Lincoln Hotel in Houston. He was twenty that spring.

He was there in the lobby of the Lincoln when a seven-foot,

six-inch man ducked out of the barber shop where he'd had his shoes shined. "It was like painting a garage," the shoeshine man said.

Stengel was talking about a new first baseman he expected when he spied the giant and said, "And there he is."

"And he's only seventeen years old," said Bethke.

McGraw struggled up and down between the Mets and Triple A until Gil Hodges and Rube Walker made him a relief pitcher in 1969. "That was the break of my life," McGraw said. "I don't think I'd be a $90,000 starter now." The Mets wouldn't have been in two World Series without him, either.

Now the brass talks about the pitchers being developed in the minor leagues. "We got guys with potential we got to think about," Yogi Berra says. "We got pitchers."

And McGraw reads between the lines. "You begin to think about what players will be around next year," he said. "You have an idea who is coming up and who is in the minor leagues. Or what left-handed relievers are around. You have to think about that. You're part of it. Especially when you've been in just one organization like I have."

There's no reassurance for McGraw here. Berra points that out when he reads the statistics of the bullpen. The Mets are 4–15 in extra-inning games and 16–30 in one-run games. Figures like that are worn like a tattoo in the bullpen. "It's been a long season," McGraw said.

Like today. The Cubs beat the Mets, 5–4. McGraw got Bob Apodaca out of a bases-full jam in the eighth with the score tied and then gave up two runs in the top of the ninth that decided the game. His earned-run average is 3.69, a bit better than last year's, but he has only two saves.

He's pitched better lately. The effect may be that the front office, which may not view the potential of the farm system as highly as it says, may find increased market value in McGraw.

That's the thought McGraw finds intruding on his mind. "My only concern—I know I can pitch—my only concern now is whether my future will be here," he said. "Everyone is susceptible. It's going to be a busy winter. I hope I'm here. I'm kind of stepping out of line by talking about trades, but I can't help it."

Hank Webb started and lasted five innings in search of his first major-league victory. He hit two batters and balked once.

SEPTEMBER 16, MONTREAL

McGraw got his third save in the second game of the doubleheader. Randy Sterling was the winner in his first major-league appearance. He was forced out of the game when his elbow tightened in the sixth inning, and McGraw preserved the 3–2 lead. Jerry Koosman was the loser in the first game, 3–2, on an unearned run.

SEPTEMBER 17, MONTREAL

With the Mets rained out tonight, an interesting parallel to Seaver's history and difficulties appeared in Jim Palmer's shutout for Baltimore. Palmer won twenty games the last four seasons. He won the Cy Young Award last year. He was a power pitcher who threw heat high and inside and defied the hitters to hurt him. He laughed about the way his fastball leaped over the bats.

But he spent two months on the disabled list this season and now is learning something about finesse. His shutout of the Yankees left his record at 7–12.

"Tonight he really popped only three fastballs," said Ellie Hendricks, who has caught Palmer since 1968. "His first game back from the disabled list he wanted to prove himself. So he extended himself too much. And he set himself back."

Until then Palmer had few doubts. He was tall and good looking and had a bright smile and quick wit. He could play golf near par with hardly any practice. His wife said he could even diaper the baby better than she could. He could learn a game in the morning and beat the teacher in the afternoon.

"What he's probably learned because of this is to put the ball in spots," Hendricks said. "He's learned he has to be a pitcher instead of a thrower. Most fastball pitchers hate to admit when the time comes. They're the last to know. I know a lot of pitchers can't cope with losing their fastball. But Jimmy is quite realistic."

It sounds so much like Seaver's struggle with himself, and Palmer just turned twenty-seven. He's almost three years younger than Seaver.

"If I have to, I'll find another way to win," Palmer said. "There's nothing that says I can't throw another way. There's nothing wrong with throwing a fastball low and away for a strike." Seaver hasn't yet come to the point of putting that kind of conclusion into words.

SEPTEMBER 18, MONTREAL

"There's a distinct possibility I won't throw a baseball again this year," Seaver said. He mowed the Expos down for five innings in the second game of the doubleheader, allowing only one baserunner on a walk. Then he "popped" the sciatic nerve in his butt again.

The Mets are mathematically eliminated from the race for .500.

Several of the Mets are trying to get out of the month-long trip to Japan at the end of October. It could be a sensational experience, but the Mets are fed up with baseball.

SEPTEMBER 20, PITTSBURGH

Baseball players as far out of it as the Mets take great delight in beating a team that's going for the championship. The Pirates are a half-game behind the Cardinals. Not that it's anything personal; the Mets enjoy beating the Cards, too. It gives some kind of incentive for playing out the remainder of the schedule.

Tonight was great fun for eight innings. Ray Sadecki had the Pirates eating out of his hand. He had three runs and they had only one. His first mistake was walking the leadoff man in the ninth. A pitcher wth a two-run lead should never walk the leadoff man. Sadecki didn't get another out.

Tug McGraw relieved and got one out. He also gave up two hits and made a wild pitch. Harry Parker relieved and got an out and walked a man. The third out never came and the Pirates pulled it out, 4–3. Another one-run loss for the Mets; another failure by the bullpen.

Dr. Parkes examined Seaver and said he might be able to pitch again in a week, after all.

SEPTEMBER 21, PITTSBURGH

The Pirates won't go into first place at the Mets' expense tonight. Jerry Koosman beat them, 4–2. It was his fourth victory over the Pirates this season. They haven't beaten him yet.

Philadelphia relief pitcher Pete Richert woke up this morning with discomfort in his pitching arm and saw the team physician. Richert's left hand was cold and pale. Tests revealed almost no circulation because of three blood clots in Richert's shoulder.

Richert was given the choice between trying to save his eleven-year big-league career and trying to save his thirty-four-year-old arm with surgery. Richert said there wasn't much choice. He voted for the arm.

SEPTEMBER 22, PITTSBURGH

Matlack pitched a dazzling three-hitter to beat the Pirates, 3–0, his seventh shutout. He leads the league in that department. "It wasn't the best stuff I had all year, but I was capable

214 THE PITCHING STAFF

of pitching the no-hitter," Matlack said. None of the Pittsburgh hits got out of the infield.

The Pirates are now a 1½ games behind the Cardinals. "The Mets," said Pirate outfielder Richie Zisk, "are the club I'm most afraid of."

SEPTEMBER 23, LOS ANGELES

Mike Marshall, who says he's taken the trouble to learn more about a pitcher's body than anyone else has, pitched in his 101st game for the Dodgers. He set the record with ninety-two games last season. "I pitched the last game of the season and wasn't tired," Marshall said.

SEPTEMBER 24, PHILADELPHIA

Hank Webb started and lasted four innings as the Phillies won, 6–3.

Yogi Berra said Tom Seaver might pitch here tomorrow night. "We're going to warm up Seavers for the second game and see how he feels," Berra said.

Berra always pronounces Tom's name with an "S" at each end, probably because Roy Sievers was one of the top hitters in the American League when Berra played. The mispronounciation is one more of the things about Berra that irks Tom Seaver.

SEPTEMBER 25, PHILADELPHIA

Tom Seaver tried. He warmed up before the first game and decided he felt good enough. But then he got that pain in the ass and his tenth loss for his efforts. "The pain kept building up," he said. "By the sixth inning, when I tried to throw a fastball to Greg Luzinski, I felt a real knot."

Luzinski doubled and scored the fourth and final run off Seaver. Nino Espinosa allowed two more in the seventh and Bob Miller pitched the eighth.

In Los Angeles, Tommy John underwent a two-hour operation on his arm. Dr. Frank Jobe took a six-inch section of tendon from John's right forearm and used it for reconstruction of his left elbow. John had a 13–3 record and was headed for his best season when his arm broke down on July 25. "It was everything adding up," Dr. Jobe said. He also said it was the most complicated surgery he'd ever performed on a pitcher's arm. He said John could expect to test the arm in January.

SEPTEMBER 26, PHILADELPHIA

In a stroke of managerial genius, Danny Murtaugh held a one-minute pre-game meeting with his Pirates. He told them to forget last night's unforgettable 13–12 loss to the Cardinals.

So the Pirates went out and scored four runs in the first inning and two more in the second to beat Jerry Koosman, who had pitched four complete-game victories over them this season. The winning pitcher for the worn and shaky Pirates was thirty-seven-year-old Juan Pizarro, who pitched in the Mexican League for most of this season. Pizarro congratulated Pirate general manager Joe Brown for his wisdom in "offering more money than Cleveland when I go home to Puerto Rico from Mexico."

In Arlington, Texas, Jim Kaat won his twentieth game for the White Sox. That brings up an interesting point. The White Sox pitching coach is Johnny Sain, whose concepts of handling a pitching staff meet with great disagreement from Yogi Berra and Rube Walker. The only other time Kaat had won twenty was when he was with Minnesota when Sain was the pitching coach there.

Sain was the Yankee pitching coach from 1961 to 1963 and had a hand in three pennants. Whitey Ford, who had never won twenty, won twenty-five and twenty-four. Ralph Terry and Jim Bouton had their only twenty-game seasons.

Sain was with Detroit from 1967 to 1969. In 1968, Earl Wilson had his only twenty-game season and Denny McLain had his thirty-one game season.

The prevailing criticism here is that Sain burns out his pitchers. They don't pitch as well after he's gone.

SEPTEMBER 27, SHEA STADIUM

It was a struggle between two pitchers who had to struggle for outs with less than their best stuff. Jerry Reuss was struggling to get the Pirates into a tie for first place with the scoreboard showing that the Cardinals had already lost in Chicago. Jon Matlack was struggling to get his record over .500. Reuss won, 2–1.

He continually baffled himself as he got hitters out. "When I was warming up, I didn't think I'd win, because I didn't have a good fastball," he said. "Sometimes it's better not to have good stuff because then you concentrate more on pitching to spots."

Reuss—tall, blonde, and twenty-five—is holding up well under the pennant pressure. Maury Wills starred for ten years and still found the race kept him from eating dinner from Labor Day until the end of the season. He'd pass up a steak, order a sandwich, take a bite, and find his mouth too dry to eat.

"Sure I'm excited," Reuss said. "But it's still the game you play early in the season. You have to put things in the proper perspective. Suppose I gave up five or six runs in the first inning—the sun would still shine tomorrow." Saying that is easy. Believing it is more difficult.

SEPTEMBER 29, SHEA STADIUM

The Mets gave gifts of tote bags to 50,563 fans on what was called "Fan Appreciation Day." And then they gave the Pirates Apodaca, which pleased the fans more. Apodaca had faced the Pirates only once before in his major-league career.

Last year on September 18, Apodaca was called up from his home in California and thrown into the fire at Pittsburgh. He walked the two batters he faced and went home for the winter "wondering if I would ever be able to face major-league batters with confidence." This time, with the Pirates going for the pennant, Apodaca wiped them out. He held them to three singles, two of them in the ninth inning, pitched his first complete game, and beat the Pirates, 7–2.

He had a no-hitter into the sixth inning, pitching with confidence that has been building slowly through the second half of this season. Apodaca got the first out of the sixth and the Pirates sent up Gene Clines to pinch-hit. "Then last September came back to me in a flash," Apodaca said, "because Clines was the first major-league batter I faced. I thought to myself, 'You're not going to get a walk this time.' "

Clines blooped a fastball into right field and the no-hitter was gone. Before the inning was over Benny Ayala had dropped a fly ball in left field and the shutout was gone, too.

But Apodaca had a 7–1 lead and was able to force his way through the last two Pittsburgh singles and a run in the ninth inning. "I got tired," Apodaca said, which was not nearly the same thing he had said about that event of last September. "I was scared that day, real scared," he reflected.

And if the Pirates were going for the pennant now, it was just enough to give Apodaca a boost. "The money is on the line and they have the incentive to beat your brains out," he said. "It was a case of asking no quarter and giving none."

Someday Apodaca may be able to look back on a successful career and remember this game as a line of demarcation, when he knew he could stand up to major-league batters.

SEPTEMBER 30, SHEA STADIUM

Jerry Koosman won his fifteenth game as the Mets beat the Phillies, 5–2. It's the most he's won since 1969, when he won seventeen in his second season and there seemed to be no limit for him.

OCTOBER 1, SHEA STADIUM

It was the best of days for Tom Seaver. A beautiful gem to remember all winter, like the long putt on the eighteenth hole that brings you back to play next time. Now Seaver can think back to one game when he had it all together. The Phillies beat him, 2–1, today, but that's extraneous. He struck out fourteen and simply overpowered them.

Seaver finished with a flourish, striking out the side in the ninth inning to raise his total to 201. It's the fewest Seaver has struck out since he was a rookie, but it made him the first National League pitcher to strike out 200 or more in seven consecutive seasons. Walter Johnson and Rube Waddell did it in the American League.

It wasn't Seaver's season high in strikeouts. He struck out sixteen Dodgers in Los Angeles on May 1 and for that moment thought he had overcome his difficulties. Now he looks back on that game and says the steep mound at Dodger Stadium made his stuff better than it really was.

This game is the one that pleases him. But this one leaves him with a double-edged thought to ponder. Did the last game—after the most helpful medical treatment—prove that Seaver can return to a new season and pitch as he always has? Or will it just obscure in his mind the fact that he pitched erratically before he hurt his hip?

OCTOBER 2, SHEA STADIUM

There's no overtime pay for playing ten innings in the last game of the season. The Mets didn't linger in the clubhouse any longer than necessary.

The 3–2 loss to the Phillies hardly mattered. The last out came and moments later a groundskeeper lowered the National League pennant that had flown over Shea Stadium all season. It is now a relic to be folded away.

The season was over and that was a relief. The players showered, and then baseball gloves, long underwear, and costly aftershave were tucked away into equipment bags. There was no need for a whirlpool bath for anybody to get ready to play tomorrow. There were handshakes and pats on the back, but no emotional parting.

"You spend months together and you become close; you have to say something," said Bob Apodaca, who had never experienced this before. It was the conclusion of his rookie year.

But there were no poignant moments. "About ninety per cent of the guys can't wait until the season ends," Duffy Dyer said.

Poignant partings are for winners. Like the time Jim Lonborg raised his can of beer to the Red Sox after losing the seventh game of the 1967 World Series and said, "One night during the winter, wherever we are, we'll sit in front of the fire, raise a glass of wine, and think, 'It was a hell of a year, wasn't it.'"

For the Mets it was a year of hell. The worst kind for an athlete. It was a total failure. They thought they were the best. They thought they would win. They thought they had the pitching to win. Every day they thought they would begin to win at any time. And they never came close.

For some of them it was the end of an era, maybe the end of something they would never have again. For some, it meant they would be swept away in the front office reaction to the flop. "I think trades run through a player's head every year at this time," Dyer said. "You have to think that maybe I'll never have on a Met uniform again."

And when the logical trades come and the inevitable end comes to some careers, the ones who remain will say, "That's too bad." And they will think, "Thank God it wasn't me."

In the end, they are all Hessians, merely hired for the duration. Then the war is over. "You live with the same people for seven days a week, seven months a year," Ray Sadecki said. "You shower together and you work together. By this time you're tired of those people and you just want to get out of here."

POSTSCRIPT

Ray Sadecki, who said, "What're you going to get for me?" was traded to St. Louis for Joe Torre.

Bob Miller was released and then taken on the trip to Japan with the club.

John Strohmayer was dropped from the roster.

Tug McGraw was traded to Philadelphia for Del Unser, a journeyman outfielder, and Mac Scarce, a middling relief pitcher.

George Stone, the surprise hero of 1973 who hurt his arm trying to have a better year, was asked to take a $7,000 cut in his $45,000 salary. He said it was no surprise and refused.

Tom Seaver accepted what he called a "healthy cut" in his $172,000 salary, as he had agreed in September. "No doubt in my mind that a cut was in order," he said.

Jon Matlack analyzed his situation and took on a professional negotiator for the first time. With Seaver's condition questionable, Matlack may be the most valuable property the Mets have. He had the third-best earned-run average in the league, 2.41, and led the league with seven shutouts. Yet he won thirteen and lost fifteen. He won only four games after the All-Star Game, all shutouts. He made $60,000 in 1974 and asked $100,000 for 1975.

Matlack came across a magazine computer study of the top forty-four pitchers in the league, broken down into sixteen categories. Matlack was in the top ten in fifteen of the categories and was rated tops in effectiveness. "Of the forty-four pitchers, I finished dead last in offensive runs scored," he said. "That's why my won–lost record is so deceiving."

So he took on an agent, named Irwin Weiner. The Mets have always discouraged taking salary negotiations outside what M. Donald Grant calls "the family." "They keep telling the players not to go out of the family," Weiner said, "and I think the players have to worry about feeding their own families."

New on the pitching roster are pitchers named Baldwin, Grose, and Tate.

Pete Richert was told after surgery the circulation was good enough in his arm for him to play golf, but he should forget about ever painting his house or doing much carpentry.

When the cast came off Tommy John's arm in January, he was told he couldn't pitch again until the second half of the 1975 season, if ever.

1974 NEW YORK METS PITCHING STAFF

Pitching	G	ST	CG	W–L	IP	H	R	ER	BB	SO	HR	SHO	SV	ERA
Aker	24	0	0	2-1	41.1	33	18	16	14	18	4	0	2	3.51
Apodaca	35	8	1	6-6	103.	92	47	40	42	54	7	0	3	3.50
Cram	10	0	0	0-1	22.1	22	4	4	4	8	1	0	0	1.64
Espinosa	2	1	0	0-0	9.	12	5	5	0	2	1	0	0	5.00
Koosman	35	35	13	15-11	265.	258	113	99	85	188	16	0	0	3.36
Matlack	34	34	14	13-15	265.1	221	82	71	76	195	8	7	0	2.41
McGraw	41	4	1	6-11	88.2	96	43	41	32	54	12	1	3	4.15
Miller	58	0	0	2-2	78.	89	39	31	39	35	2	0	2	3.58
Parker	40	16	1	4-12	131.	145	64	57	46	58	10	0	4	3.92
Sadecki	34	10	3	8-8	103.	107	49	39	35	46	7	1	0	3.41
Seaver	32	32	12	11-11	236.	199	89	84	75	201	19	5	0	3.20
Sterling	3	2	0	1-1	9.1	13	8	5	3	2	0	0	0	5.00
Stone	15	13	1	2-7	77.	103	57	43	21	29	10	0	0	5.03
Strohmayer	1	0	0	0-0	1.	0	0	0	1	0	0	0	0	0.00
Swan	7	5	0	1-3	30.1	28	19	15	21	10	1	0	0	4.50
Webb	3	2	0	0-2	10.	15	9	8	10	8	1	0	0	7.30
Totals	162	162	46	71-91	1470.1	1433	646	558	504	908	99	15*	14	3.42

* one combined, shutout